SAME-SEX
LOVE

SAME-SEX LOVE

And the Path to Wholeness

EDITED BY ROBERT H. HOPCKE,
KARIN LOFTHUS CARRINGTON,
AND SCOTT WIRTH

SHAMBHALA • *Boston & London* • 1993

SHAMBHALA PUBLICATIONS, INC.
Horticultural Hall
300 Massachusetts Avenue
Boston, Massachusetts 02115
www.shambhala.com

Printed in the United States of America

Distributed in the United States by Random House, Inc.,
and in Canada by Random House of Canada Ltd

LIBRARY OF CONGRESS CATALOGING-IN-PUBLICATION DATA

Same-sex love and the path to wholeness/edited by Robert H. Hopcke, Karin
    Lofthus Carrington, and Scott Wirth.
        p. cm.
    ISBN 0-87773-651-0 (acid-free paper)
    1. Gays—Psychology. 2. Jung, C. G. (Carl Gustav), 1875–1961.
    I. Hopcke, Robert H., 1958– . II. Carrington, Karin Lofthus.
    III. Wirth, Scott.
    RC558.S35   1993   92-50443
    155.3′4—dc20   CIP

BVG 01

For Elizabeth K. Osterman, with loving gratitude   K.L.C.

To all gay, lesbian, and bisexual people in analysis—may they find acceptance and understanding each step of the way
R.H.H.

To David and Jessica, with affection and gratitude   S.W.

Contents

ACKNOWLEDGMENTS ix

EDITORS' INTRODUCTION 1
  Robert H. Hopcke, Karin Lofthus Carrington, and Scott Wirth

HOMOEROTIC RELATIONSHIPS BETWEEN MEN
  IN INDIA AND IN WESTERN MYTHOLOGY 8
  Robert A. Johnson

COMING HOME: THE LATE-LIFE LESBIAN 28
  Christine Downing

INDIVIDUATION AND EROS: FINDING MY WAY 38
  Caroline T. Stevens

HER RADIANCE EVERYWHERE: POEMS FROM
  A MIDLIFE AWAKENING 51
  Morgan Farley

HOMOPHOBIA AND ANALYTICAL PSYCHOLOGY 68
  Robert H. Hopcke

WOMEN LOVING WOMEN: SPEAKING THE
  TRUTH IN LOVE 88
  Karin Lofthus Carrington

DREAMING THE MYTH: AN INTRODUCTION
  TO MYTHOLOGY FOR GAY MEN 110
  Will Roscoe

HOMO/AESTHETICS, OR ROMANCING THE SELF 125
  Lyn Cowan

HOMOVISION: THE SOLAR/LUNAR TWIN-EGO 136
  Howard Teich

TOWARD AN IMAGE OF MALE PARTNERSHIP 151
  John Beebe

BROTHER LONGING AND LOVE: THE EXAMPLE
OF HENRY JAMES   170
   Suzi Naiburg
NOT "A ONE-SIDED SEXUAL BEING":
CLINICAL WORK WITH GAY MEN FROM A
JUNGIAN PERSPECTIVE   186
   Scott Wirth
THE ROLE OF THE ANIMA IN SAME-SEX LOVE
BETWEEN MEN   219
   Donald Sandner
REFLECTIONS ON HOMOSEXUALITY: AN
INTERVIEW WITH JOSEPH HENDERSON   231
   Scott Wirth
HOMOEROTICISM AND HOMOPHOBIA IN
HETEROSEXUAL MALE INITIATION   246
   David J. Tacey
INDIVIDUATION, TABOO, AND SAME-SEX LOVE   264
   Robert Bosnak
MIRRORING AFFIRMATION: WITH SPECIAL
REFERENCE TO PSYCHOANALYSIS
AND TO MEN   273
   Eugene Monick
THE UNCHARTED BODY   284
   Susan Griffin

ABOUT THE CONTRIBUTORS   291

Acknowledgments

We three co-editors wish to honor and thank each contributor to this collection for lending her or his distinctive voice to the chorus which this volume comprises. We also wish to acknowledge each other for our mutual honesty, tolerance, energy, humor, and commitment, all of which brought this work into being.

I wish to express my gratitude to my patients, who open themselves in vulnerability, seeking their integrity; to my personal guides over two decades: Arthur D. Colman, Geraldine Spare, and David Stockford; to my consultants who have helped me find my depth in analytic work: Charles H. Klaif, Donald F. Sandner, Mary Jo Spencer, J. Michael Steele, and Louis H. Stewart; to John E. Beebe, Robert H. Hopcke, J. Michael Steele, and David Stockford, gay men who broke new ground in the Jungian world; to friends and colleagues, each of whom has made a particular impact on generating this volume: Shira Barnett, Susan Bostrom-Wong, Mondi Bridges, Florence P. Grossenbacher, Naomi Lowinsky, Carol McRae, Ruth Palmer, Saralie B. Pennington, Ellen Siegelman, Patricia Stamm; Philip A. Tecau; to the entire community of the C. G. Jung Institute of San Francisco for providing an atmosphere for dynamic learning and individuation; to Nancy Berry and Judy Matthews for invaluable help with preparing manuscripts; to my parents, Arthur and Marian Wirth, and my sisters, Vicki Legion and Patricia Wirth; and to all people facing and living with HIV disease.

S. W.

My contribution to the vision and actual creation of this volume was made during a period in my life when the likelihood of my creating anything was against all odds. I want to express my deep gratitude for the wild, natural beauty of West Marin County, Orcas Island, and Northern New Mexico, which has contained, nurtured, and reflected my true spirit during this challenging time. Morgan Farley's love, steadfastness, and brilliance have been essential to me during the final stages of this project. I thank John Beebe from the bottom of my heart for his integrity, sensitivity, and wise guidance "through it all." Kathleen Meagher, Cornelia Schulz, Arlene Reiss, Oliver and Corey Cooperman, Critt Brookes, Mauna Berkov, Sylvia Brinton Perera, Ruth Palmer, Anne Stine, Dominee Cappadonna, David Anderson, David Ross, my brother Michael Lofthus, and my parents Lloyd and Francesca Lofthus, have been loving, constant, and deeply supportive. In addition, Caroline Stevens and Rosemarie Chrapkowski, Suzi Naiburg, Amy Rennert, Mondi Bridges, Ruth Anthony, Suzy Spradlin, Jack Kornfield, Patrick Tribble, Anne Heller, Rogers Carrington, Rosemary LePage, Marny Hall, Steve Joseph, Jean Shinoda Bolen, Arthur Colman, Sarah Janosik, Jessica Radin, Medora Perlman, June Kounin, Bill Gray, Judah Betz, Susan Griffin, Bryan Wittine, Florence Grossenbacher, and Donald Sandner offered openhearted personal and professional encouragement for my work. And my beloved women friends and colleagues from the Branham Ranch Gatherings held me through the deepest grief and hardest rebirth of all—with fierceness, tenderness, patience, and humor. Finally, Nancy Cazaux Nordstrum has my eternal gratitude for all we rejoiced in, endured, and opened to—together and separately—in the years that this book was in the birthing. My contribution to this volume reflects, without doubt, endless communal generosity.

K.L.C.

Those who have been most helpful in my efforts to raise consciousness around homosexuality for the last few years within Jungian circles are, to my great pleasure, among the many contributors to this volume, and among those, John Beebe, whose courage and intelligence has been an invaluable help to me along the path of my own professional growth as a writer, deserves my special appreciation, along with Mark Thompson and Mitch Walker, who for various reasons could not be a part of this volume. All the gay men and lesbians I work with week after week at Operation Concern in San Francisco form a support group of a sort unique for many gay, lesbian, and bisexual therapists, and for this community, without which my thinking and actions around the issues as addressed in this volume would be decidedly more impoverished, I would like to extend public gratitude. For a book whose birth has been more demanding and complicated than most others for me, I would especially like to acknowledge the patience, understanding, and support of those with whom I share my everyday life and who have followed me through the trials and tribulations of this volume: Paul, Bianca, Minou, Mark, Jennifer, Anna, Jill, Rich, Steve C., Steve E., Ray, Sharon, Jesse, and Chelsea.

R.H.H.

We wish to extend our sincere gratitude to the editorial staff of Shambhala Publications, in particular Emily Hilburn Sell, Kendra Crossen, and David O'Neal. They have joined with us in the intensive labor which gave birth to this book.

SAME-SEX
LOVE

Editors' Introduction

To introduce the first collection of papers from a Jungian perspective focused exclusively on same-sex love is a joyful task. The wide variety of writers who have contributed to this volume, the depth and breadth of their perspectives, the rich insights they bring from their personal and professional lives, all make this collection a unique event in the Jungian literature. However naturally this collection may seem to unfold, and however timely its appearance, this coming together of diverse minds and hearts around the "who," "how," and "why" of lesbian and gay lives is not an event that occurred either easily or outside of a larger context. To discuss that context, both personal and collective, in the introduction to this book is fitting, so that the contributors to the book may be appreciated for their courage, originality, and thoughtfulness.

The early 1970s ushered in the women's and gay/lesbian liberation movements alongside a broad mix of other social currents pulsing at various levels through culture, academia, and political structures. Through the ensuing decades, these movements, in their refusal to accept patriarchal separateness and division between personal and political life, have attempted to bridge the separation between mind and body, the outer structures of society and the inner world of psyche, and between Self and other. The challenges to traditional psychological thought made by feminism have brought about extensive dialogue and changes to both theory and practice. In Jungian circles there has been a steady stream of publications, conferences, and other expressions of raised consciousness about women's issues. Indeed, in the course of two decades, in some American Jungian training institutes, women have gone from being a small minority of analytic candidates to a three-quarters majority.

In contrast, no comparable significant integration has taken place vis-à-vis homosexuality. As with racial and ethnic minorities (with the possible exceptions of Jews), gay and lesbian people as a minority group have not taken their rightful place in Jungian psychological circles. Until the 1990s, there were virtually no Jungian conferences, seminars, or lectures on homosexuality, no special issues of journals on the topic, no books having to do with lesbianism or male homosexuality, even though many Jung Institutes are located in major centers of gay and lesbian cultural life, such as San Francisco, Los Angeles, Chicago, New York, London, and Boston. The logic of demographics would lead one to expect by the 1990s to find an abundant, fertile intellectual outpouring from Jungians in the study of same-sex love. Yet such a development has not occurred.

In response to this paucity, a group of us began coming together five years ago on a monthly basis in order to explore, discuss, and support one another in creating a new body of Jungian-oriented writing that would give voice to our particular experiences and understanding, both personal and clinical, as men and women who identify ourselves as both homosexual and Jungian. We were acutely aware of how little had been spoken or written about same-sex love by Jungians. Our work was to begin, through personal support and professional commitment, to synthesize for ourselves, our clients, and hopefully our colleagues and friends the two sometimes seemingly disparate realities of "union of sames" and Jungian theory and practice so centered as it is on the tension of opposites. We met, we talked, we cried, we laughed, and slowly we sorted our way through hours of confusion, anger, inspiration, and fear. In the end, three of us remained. At this stage, having come to know and respect one another, we began to talk about publishing an anthology that would address homosexuality and the homoerotic from a Jungian perspective and give voice to both the differences and points of connection between man-to-man relationships and woman-to-woman relationships.

For one woman to love another, to make love with another, to share a life with another, demands that she radically alter her relationship to patriarchal culture. Some women may choose to be separatists as a way of containing and preserving the precious new life they find with one another; others continue in the heterosexual mainstream. Rules break clear and forever in such a radical move, and women in love with women must "re-create the world." In this new world, gender roles no longer hold, and though the butch/femme paradigm is often engaged by lesbians, even that does not replace the gender roles of heterosexual culture. Women as lovers are not (as so many Jungians have suggested in their effort to make sense of lesbian experience) merely living out a complex centered on the Feminine, exhibiting an aversion to the Masculine, or expressing in their love unresolved mother issues. Relationships between women are complex and do offer the potential for a deep grappling with the instinctual feminine and internalized masculine sides of a woman's nature, as well as with developmental issues centered on early mothering. Yet the special emphasis in erotic and sexual bonding between women focuses more on an individuation through the refinement of sameness rather than strictly through the tension of opposites. In sexual union between women, the embodied likeness as well as differences are profoundly experienced and often contribute to a woman's reunion with her own body after years of living in an androcentric culture that separates body and soul, matter and spirit, and has often violated, demeaned, and mutilated the body and women's bodies in particular. For a woman to be compelled toward another woman in love is ultimately to be compelled to her Self in a new and deeply instinctual way, in a way that individuates, not so much through difference, opposition, and disparity as through mutuality, complementarity, subtlety, and sameness. These paths of sameness which lead women in love with each other to the Self have different textures, feeling tones, shadows, visions, aesthetics, and problems than those which lead to the Self through difference.

The articles and poetry in this collection by women are largely personal and deeply reflective. Because the contributors have gone down into the well of their particular experiences in love with other women, the richness of their stories touches archetypal levels that are significant for our collective understanding of lesbian life. One cannot help being struck by the expression of extremes of experiences often inherent in women's love of women, the extremes of darkness and pain as well as of light and ecstasy. There is something essential, so near the source of life and death, which women come to know in intimacy with one another and the extremes are inevitable, the risks correspondingly great. The areas of primary vulnerability and of woundedness in a woman can become raw as she opens her body and soul to another so like herself and, in an embodied sense, so reminiscent of "the mother." The possibility exists in such a relationship for deep healing or equally deep rewounding, for a return to a place of pure knowing and pure being behind the wound, or for a thickening of the scar tissue over this wound so that any penetration becomes impossible. The journey is often precipitous as well as abundant, ordinary as well as ecstatic, dark as well as filled with light. The writings by women in this book address all of these issues—containment, gender roles, extremes of experience in love, reclaiming and redefining boundaries, individuation through sameness, subtlety and nuance, archetypal patterns, mutuality, the remembered body, ecstasy, destruction, and the erotic.

Men's experience of love for other men within a patriarchal culture carries a similarly revolutionary effect psychologically and socially. To see another man as an object of erotic attention, rather than a rival or a stranger, to own and act upon the oneness that men sense as men in another's masculinity, is to overcome that peculiar self-alienation inherent in the patriarchal split between men and women and its single-minded insistence upon heterosexuality. The essays by men in this book give voice to the mythic dimension of men's love of other men, recount the transformative effect of homoeroticism realized in the course of individuation, and attempt to put into more theoretical terms just what it is about homosexuality that is at once so frightening and so sacred.

In some ways, this collection is looking in two directions at once, hoping to provide the world of analytical psychology as well as the contemporary gay and lesbian community with broader and deeper ways of understanding the passionate mysteries of sexual orientation. The question, "Do homosexuals individuate, or come to psychological wholeness?" has been a bone of contention within Jungian circles. Some analysts argue that homosexuality is a case of arrested development, while others, fewer in number, see a special kind of individuation process for gay men and lesbians, one that emerges not in spite of but precisely through their homosexuality. Jung's own writings suggest clearly that he regarded homosexuality as having an individual meaning, which must be made conscious for wholeness to occur. Thus we have assembled here a diverse group of psychotherapists, writers, and others—homosexual and heterosexual, women and men—whose stories and ideas demonstrate the beauty and significance of same-sex love and its contribution to the expansion of personal and collective consciousness.

Just as the Jungian community can benefit from a reformulation of ideas on homosexuality and the homoerotic, so can the lesbian and gay community profit by embracing a more symbolic, depth-oriented, psyche-honoring way of life. One of the most tragic aspects of our oppression as gay men and lesbians has been the fact that we have had to devote so much of our time to social and political action on the most basic level—from fighting the criminalization of our love to assuring our fundamental human rights to privacy, work, parenting, public safety and housing, not to mention the decade of effort required to combat the AIDS epidemic. Our political action, while necessary in many cases, has resulted in a kind of forced extraversion, leaving us little time, patience, and energy for the equally necessary inner work around what it means to be lesbian or gay. Thus, the editors and contributors to this volume see our collection as a gift to the inner life of the lesbian and gay community.

As we sat and looked at the contributions we had solicited and received, a certain organic flow of the material gradually became clear. Hence, we start with personal stories, in which individuals relate their own experience of the transformation wrought by the welcoming of the homoerotic into their lives. A broadening of that vision to include what can be found in the culture, in art, literature, film, and myth, seems to follow quite naturally, further supporting and encouraging us in our quest for meaning. Finally, we begin to elaborate theories, become more abstract, find ways of articulating not just what we have lived but how what we have lived and are living can be clinically and philosophically understood and manifested. Though somewhat wary of theories and the generalization inherent in them, we feel it important to show how Jungian thought can indeed expand to hold lesbian and gay lives, and offer a container for a bewildering wealth of experience, both inner and outer, that faces each individual on this particular path to wholeness.

We have sought also to provide balance with the assemblage of voices, balance between women and men, between gay and straight perspectives, between different philosophical perspectives. We have sought above all to create a collection that is not an end point but that will serve as a beginning for readers, stimulating them to think, to write, and to work clinically from their own well of homoerotic experience. Our hope is that this volume will contribute to the healing for both individuals and the culture, which a fuller understanding and recognition of same-sex love can offer. We further hope this collection will provide a deeper and more expansive container for men and women who through choice and fate find themselves in love with someone of their own gender. Such results can only enrich us all.

Homoerotic Relationships between Men in India and in Western Mythology

ROBERT A. JOHNSON

I have been immensely impressed that Sanskrit-based languages have ninety-six terms for love, the ancient Persian texts eighty, the ancient Greeks three, and we one. So to talk of love for an American means we are in trouble already. When there is no differentiated language for a subject, it usually means that it is an unconscious area in the culture of that people, and so the very fact that we have such a poverty-stricken vocabulary for things of relationship speaks of the poverty-strickenness of that faculty in ourselves. It is said that Eskimos have upward of fifty terms for snow, because snow is important to them. They have to talk about different kinds of snow because they have to cope with different kinds of snow, and it is important. As a people needs or values a particular faculty, it will develop a terminology for it. It is a dead giveaway that we have not developed a terminology for relationship and for love. Thus, when we launch into talking about homoerotic relationship, we are in deep trouble because we have no language for it. Partly this is because feeling is the inferior function of most of our Western world, and particularly the English-speaking segment of the Western world, so we are talking about inferior function phenomenology, a notoriously sticky and difficult subject.

This article is about homoerotic relationship as I experienced it in India. Unlike our country, India is an introverted-feeling society, hence this wonderful flexibility of terminology, and a tremendous deep insight which they have in relationship. They are as much masters of relationship as we are of mechanics. We trade shadows in going back and forth between India and America. We build such wonderful bridges and computers and the like, and they work; and India builds such wonderful relationships, and they work.

When I first went to India I was simply overwhelmed by a certain kind of joyousness which those people have, a joyousness notably absent in our own society. I thought that loneliness and alienation and the sense of separateness—the sense of disconnectedness, the whole twentieth-century phenomenon of our Western world, which novelists and poets spend so much time with—were simply the lot of man. That is what it meant to be born; that is what it meant to grow up and take your place in the world. I found out in India that it did not mean that. India has a differentiated feeling faculty which is one of the finest arts that one would ever find. It was an absolute delight to me.

I determined to learn as much as I could about it, even as a Westerner, carrying a Western unconscious. I have never repudiated my background because that is what I am; it is as indelibly imprinted into me as my blue eyes, the shape of my nose, and the color of my hair, so I never tried. Many people who go to the Eastern countries or adopt Eastern ways try to repudiate their Western unconscious, and only compound the difficulty that they are in.

Rather than repudiate my own Western characteristics, I set out to learn as much as I could. In preparing this piece, I tried to find a word for a particular kind of relationship which India is capable of that was an absolute joy and a delight in my two hands, but I had no word. *Homoerotic* is the nearest I can come to it, and yet it grates on my nerves just a little because the word *erotic* is suspect in any context that one uses it, one of those clinical things that smells slightly of disinfectant. I do have some slight justification, though, because when I got back to looking at Eros and the erotic structure which we draw from his example, I found out to my immense pleasure that when that wonderful, terrible, divine mischiefmaker god pulls back his bowstring and lets an arrow loose, he aims at the heart. He does not aim at the genitals. So *erotic* is not something necessarily sexual; it is not interchangeable with *sexuality*. The erotic quality is the quality of relatedness. It is the quality of belongingness. It is the quality of identity.

In this sense I want to explore that particular homoerotic quality which springs up with such great beauty in India between man and man or woman and woman. However, I first want to make it plain that I am not extolling the virtues of this quality above anything else. I am not turning moralistic and saying this is better than something else. I am not implying that if we just had some sense, we would make our exchanges homoerotic instead of homosexual or heterosexual. I am not saying any such thing. If I am moved to speak of the homoerotic quality, it is because I want to differentiate that specific faculty out, for it is a noble one; and when used intelligently, in a differentiated way, it brings an enormous amount of pleasure, stability, and warmth.

I was in for many surprises in India. People warned me, "Robert, you've got to steel yourself before you get there or it will just sweep somebody like you off your feet. You are going to be stepping over dead corpses on the street. There are going to be lepers after you. People are going to throw dead babies into your hands. Amputated arms and legs are going to be poked into your ribs. You are going to watch people starving to death right before your very eyes," and so on and so forth, all of which was true. All that I survived. I had some bad moments, but somehow my sense of reality expanded sufficiently to take in this dimension of life. What no one had prepared me for was the immense deep happiness of almost everybody in India, people who have no *reason* to be happy. They are starving to death, on the edge of disaster, living for all intents and purposes unprotected, outdoors much of the time, with no idea where the next meal is coming from, watching their children die in their hands. But they are happy people, with nothing to be happy about.

That observation set me off, and gave me the clue I needed. I found out that you are not ever happy *about* anything, you are just happy. Consulting the dictionary, I found out that the word *happy* comes from the verb *to happen*. You are happy about what happens, as simple as that. But not, perhaps, if you are an American.

Yet another qualification here is in order. When I speak of this specific kind of relatedness, the homoerotic tie or relationship, all of what I am talking about is the traditional Indian. The Westernized Indian is as neurotic and as unhappy as we are, and it only takes a half generation to do it. Westernized, urban Indians are so much like us it is painful. Mostly the Indians who make their way here, the educated, English-speaking Westernized Indians, share all of our difficulties, and they are really not much different from us and are in general not very happy people.

The traditional Hindu is married twice in his life. The first marriage happens quite early, in late boyhood, in earliest manhood. He makes a blood-brother pact with another of his own sex, his buddy, so to speak. They wound themselves in a ceremony, they mix their blood, and they belong to each other for the rest of life. This is the blood brother; it has nothing to do with blood relationship as we speak of it. It is a tie as deep and as lasting and as rewarding in its own dimension as is a marriage.

When a boy is sixteen, the parents bring home a bride for him that they have chosen. Economic matters, family matters, caste, and most of all the astrologer determine who would be a suitable wife for the boy. The bride, so bedecked in flowers that when the ceremony begins neither sees the other for the five days of an Indian marriage, and when finally the last of the wedding rites take place, the flowers are taken aside and they see for the first time whom they have married. This is the second marriage of his life.

These two relationships buffer that man on both sides of his nature for the rest of his life. Each brings a safety, a security, a sense of belongingness, a rootedness, a beingness almost unknown to a Westerner. I have come to the conclusion that we Westerners have all of these capacities and all of these hungers no less than an Indian does, and I watch futile, abortive, often guilt-stricken attempts of Westerners to accomplish this kind of buffering, this kind of surroundedness, containedness, and safety. Sadly, it does not work very well.

With some Indian insight, I watch painful episodes going on at the locker room at the YMCA, where two men are trying to strengthen each other, buffer, surround, protect each other, and they are so guilt-stricken they cannot do it. Such efforts are mostly couched in the terms of their opposites. People so often, when they are trying something that is very, very delicate, will use the terminology of its opposite, almost as a disguise or subterfuge. So the towel-flipping and the punch on the shoulder, the kidding, the razing, and the putting down and all such things, I see as affection, as homoerotic attempts, offers, and pleas, which more often fail or misfire than accomplish what they were intended for. Western men seem curiously impotent and frightened, and are suddenly left without any energy or any courage when they want to make a homoerotic relationship with someone. We do not know what we have lost!

Here we are in the realm of feeling, a realm in which Westerners, especially English-speaking Westerners, are especially inept. To theorize much about feeling, however, would kill it. In his article on the feeling function, James

Hillman says that it is an anachronism that a thinking type should talk about feeling, but he proceeds to do it anyway. Feeling has to have feeling language. If one is a poet or an artist, there is the possibility of dealing with feeling. However, the only possibility I have at hand, since I can do none of those other things, is to tell you stories. Stories are consistent with feeling, and I will rely heavily on them to make my points. Here, therefore, are stories of the homoerotic quality of India. It delights me to tell them; it warms me immensely.

I arrived, knew no one, and quickly discovered that wonderful magical language in which, if you want to make friends with somebody, you stand beside him, just a little bit in back of him, and wait. You don't say anything. You don't do anything. You wait. And he won't look, but he is aware. Indians never look each other, or anybody, straight in the eye. That is much too crude a language. Indians never have that direct, straightforward gaze or glance in conversation, so it gives something of the feeling that they are not noticing, but indeed they are noticing.

If you want to make friends with an Indian, you edge up just beside him—this is always with somebody of your own sex, you never do this cross-sexually—and wait. If he consents to something with you, he won't go anywhere. He will just stand there, and after what seems like a terribly long period of time, somebody says something or somebody does something, and then you are probably friends for as long as the two of you wish or intend, likely for life. This is not taken lightly. If the other person does not want that close tie with you, he will find occupation someplace else, and nothing is said.

I was too shy to do this; I didn't know my way around that intricate, wonderful world of feeling, though it is my native language. But others did it with me, and I ended up with friends amazingly quickly. Then I got sick, nothing permanent, nothing of any moment, but very sick. I was in an Indian hospital—a nightmare. They explained to me, it was a truly modern, Westernized hospital. They had one thermometer, which all of us patients had in succession, one after the other. I objected, and they said, "It's all right because we rinse it off under the tap." Somehow we all survived.

The point of this story was that my Indian friend who had taken me on as blood brother—for what reason I'll never know, it's futile to ask—came and slept under my bed at night. He said, "I'm not going to have you there alone," so he or somebody assigned by him slept under my hospital bed every night. Now, if I go to the hospital in America, I can't get anybody to sleep under my bed. It's just not possible. One day when my fever was 104, and I was just slightly out of my head, Amba Shankar, that was his name, stood at the foot of my bed and told me the story of Baba.

Baba had a friend, and the friend was ill. It looked as if Baba's friend might die. So Baba came to his friend, and said, "I wish to die for you, and you have only to say the word and I will go and die that you may live. This is my wish, this is my friendship, this is how it is." The friend agreed, so Baba went away and died, and the friend lived.

Being told this story, which was like something out of *The Arabian Nights*, snapped me into focus, because Amba Shankar then said, "You say the word and I will go and die, and then you will be all right." I was speechless. I don't understand things like this. My heart understands and resonates instantly, but none of my Americanism, none of my Anglo-Saxon verbal concepts, can cope with this. So I managed to say, "Amba, I don't think I am that ill. Don't do anything now, please. I think we will both pull through." And as it happens we did. But that man had offered me a priceless gift—his life.

In India nothing is "one's own business" and this is especially true between blood brothers. I found out to my astonishment and bewilderment that my pocketbook was common property with my close friends. Without saying anything, a friend would take my wallet and return it a few minutes later, slightly depleted. I never resented this as I could not have found any other way of repaying the kindness that my friends constantly gave to me.

One day I was riding my bicycle, minding my own business—though nothing is ever entirely one's own business in India—when a young fellow came along paralleling me. In good Anglo-Saxon style I moved over slightly and dutifully looked straight ahead. The young fellow remained parallel to me, so I moved over a little farther—but he was still there. Presently he reached out, took my hand and we proceeded for a block, riding together hand in hand. He turned off at the next street and I never saw him again. But feeling was engaged and a bond was made that is the genius of India.

What this made clear to me as an American is that one of the great barriers to us, with our Western mind of understanding, is that some of the forms of love which are not common to us we tend to sexualize, and we ascribe sexuality to things which aren't necessarily attached to that part of our nature. I am in no way diminishing sexuality, but it's not everything. To ride a bicycle holding hands with a stranger, this is the homoerotic world. It is affection, devotion, one of the ninety-six kinds of love which we cannot comprehend.

A story that illustrates this sexualizing tendency of Western mind:

I was taken off to a small village, for a wedding. I was guest of honor because I gave prestige to the ceremony. There had never been a white man in that village before, and most people had never seen anyone like this Occidental. The wedding was specially graced because they had a distinguished foreigner from far, far away as guest. They were happy with that. When I went back two years later, to the same village, here was the baby, and they came and asked me with great joy and with great delight (there were one or two people in the village who spoke English) please to observe how light-skinned the baby was, lighter-skinned by far than either its father or its mother.

They coolly and proudly announced that it was my influence. Of course there is not a Western mind that hears such a story without attaching an off-color joke to it. Such an attitude does not exist in India, and an Indian wouldn't think like that. He thought of the influence of the light-skinned man on the whole village, and the lightening of the village because of the presence of the light-skinned man.

I am embarrassed when I see what my Western mind does. It sexualizes, instantly, almost everything it touches. And yet I don't think that this is a natural faculty, but rather a product of our jokes, our attitudes, our billboards, our advertising.

In the same village every evening a young fellow in his early twenties walked four miles from his farm to sit with me at sunset. We had not one word of language between us. I had learned his name and nothing else. But every night he came in just to sit with me, for a half-hour. He would sit so that he touched me—a foot, or a knee, or a hand. Then he would turn around and walk four miles home again. Such things are inexplicable in our Western world. Of course, we are capable of these things, and as I expanded my concept of honesty out farther and farther in my own inner work, I found out that I was capable of things like that but had never dared. Shankar did. He came and he sat. He wanted to sit near me, I was pleased, and that's all there was to it. Not really "that's all," for that was everything. He lived, I lived, and feeling was served.

The youngsters found that I liked to go walking a little bit before sunset time. So about twenty of them would arrive, and they all wanted to touch me. So I had a child on each finger, and I had two or three on each belt buckle, and they would pull my shirttail out so that six or eight of them could hang on. This was the procession before sunset every evening. What nourishment to one's feeling function! What devotion was implied and shamelessly portrayed in all of that!

Then the youngsters found out that I had fillings in my teeth, which they had never heard of. So each in turn had to make a private exploration of this mystery. It was a great delight. Nobody but my dentist had been in my mouth ever before.

Bargaining, too, is a relationship. If you don't bargain for something, you have cheated the person in question, even if it is only the shopkeeper, whom you may never see again. As you bargain, you acknowledge him and he acknowledges you. It has very little to do with how much you are going to pay for something. You have bargained, and this is a particular kind of relatedness. Having gone to India to get spiritualized, it is probably the largest joke of my life that I came home humanized.

Amba Shankar employed rickshaw drivers for me, a standard transportation in small to medium Indian cities. The rickshaws were bicycle-driven, not hard on the rickshaw-walla, so this was fine with me. When they are pulled by a human being, like an animal in between two poles, this is too hard on him. Those people die young. I wouldn't take such a rickshaw. But the bicycle-driven ones were fine.

Amba Shankar paid the rickshaw driver. You could go anywhere in Pondicherry for half a rupee. I got brave after a while and got my own rickshaw. I paid him a whole rupee, and he howled. And I gave him a second rupee, and he howled. And I'd walk off down the street and he was howling at me as long as he could see me, which embarrassed me. One day I got angry at this, so I paid him a rupee and he howled, and a second rupee and he howled, and a third rupee and he howled, and a fourth, and a fifth, and a sixth. So I barked, which I had heard other people do, and he quieted down and walked off. Thereafter I paid him one rupee and barked, and he went off. I had learned something. The bark is just that, a sound that would come out of an animal. My muscles are incapable of making that sound on American soil, but it works in India. In part, you go to India to learn to bark.

I began thinking about this. The rickshaw people are untouchables, totally uneducated people, and one was providing form for those people who had no form and no capacity for form. This is one of the acts of love, to give form to another person. If he is not capable of engendering the form which he needs for himself, someone else has to provide that form. This is true of children. They will test the limits to make sure there are limits. The rickshaw drivers had to have the limits set for them, not as an exploitation but as a gift of love.

The members of the family in the village that had adopted me managed an education and about ten of them (there were something like two hundred in the extended family), who had gone off to Bombay and gotten professional jobs, mostly as engineers. When I was in Bombay I was guest in that house. Ten people in a tiny, tiny apartment. Dinnertime was a trial and difficult for me. They got into a silly game, which irritated me, that when I was not looking, they would heap some more food on my plate. I would be talking to someone on my right and I would find more food on my plate from my left. And I would be over here, and somebody over there would find occasion to get more food into my plate for me. I hate to waste food, but I also hate to overeat. Moreover, it is impolite not to eat what is on your plate, so I really was angry at this. I didn't know what to do. After one of these dinners, one of the young men, I think, perceived my difficulty, and he said to me, "You must forgive us, because in the city now we have so little feeling and our days are so arid that all we have left to do is pile food on each other's plate in the evening." My heart melted, and I understood.

I realized then that Old India is vanishing. The feeling nourishment which one got at every turn of the way in traditional India is breaking down for those people, and they have to do silly things, remnants of feelings, foolish things, in order to get some feeling between them. So many symptoms in them, and in us too, are much more about wounded Eros than about wounded sexuality.

I made friends with a doctor. I began doing analytical work

in India, partly because I was pressed into it and partly because it was so interesting and I learned so much. Analytical work, as taught by Jung and his school, works superbly in India. They understood immediately, instantly. So this doctor gave me an office in his clinic, and I saw my people there. I learned much more than I ever taught anybody.

I made friends with the doctor, he was a heart specialist, and one day he came in and he said, "Robert, all right, now, you're the psychologist, you must explain something to me. Why is it that when I go up to the second floor to see some of my patients, I always get palpitations of the heart"—he had a quite serious heart ailment—"but when I go up to see you, I have no palpitations? Now, explain." So I drew a deep breath and launched off on the psychosomatic effects of healing states and such things, and halfway through there was a glazed look over that man's eyes which I had learned to recognize. He had made blood brother with me and there was no use finishing my sentence because he wasn't listening. He was answering his own question.

When I stopped talking, he said, "You must come home with me now." He took me by the hand; a man always walks hand-in-hand with a man friend in India. He took me to the shrine in his house. Every day he took me there to worship, because we were blood brothers, and he didn't have palpitations of the heart anymore on the stairway.

Another example of Eros:

With Muslims if you stand more than six inches away from the face of your friend whom you are talking to anywhere on the street, it is a public, blatant indication that you don't like the man. If you are within six inches of a Westerner when you are talking to him, the most violent backing-up process begins between the two of you.

All of this culminates in an Indian custom sufficient to silence a Westerner. It is a custom in India that you can go to another person—anyone, man or woman, young or old, stranger on the street, trusted friend, anyone—and ask that person if he or she will be the incarnation of God for you. If he or she agrees, there are very strict set laws for what transpires. Nothing personal thereafter may ever exchange between the two of you. You cannot make friends, you cannot court, you cannot touch, you cannot just be around; you may only worship that person. You have elevated him to the status of the incarnation of God.

Fortunately I knew this custom, I had read Rabindranath Tagore before I first went to India, and he tells of such an episode in his own life. So when somebody came to me (largely because of the color of my skin, I think, no other virtue was necessary) and asked if I would be the incarnation of God for her, I had some understanding, and could make my way through the extraordinary request. Soon it was my turn to need this extraordinary healing experience of India and I was grateful to have the tradition at hand.

A friend took me to Calcutta, the darkest city of India, dedicated to Kali, the goddess of destruction, the most horrible of the goddesses. My friend left me there for three days alone while he went to visit his parents in a section of India forbidden to foreigners. I was not afraid of India by that time but I had not reckoned on the terrors of Calcutta. Soon my courage was eroded away and I could not stand one more amputated arm thrust into my ribs or another corpse to step over on the street. The final straw was a woman who thrust a dead baby into my arms in hopes that I could restore it to life for her. I have rarely been totally defeated in my life but this was such an event.

I started to go to pieces, and it was the only time in India I have ever been overwhelmed by the darkness of it. In my anguish all I needed was somebody—somebody to be close to, somebody to hear me, somebody to talk to. I knew what to do, for Indian custom informed me how to get the help I needed. You go find somebody, ask him if he will be the incarnation of

God for you, and treat him as such. So I went off to the park, began looking around, chose a middle-aged Indian of serene face, dressed in traditional Indian clothing, and went up to him. The first question was, "Do you speak English?" "Yes." Second question, "Will you be the incarnation of God for me?" He looked me straight in the eye—rare—and said, "Yes." So for twenty minutes the dam broke and I poured out my fright and my misery and my loneliness, and the anguish of three days of Calcutta which had been accumulating in me. I felt better. I just needed somebody, some human being to parallel or to understand or to walk with me for a minute, and bear this anguish of an intensity that I'd never known before. Being the introvert that I am, I can take inner anguish very well. It hurts, but I know what to do with it. But outer anguish is not my world and it is alien to me.

He helped, just by listening. He was the incarnation of God for me. I thanked him and told him that I had recovered my manners and was sorry about this outburst. I said, "And now please tell me who you are." He gave me his name, which was interminable and unrememberable, and said, quite simply, "I am a priest."

Now, there are very few Christians in India, and certainly very, very few priests. And of all the people in Calcutta I could have asked to be the incarnation of God for me, I had picked out a Roman Catholic priest. When I write my book on synchronicity, that story will most certainly be in it. I was just astonished. He took me by the hand, got lunch for me, paid for it before I could function, bade me good-bye, and walked off.

This is the homoerotic capacity in humankind. It is that specific quality, essentially indefinable, which happens between man and man and woman and woman. Other kinds of magic, not less by any means, happen between man and woman, or woman and man. But these others are specific man-to-man or woman-to-woman exchanges. They are the art of connection, the art of identity, the art of sympathy. At best, this art functions man to man and woman to woman. If this is an archetype, and I think it is, it must exist at least in story or myth form in the Western world, so I began looking, and yes, indeed, we have a wonderful homoerotic story from Greek mythology. It is the story of the Dioscuri, the divine children, better known as Gemini, the twins.

The story goes something like this: Leda, a mortal woman, lay with her husband one night and conceived identical twins, but in the same night Zeus, having fallen in love with her, came in the guise of a swan and also lay with her, and engendered another pair of identical twins. So here is a pair of pairs. They were all born in due time, and the earthly pair, fathered by a mortal man, is Castor and Helen, a boy and a girl, while the divine pair, sired by Zeus himself, is Pollux and Clytemnestra. There are many stories about these four people and their exploits, but the two boys make a friendship, become "buddies" (if such a slang term can bear such weight). They are bosom friends, blood brothers.

Together, their exploits are legion; they do wonderful things, they do terrible things. They get through all kinds of battles and scrapes. Then, heaven forbid, Castor, the mortal one, is killed. Zeus comes and tries to get Pollux, his son, to go off to Olympus and live with the gods, because he is indeed a god. Pollux refuses, saying stoutly, "If my beloved Castor can't come, I won't go." Zeus is beside himself, faced here with a terrible conundrum. Finally he relents. "All right. We will arrange it that the two of you shall live in Olympus one day, while the next day the two of you live in Hades, the underworld."

Pollux accepts this, and so they alternate, day by day. They go from heaven to hell one day, and then from hell to heaven the next.

However, the arrangement becomes quickly untenable, and they are both so miserable that finally Zeus, wrung to the heart by all of this, solves the dilemma by making them both immortal and putting them in the sky as the sign of Gemini. The twins live in perpetual embrace, reminding all of mankind throughout all of eternity of the nobility of friendship.

This is a classic Western story of the homoerotic way, of two men who love, alike enough to be very close and yet different, one mortal, the other immortal, opposites speaking to each other. I would like to suggest the possibility that this myth reveals a pattern of homoerotic, even homosexual relationships. Every pair of men is like this, be it the homoerotic relationships such as I describe in India or the homosexual pair, which is also known in India but is differentiated from the homoerotic. These relationships are a kind of Castor and Pollux story. Early in the relationship between the two men, they are delighted with each other and immediately go off to exploits. They will build something, set up something, make a project, Castor and Pollux out on the battlefield enjoying each other. Simply, the cooperation and the exchange between the two of them is lifeblood to them. Then one of them gets killed. The mortal side of the relationship is struck dead, and the relationship comes to a grinding, painful halt.

The halfhearted solution, which has some logic in back of it but doesn't work, finally, is that the relationship alternates between heaven and hell, almost alternate days. Things are good one day, bad the next. They get patched up and they are good the next day, and then they fall apart again. This is that painful section of relationship which few survive. If one will stay with it, finally the gods translate both elements, both people, into the sublime relationship of high consciousness or immortality, the truest possible between men.

It has been surmised that this Dioscuri quality turns up on many, many different levels, some of them entirely unexpected in our human affairs. One of them is the difference between the king and the high priest. One is heavenly, the other mortal, and it is said that they draw their archetypal validity or pattern from the twins, one mortal and the other immortal, like the pope and the emperors of the Middle Ages. This is in every male-to-male friendship. No matter who they have been before they touch each other, they unconsciously and unwittingly apportion out their lives to divinity and mortality. One of them takes charge of one of these aspects, and the other takes the opposite. For a time there is a wonderful exchange; then one side of it breaks down, and at best then they are alternating heaven and hell for a time. If they stay with it, finally relationship comes to its archetypal strength and is secure.

This pair, one mortal and the other immortal, turns up all over the world, from Jacob and Esau, to David and Jonathan, to Christ and Saint John the Divine, to Abbott and Costello, to Mutt and Jeff. The archetypal intrigue of the comic-book characters, these pairs which entertain us so much, stems from this archetypal structure. Years ago a friend and I were in Strasbourg in eastern France, ordering a meal. The waitress came, and we were halfway through our order when she suddenly broke into uncontrollable laughter and dashed for the kitchen. In two or three minutes she came back, tidied up, under control again. We got halfway through the order and she broke down again and dashed for the kitchen. Two or three minutes more and she came back and didn't even get started before she began giggling and fled once more. Five minutes later another waitress came and took our order. That's fine. My friend, who is more audacious than I was, called for the manager. He explained in excellent French, "There's nothing wrong, we are not in the least angry, we are not complaining . . . we're just curious: what happened to the waitress?" The manager said, "Oh, no, no, nothing," and tried to smooth it over. My friend said, "No, we're not angry, we're just humanly curious." So the manager went off and got the poor girl out of the kitchen, who was in convulsions of giggles by this time. "Mademoiselle, what was so funny?" And finally she blurted out, "They are just like Laurel and Hardy," and dashed to the kitchen again.

There's the archetypal structure of the tall, lean one, who is generally the divine one, and the short, round one, who is the earthy one. Of course you have Don Quixote and Sancho Panza before you. But it can go quite well the other way, so there is no corner on divinity for tall people.

I have exhausted my stories, but a final point is in order: unless one understands the degree of woundedness of the feeling function of Western man, especially the English-speaking world, one will not understand relationship in any aspect, homoerotic or otherwise.

Our superior function in the West in chiefly thinking, with sensation in accompaniment. So our inferior function is feeling.

I have wanted to talk about this situation in our culture for a long time, but had no structure, no framework to hang it upon. Finally I found the structure: the wounded Fisher King in the Grail legend. The Fisher King in his youthfulness blundered into a camp. No one was there, but a salmon was roasting on a spit over the fire, and the youth, being impetuous and very hungry, reached out to take some of the salmon. It was exceedingly hot. He dropped it, thrust his burnt fingers into his mouth to assuage them, got a little bit of the illicit salmon into his mouth, and groaned and shrieked in agony the rest of his life, but for three days. That is the wounded Fisher King in all of us modern people.

Another version of it is that he was found pilfering the salmon, and somebody shot an arrow which transfixed his two testicles, and it could not be pushed through and extricated, nor could it be pulled out. Yet another version, probably more to the point than any of these. The Fisher King had a half brother, sired by his father in the Orient, who was as dark as he was light. The two half brothers met, pulled down their visors, and went at each other, as good knights always do, and at the crash between these two opposing forces the Oriental brother was killed and the Fisher King was castrated. It so happened that the two were out and probably met each other because the Oriental one, pagan that he was, had had a dream of the Grail and was hunting for the treasure, and the Fisher King, the Christian one, was out on a foray to see if he could find fair damsels to exploit. He was off on the pagan journey. And these two things (please try to recognize them inside yourself, if you can, because that is where the story is pertinent) crashed head-on, and instinct died, and idealism was castrated. That's what has happened to our feeling function.

The story goes on. The Fisher King lies too ill to live, and yet he cannot die. Parsifal comes into the Grail castle, charged with a task to complete, but fails to ask the right question. In psychological terms he fails to make the matter conscious. Innocent fool (which is what the name *Parsifal* means), he does not do his duty because he does not insist or make his action conscious. So he goes off and spends twenty years rescuing fair maidens and lifting sieges and doing dragon battles. Finally, on Good Friday, somebody reminds him that he should go to the old hermit to make confession. The hermit gives him a bad time but finally gives him confession, and says, "Oh, by the way, the Grail castle is just down the road a little way. Turn left at the drawbridge, and there's the Grail castle." The awful wound of the Fisher King is that when the Grail is passed about and nourishes everyone, according to his wish, the Fisher King, the wounded feeling function, cannot partake of the Grail. There is no torture, no suffering, greater than being in the presence of beauty and enlightenment and not able to take it. That is the highest refinement of torture that there is. And that is the torture of the feeling function, as it exists in twentieth-century man.

Parsifal finds the Grail castle a second time and asks the question, "Whom does the Grail serve?" The answer immediately comes, "The Grail serves the Grail king." Not Parsifal, not the Fisher King, not the wounded one, but the Grail king who lives in the center of the Grail castle and whom we have not heard of before. The Grail king is healed at that moment and rises in a great triumph. The wounded Fisher King, Amfortas in Wagner's opera, rises and sings the most triumphant aria, because he is healed, and the whole kingdom is healed. He has only three days to live, which means that particular constellation of innocent fool and wounded Fisher King will simply be swept away because its usefulness in that dichotomy is over, and Parsifal continues on. This doesn't mean that you die three days after your enlightenment, but that particular constellation of things dies at that moment.

From our Western tradition, therefore, we have this final story of how wounded the feeling function is, a story of homoerotic relationship and its healing potential.

Enough.

Coming Home
The Late-Life Lesbian

CHRISTINE DOWNING

There are many different forms of lesbian love, each with its own etiology, mythology, and archetypal significance, each with its own gifts and dangers. In writing my book *Myths and Mysteries of Same-Sex Love*, I discovered how the Greek mythological traditions about Demeter, Hera, Athene, Artemis, and Aphrodite bring into view the beauty and power inherent in female bonds—and some of the darker, more fearful aspects as well. The stories in which these goddesses figure illumine the multidimensionality and diversity of the erotic relationships that exist between women.

In this essay I want to focus on the late-life lesbian. I choose this focus in part because her story is my story—though, actually, I know and celebrate that each of us who make our pull to women central in our lives only at midlife or later has her own individual story to tell. But there are many of us—and that in itself has implications that compel attentive consideration. For the prevalence of the pattern implies a radical critique of the dominant Jungian view of homosexuality, which sees it only as a phase preliminary to mature heterosexual adulthood. Reflection on this phenomenon may also reveal some of the most salient ways in which the archetypal meaning of women's love of women differs from that of men's love of men.

Looking back, I can say I have always loved women. My

mother, of course. She and I drew very close when I was two and three and four. My father had left Germany because of Hitler, and it was several years before we were able to rejoin him in America, though he did pay us two brief visits during those years, and my two younger siblings were born while he was gone. During that time we shuttled back and forth between the homes of my two sets of grandparents, both of whom were pressuring my mother to get a divorce, have an abortion, free herself of him. I was her only confidante. And though in surface ways she and I have sometimes been close, sometimes distant, in the intervening decades since those events the intensity and centrality of our bond have never been in question.

My sister, born just before we left Germany, has been my most important lifelong same-sex peer, the primary foil for my discovery of who I am and of what it means to honor and love another as *other*. Other females I have loved include the girl friends with whom I was intensely bonded during latency and adolescence, the teachers on whom I had crushes, the young woman with whom I was sexually involved while I was in college, and the women friends of my early adult life, some of whom on rare occasions became lovers as well. They also include the younger women who were formally my students and have often more truly been my teachers, and, perhaps more important than any of these, my daughter, who is herself a lesbian.

So I have always loved women, but I wasn't always fully conscious of how important a role this love has played in my life. I see that only retrospectively because of how central that love has become since I went through menopause a decade ago.

Odd, how the beginnings of my life as a lesbian and as a crone, a postmenopausal woman, have coincided. I had already begun to imagine that the love of women might become focal when, in my mid-forties after our children were grown, I'd left my husband and begun to live alone. But it hadn't happened then. I hadn't met the right *her* (or hadn't yet

become the right *she*). But then suddenly, surprisingly, unde-
niably, she was there. I fell passionately in love. We moved
toward one another gradually, gently, but from very early on I
knew I hoped to spend the rest of my life with her, to make love
with her and to share a home, to tell her my dreams and have
her tell me about hers, to read her poetry before anyone else
and to let her be my first reader. I was lucky. She had the same
hope and longing (or nearly so)—and some of the same fears.
We've been together ten years now, though I guess it depends
when you start counting. We've known each other for ten; we
began our courtship nine years ago, moved in together eight
years ago, celebrated our commitment in a ceremony seven
years ago, have just this year bought a home together on an
island in the Pacific Northwest. In the process of planning how
we'll shape our lives when we move there, we are discovering a
whole new level of commitment and love.

But although it is true that on looking back I am now more
aware of how I have always loved women, I do not mean that
the years I spent in a heterosexual marriage or the years I spent
ardently involved with male lovers were in some sense a
mistake or a misunderstanding—or even a detour. They were
as essential a part of my way as what I am living now. And I
still love men—though I do not imagine I will ever make love
with one again. I still feel drawn to sometimes, when I am with
men who have been lovers and whom I still love, or in my
dreams—but to respond to that pull might risk hurting the
woman I love in a way I could not bear. So (strange for me to
acknowledge, given my history) I suspect I will be monogamous for the rest of my life.

My turn to women is not a rejection of my heterosexual past
nor of men, but a moving beyond, part of my moving consciously into the last third of my life. It feels like a *return*—to
mother, to sister, to self—which may simply be a way of
saying that I feel myself in touch with the archetypal dimensions of this turning. I see my turn to this woman as a turn not

only to her but to women and in a sense also to "woman," and thus to self as woman. It feels numinous, sacred, necessary, almost fated. It feels like gift and blessing and culmination.

I see myself as now engaged in a continual circling and recircling around the images that have appeared and reappeared in my dreams and fantasies ever since I can remember—images of a numinous She awaiting my presence in a richly furnished secret chamber or in a dark underground cave. Honoring these images has become the central task of my life and now shapes not only my inner life but my outer life as well. What has come to matter is entering deeply *into* that life, not accumulating ever-new experiences. There is a sense in which being with the woman I love is not so much another episode to be added onto a narrative account of my life as it is a discovery of life as poetry, as shaped by the ever-recurrent image of Her.

It also feels as though this turning to women, this returning, is not simply personal or accidental, but rather that the pull to intense, focused, centralized engagement with women might become conscious and urgent for many women during their later years. In the postmenopausal phase of life, many of us seem to be pulled toward reflection and integration, to introspection and to a more introverted kind of intimacy. We long for a relationship with another drawn in the same direction and have learned that such another is much more likely to be female than male. We long for this relationship to involve us with all our being, body and soul, and so we hunger for something more than friendship, for love, for sexual as well as emotional intimacy. I know it was becoming conscious of this longing that prepared me for my present relationship.

I have always experienced sex as having a sacred aspect in its capacity to take one truly out of oneself, into an ecstatic meeting and merging—but in sexual intimacy with a woman the sacred dimension becomes for me almost overwhelmingly powerful. The entrance into another woman's body is the entrance into that sacred cave where Her presence is inescapable. As my fingers and tongue explore my beloved's vagina and approach her womb, I know myself to be returning to the place from which life emerges, the place from which I came and which I also carry within myself. This is an experience of *the* sacred, of the very source of life. Perhaps this is why women's turn to women may often happen later in life when it is time to engage life's deepest mysteries. Of course I know that many women experience their pull to women as having always been primary or even as the only form of sexual attraction they have experienced—but I would venture that the pull to women may have a specific soul meaning when it happens later.

That lovemaking among women may signify this reunion with the maternal source marks it as different from what lovemaking among men is likely to mean, and may relate to why most of the gay men I know feel they have always and inescapably been gay (whereas many lesbians I know tell their story with an emphasis on *choice*) and why most of my gay friends emphasize their sexual pull to men (whereas many lesbians emphasize emotional closeness).

As I reflect on my own experience, I am not at all sure how focal *sexual* preference is in my conviction that I, my soul, my body, are in a primary way now dedicated to being with women, and in particular with this woman. I imagine that among late-life lesbians there are many different responses to this question. In my own case, urgent, almost irresistible sexual attraction surely played a central part in pulling me into the relationship—in giving me the feeling *this* is the one with whom I want to spend the rest of my life, in giving me the courage to make a commitment to another when living alone had been so comfortable and when I knew so well that being in relationship is always challenging and difficult.

When my partner and I became lovers I was deeply moved by the discovery of how this was indeed a different sexuality— a truth that had somehow been less evident to me in my earlier sexual encounters with women. Now I learned not only how different it is to caress a woman's breasts and vulva and clitoris and to enter another's vagina with my fingers and lips than it is to make love to a man's body, but also how different it is to be caressed and entered *by* another whose body and desires are also female. The rhythms of touching are different, the place that orgasm plays in lovemaking is different, the taking the time to focus fully on one partner's longings and then the other's was different. When Adrienne Rich speaks of "a whole new poetry beginning here," I know what she means. I was learning a whole new language of love and, for someone who had thought of herself as an adept lover, this was not always easy. It involved unlearning; it seemed also to involve relearning almost forgotten but remembered-in-my-body modes of physical touch.

I also discovered that same-sex sex does not mean making love with another just like oneself. I learned to my initial confusion that what she desires is subtly different from what I desire, that what stirs her most deeply is different, that her rhythms are different. Over the years it has become clear that she (who is more than fifteen years younger than I) feels sexual longing more intensely and more frequently than do I, at least than do I now. This, too, is a surprise; I had always thought of myself as *so* sexual. . . .

As domestic rhythms have become more central to our relationship during our years of living together, I have come to question how pivotal the sex part is after all. Was it mostly just the path? The choice to be with her no longer seems exactly a sexual choice, at least not in the genital, orgasm sense of sex—though in the more expanded understanding of the poly-morphousness of human sexuality, which I learned from Freud, perhaps it *is* a sexual choice. Physical closeness, emotional intimacy, trust in one another, the sense of being fully relaxed in one another's presence—these are so important. Because I recognize much of this as characteristic of what we think of as "infantile sexuality," I could agree that there is a *regressive* aspect to the sexual dimension of our relationship. Yet by "regressive" I would intend to invoke not pathology but once again the theme of return, recircling, homecoming. It seems evident to me that really we go forward, not back, that we turn to one another as the persons we've become through all our years of living. An inexpungible nostalgia for our beginnings is not incommensurable with the recognition that we cannot literally return.

Of course, lesbian relationships, almost irrespective of how central sexuality is to any particular couple, are *transgressive*, socially-tabooed relationships. To enter such a relationship relatively late in life may entail the taking off of yet another *persona*, yet another mask. We may come, perhaps even more clearly than before, to know ourselves as we are apart from conventional gender roles. Our whole sense of personhood may be transformed as we discover the irrelevance to our self-understanding of conventional notions of masculinity or femininity. We are not simply making a different "object choice," but we experience ourselves differently. We may even discover that neither *heterosexual* nor *homosexual* nor even *bisexual* adequately describes what is now a much more fluid sense of our sexual identity, or that of others. I have come to question not only the masculine-feminine polarity but also the very notion of opposite sex and same sex. The "opposite" sex is not really opposite, but neither is a same-sex other the same.

Perhaps the *joy* of discovering a different, more subtle, perhaps more vitalizing kind of "difference" is especially vivid when it comes as a gift late in life. I certainly know how amazed I have been to discover how new my relationship with my partner still feels after ten years, how unknown *and* known she still seems, how much about ourselves and one another we keep discovering.

Of course, the turn of woman to woman inevitably reactivates the Mother-Daughter archetype. Women loving women may feel free to acknowledge our unstilled longing to nurture and be nurtured, to be mother and child, to be mothered and be daughtered—and to indulge those longings as best we can. But because of all we have learned elsewhere in our lives, we may be able to do so without being caught in fantasies of giving or being given a fully sufficient mothering, and without falling into a pattern of interaction where one is always the mother, the other always the child.

Nor is the Mother-Daughter archetype the only one that may inform our relationships. Just as salient is the archetype of Sister-Sister bonding, felt primarily in the ways we challenge one another to be all that we are capable of being and seek to engage one another in ways that are truly egalitarian, mutual, reciprocal. I feel the Sister archetype at work in my partner's demand that I be there toward her as all that I am, that I risk sharing my powerfulness and my vulnerability, my desire and my fear, my appreciation and my anger—and that I encourage her to do the same. Almost every lesbian couple I know struggles to find ways to cultivate intimacy and yet respect one another's *otherness* and need for some distance, some life apart from the relationship. We struggle to find ways to sister one another well, to bless rather than resent the differences, competition, and conflict that inevitably emerge as the "archetypal haze" induced by the initial hegemony of the Mother archetype begins to dissipate.

Our relationship is certainly not all harmony and fusion. I know it would not satisfy my soul needs if it were. Yet I also know that I usually don't like at all the particular ways in which disharmony manifests. I still fear her anger, and my own. I wish she didn't envy me my worldly accomplishments and recognitions, didn't resent my involvements with my children, didn't fear that I might someday after all abandon her. There are times when the demand that I fully and honestly open my soul to her seems to ask for more than I can give. At times I experience her as a "soulsnatcher" and do everything in my power to protect myself from her. But it is precisely through these only half-welcomed challenges that the relationship activates the archetype of the Self. I am brought into touch with so much that is *me* and yet unfamiliar and almost inaccessible. All truly vital relationships do this, but I believe a relationship with an intimate same-sex other does so in an especially powerful way. For she seems to know my potentialities and my defenses almost as though from within. She can get *through* to a hitherto impregnable core. I had not consciously wanted that from this relationship, had felt satisfied with the me I knew, had not imagined that so late in life I could be so flooded with renewed life energy.

Indeed, part of what makes this turn to her feel like a homecoming is the heightened sense of energy, the experience of renewal, that has accompanied it. The sense of being in the world in a new way is comparable to what Jung says happens when we integrate the "transcendent function" and move beyond our familiar reliance on feeling or thinking or whatever has been our dominant function and respond instead on the basis of our "inferior" functions.

Yet, like all relationships, this late-life lesbian attachment has its "shadow" side. One aspect of this is simply the inevitable "coming down" from the elation that characterized its beginnings, the ebbing of the exhilaration that seems almost always to accompany a reengagement with the archetypal. I call this "learning again about finitude." Certainly I have had to learn again the limits of any relationship to fulfill me, have had to learn again to rebalance the pulls of intimacy and solitude, love and work, or, as we might say, of Aphrodite and Artemis, Aphrodite and Athene. More painfully, I have had to learn anew the limits of my capacity to change, even when I might wish I could be different in the ways my partner wishes I were different. I am stubborn, resistant, fearful, and controlling. I am me, and though still in process and profoundly affected by this woman I love, I am in some ways stuck with being *this* me—and stuck, too, with *this* her (for I could imagine her as different, too!).

In a deeper sense, the shadow side of the homecoming comes from the fact that everything that I consciously attend to during this last third of life becomes part of my preparation for death. My partner and I have known this ever since we first came together. I remember so vividly how, when she first realized that I wasn't already making plans to leave after our first real moment of intimacy, but rather hoped to be with her for the rest of my life, she cried out, "But then you'll die and leave me anyway." We laughed, but it is likely to be true—not for a long while, probably, given the longevity of my parents, but someday nonetheless. That recognition, of course, would very likely enter into any late-life relationship and perhaps especially into a relationship where there is a significant disparity of age. But I believe there is more to it than that. I believe that there is an intrinsic connection between my coming to love this woman and my awareness of death's approach, though I did not see this until I was already deeply in love with her.

For directing my love to a woman feels like a homecoming in the most profound of all ways. My turning to her, this very particular, flawed, beautiful woman whom I love, signifies, among so much else, a return to the womb that gave us birth and which also welcomes us when we die, a return to earth, to Her, and to all those human women who in some way serve Her and represent Her.

Individuation and Eros
Finding My Way

CAROLINE T. STEVENS

As I have become more conscious of personal possibilities, aware and accepting of the variety I harbor, I have been less and less concerned about my culture's definition of me. Thirty years ago, the mother of young children, I wanted to go back to college, though this was not what mothers did in the fifties, and I wondered about my "womanliness," my feminine identity, the status of my wife- and motherhood were I to honor my wish. But the urge was stronger than the self-doubt, and at last I realized that as a woman, an obvious and inescapable physiological fact, I defined womanhood. What I did, I saw, was what a woman did.

A woman may love men, may marry, may bear children, or she may not. A woman may work in the home, the office, the factory, or the lab. She may acquire a Ph.D. and a profession. She may write a novel or a grant, paint a house or a painting, run a race or a business, or she may not. Some of these I have done, with struggle and with gusto, and others I have not. Past sixty, I have fallen in love with a woman, and this, too, is what a woman does. Not every woman, obviously, but it is no less an authentic possibility for that.

The Jungian understanding of psychological well-being involves progress on a path called individuation. We are to become more and more fully what each of us uniquely is.

Along the way we are required to recognize and embrace aspects of ourselves not previously known or welcomed into the conscious identity, perhaps not well received by the family and culture in which we have grown to adulthood. Certain of these aspects, called "shadow," appear as same-sex figures in our dreams or in same-sex others in the day-world, for whom we may feel both fascination and repulsion. The qualities these shadow figures reveal, as unpleasant as we may find them, are likely to be within the realm of possibility that our culture defines as belonging to our own sex.

If we have been raised to be demure and dignified, a wanton, vulgar shadow may haunt our dreams, wearing bright, cheap clothes, flaunting her sexuality. If we repress an "unacceptable" anger, our shadow sister is likely to rage, striking out at those who wrong her, while the dream ego stands by wringing her hands and trying to restore the peace. Self-forgetfulness and generosity, too blindly and earnestly practiced in the day-world, may bring a greedy and demanding young girl to life in our dreams, where she will steal from the fancy clothing store we cannot afford to patronize and devour the last helping of the wonderful dessert we have prepared for the family.

The brighter and more virtuous our conscious identity, the darker the shadow will loom. At first we may try to strengthen our defenses against unwelcome self-knowledge, but the more rigidly we cling to the light, the more urgent and threatening become the appearances of shadow in our dreams and the more likely we are to betray our ideals by our behavior. Perhaps we will fall into an affair or rage at a helpless child; perhaps we will find ourselves indulging in pastries when no one is looking or even, compulsively, shoplifting. With luck and support, however, we may find it possible to open our awareness to our "imperfections" before too much damage is done to our lives, becoming in the process more charitable toward the failings of others, and even discovering that these shadow aspects of ourselves conceal vital possibilities for our own development. We may find a capacity for passion that enriches and challenges ourselves and our mates, an ability to defend ourselves against abuse, an acceptance of a legitimate personal need for emotional and physical nurture.

In some ways more difficult for a woman to accommodate or assimilate are encounters with contrasexual others, those who image and embody the qualities our culture defines as belonging properly to men. In the classical Jungian understanding, these "animus" figures appear in our dreams to announce the presence in the woman's psyche of masculine qualities. It then becomes the task of the dreamer to develop a constructive relationship with these figures, so that the possibilities they reveal may find appropriate expression in the outer world. When a woman has a "powerful animus," she is urged by traditional Jungians to "put him to work." It is said that her failure to do so will cause him to turn negative, attacking both ego and others. If she does not develop her conscious contact with animus figures, her creative abilities will be unrealized. Her capacity to initiate action in the world will be paralyzed by the barrage of judgments and denigrations laid down by the frustrated animus. Now and again she will be possessed by this masculine spirit, becoming unpleasantly argumentative and opinionated, losing for the time her "feminine" capacity for relationship.

It is tricky work to accomplish an appropriate relationship with the animus, of course, and for two reasons. First, as noted by Jung, the woman who attempts to make room in her life for expressions of "masculine" abilities runs the risk of losing her feminine persona.[1] That loss, we fear, may carry a high social price. A woman who "puts the animus to work" may be defined out of socially acceptable womanhood by both inner and outer voices. She may fear loneliness and rejection, not always without reason.

But even if we find the (manly?) courage to court these

dangers in the higher pursuit of individuation, we face a deeper difficulty. In order to establish a creative relationship with a powerful animus, we must find a source of authority in the feminine that is equal to or greater than his own. As Irene Claremont de Castillejo observed, the animus may function beautifully as the torchbearer, the one who lights the way with his focused masculine logos, but it is up to the woman to choose the goal, to choose the path he will illuminate.[2] If she does not exercise this power of choice, the animus may lead her astray, into realms of activity and modes of behavior she would not otherwise select: the dreaded "animus possession." And at this level, more than an acceptable persona is threatened; we feel our very identities as women at risk.

The character of this double-bind is expressed in the common Jungian opposition of love and power, with love regarded as the realm of the feminine and power belonging to the masculine. Here, too, the task of individuation requires that the powerful animus be encountered and so far as possible integrated; and yet, if power is thought to be "archetypally" masculine, it can never be fully integrated by the conscious feminine personality. To be primarily and exclusively identified with the capacity for loving relationship, as women often are, renders women ill-suited to the owning and expression of power. As Marion Woodman observed of Lady Macbeth, power concerns are "alien to feminine identity" as such identity is defined in traditional Jungian (and cultural) terms.[3]

And so: women are to individuate, that is, to become more and more fully what each of us uniquely is, which requires the appropriation of the powers and talents of the animus. But women are also told that we should express that development only within the bounds of a traditionally feminine identity, presenting an adequately feminine persona; that is, it would seem, not at all. The way out of this box for many Jungians has been to espouse, too often rather vaguely, the notion of androgyny. We may be women, but we are "really" both masculine and feminine. This approach begs the question of authority. Which "half" is the "better" one when we come to definition, decision, and action? In our culture and in our theory, the answer has been clear. Omnipotence, omniscience, and creative power belong to the Father and Son and, in somewhat diluted form, to men and to the animus. Perhaps it is no wonder that many of us are inclined to leave the expression of "masculine" logos, creativity, enterprise, and power to men.

After many years of study and personal analysis, I came to an impasse, expressed especially in my inability to get on with the task of writing my diploma thesis, the final task in the completion of my Jungian training. I want to make it clear that prior to training I had become free to own consciously and explicitly some of the abilities defined by Jung as masculine. I had written a dissertation on the philosophy of psychology, gotten my Ph.D., moved rather bravely into unfamiliar regions of the world and of psyche. The diploma thesis, however, involved a claim to my own vision and to full authority in my profession, and here I got stuck. Then I had three dreams:

> Having finished my meal in a restaurant, I wish to leave. But the waiter will not bring me my check, and fearing the watchful eye of the manager, I cannot simply go.

> In a parking garage, and unable to leave because the attendant will not validate my ticket.

> I am offered the opportunity to live and work in an experimental colony on Mars. I ask "my man" what he might find to do there; he looks sad and says nothing. And I say to him, "Then I won't go either, because our relationship means more to me than this opportunity." Then I am on Mars in a large, protective bubble, observing the residents outside coming and going, absorbed in their tasks. I feel an intense physical longing to be among them, breathing that new air, but the woman in charge says I may not because I am only a visitor, and only those committed to the task can leave the protective bubble.

The ego depicted in these three dreams is bound by a "feminine" lack of assertiveness and a "feminine" willingness to put relationship before personal enterprise. As I pondered the dreams, I realized that my reliance on the masculine to take the lead, to provide the means, and to give permission to proceed with my task was the real problem. The "woman in charge" made it plain that further movement depended upon my conscious assumption of the risks and burdens of commitment to my work. I had to be willing to live on a world named for the god of war and let the animus follow me and assist me if he could and would. The authority for this action was mine, whether I liked it or not, and was derived from a superior female being in psyche, called in the dream "the woman in charge."

In Jungian theory, all of the psychological movement called individuation is under the guidance and impetus of a power called the Self. As a theoretical construct, the Self is "a borderline concept, expressing a reality to which no limits can be set."[4] Jung chose the term, he tells us, because it is "definite enough to convey the essence of human wholeness and on the other hand indefinite enough to express the indescribable and indeterminate nature of this wholeness."[5] The Self "cannot be distinguished from an archetypal God-image."[6] Moreover, "since man knows himself [sic] only as an ego, and the Self, as a totality, is indescribable and indistinguishable from a God-image, self-realization amounts to God's incarnation."[7] Jung further states:

> Every force and every phenomenon is a special form of energy. Form is both an image and a mode of manifestation. It expresses two things: the energy which takes shape in it, and the medium in which that energy appears.
>
> I am therefore of the opinion that, in general, psychic energy or libido creates the God-image by making use of archetypal patterns, and that man in consequence worships the psychic force within him as something divine.[8]

Or, to put it more directly, as playwright Ntozuke Shange exults, a woman may find god in herself and love her fiercely![9] And I began to see in "the woman in charge" a female image of divine energy, a feminine Self figure challenging me to move beyond the "protective bubble" of an old and limiting gender definition.

Now, as a collection intended to lift same-sex love into focus, this volume addresses the question: what contributions to the understanding of individuation may be provided by those whose love, including sexual love, for same-sex others is central to their lives? A general response to this question is that those who know themselves as gay or lesbian have known themselves defined as Other: other than either of their parents, who have lived and loved, most commonly, as heterosexuals; other than the dominant models and myths and expectations of the culture in which their lives unfold. When the collective does not mirror and support self-perception and personal experience, one must be willing to sacrifice the comfort of collective approval. One must turn, instead, to the source which in fact lives beneath all cultures, beneath all the manifestations of culture that appear in the lives of individuals. In Jungian terms, we must look to the Self.

We are required to look within and to affirm the truth of what we find, whether our discovery is of talents and ambitions not "normally" assigned to our gender, or of a passionate longing for physical and emotional intimacy with a member of our own sex. As human beings, we are all of us necessarily pathfinders, though it may be that gay men and lesbians are among the most conscious of that human necessity. Between this most general of observations, however, and the individual journey, between the core concepts and their application to an individual life, what can be said? I have asked myself, what can it mean to anyone else that I choose to love and live with a woman in these latter years of my life? It seems to me that generalizations about love are as risky as generalizations about individuation; to put it another way, both love stories and individuation stories are first and foremost personal stories. You may find your own story reflected in mine or you may not, while psychological theories tend to claim a general truth.

This claim to general truth is especially sweeping when we speak of archetypes, those universal and eternal patterns of human possibility which Jung found to underlie all human experience. They are discovered at work in every life. They are celebrated in myth and fairy tale and legend around the world. The Hero, the Child, Mother and Father, the Wise Old Man and the Witch, Anima and Animus, the multitude of gods and goddesses that inhabit the religions of the world, all these can be expressed in the lives of persons and of the cultures they create. And yet, in times of great public or personal change, however eternal the archetype, the image through which it manifests can fade, can alter, can sicken and die, and with it the world it enlivened. A dominant archetype can fade from a life or from a culture, but in either case someone who hopes for an authentic life, for individuation, must let go of the old and wait for the new guiding image to emerge.

You may recall from the dreams reported above that such a transformation of image did emerge for me after some years of confusion and uncertainty, a Self image called "the woman in charge." Indeed, there had been other such feminine authorities in my dreams, but their central significance for me had not before been so plain. In Zurich, years before, I had dreamed of a warrior queen who deployed her troops and her male advisors with ruthless efficiency; of an abbess who gave me an orange and advised me not to enter a convent; of the Holy Virgin, who suggested that my readiness for self-sacrifice was uncalled for. I stepped into a fire nevertheless; she led me out and applied a balm to my burned right hand.

I now see that all I had been reading of masculine logos and feminine eros had blocked me from understanding these feminine figures. I was, after all, busy at work interpreting fairy tales whose denouement was the wedding of prince and maiden. I was studying Jung's interpretation of alchemical images, discovering the *coniunctio*, the *hieros gamos*, the coming together of Sun King and Moon Queen to form the androgyne, the ultimate image of wholeness. The feminine powers in my dreams, never mind their expression of both spiritual and temporal authority, according to the theory I was imbibing must express only the feminine half of my whole-ness, and this eminently heterosexual image of interior one-ness was reflected and reinforced by the image of the heterosexual couple as the acme of personal fulfillment in the outer world. The historical resonance given to heterosexuality, I believe, explains much of the androgyne's hold on my own imagination, and on Jungian theorizing as well. And yet, Jung himself spoke of the androgyne as only one symbol of the Self among others, only one imaginal expression of something in itself essentially "indescribable and indeterminate."[10]

Given my dreams and the burgeoning experience of the Self as feminine, two problems confronted me in the acceptance of the androgyne as the image of inner wholeness. In my dreams, the masculine ruled the moon, not the sun. My animus figures were dark and Dionysian, erotic and earthy; they did not express the logos and spirit that "archetypally" it seemed they should. But this reversal was a minor difficulty compared to the second: the androgynous image of the Self clouded the issue of whence the ultimate authority for my life as a woman derived. Nevertheless, in spite of these problems and perhaps because of my continuing spiritual and intellectual interests, the insistence upon a masculine element in the Self reinforced the culture's teaching that creativity, initiative, and power belonged to something which for me as a woman could only be other, something which I could not truly own as my deepest self: "the masculine."

I returned to the States from Switzerland with this burden and fell once more "madly" in love with a man of sorrows, of unfulfilled potential, a man who could not bring to full expression his evident writing talent. I continued my training and my struggle with the theory and practice that had seemed to offer a freedom of growth and expression I had not yet fully experienced. I tried to write a thesis on Dionysus as a Self image, for he was the god above others I had come to know and revere. But the thesis wouldn't come.

Meanwhile, my personal analysis was at last returning me to the girl-child I had been, to the active eros, intellect, and spirituality she had once embodied and never found fully received in her world. At last I began to realize that the Self of which Jung had spoken had been and continued to be made manifest for me in feminine images. The Queen, the Holy Virgin, the Witch, the Woman in Charge, and all the goddesses began to live more and more vividly for me and came to express the "superordinate personality" Jung had identified as the ultimate guide and motivating power on the path of individuation. The child in me was finding her validation as a daughter of the Goddess, and she began at last to find expression in my life.

I began to write, at first in great anger, of the failures of the mapmakers, most immediately of the failure of the Jungian map more fully to illuminate my journey and those of the women who were beginning to come to me as a student analyst. I saw how they and I had projected the authority of the Self upon men. I saw how they and I struggled to claim and express intellectual, creative, and spiritual abilities in a culture that allotted these gifts to men, in a theoretical community that named these qualities of mind and soul as archetypally masculine. I began to work out an understanding of our journeys which was certainly grounded in Jungian thought, in the Jungian understanding of psychological growth and fulfillment and in the Jungian concept of the Self as their source and goal, but with this difference: however important the role of men in our outer lives and of the animus in our inner lives, the Self,

containing all my potential and authority as a woman, is not
fundamentally androgynous, certainly not masculine, but
wholly and unequivocally feminine.

I had another dream:

> I am on a treasure hunt with others, including a strong, blond,
> somewhat younger man. He and I embrace, confirming our spe-
> cial relationship. The treasure we seek has been seen before, but
> now its location is unknown. A river's course has been altered,
> making the landscape unfamiliar, but I realize we can follow the
> river to its source and so come to the cavern where the treasure is
> hidden. As we approach, the cavern becomes a place of purifica-
> tion for men and women, with separate sections for each. I will
> enter the women's side.

As I wrote my thesis, at last, on the treasure of the feminine
Self, my anger at the misleading, masculine mapmakers of
culture, religion, and theory fell away. They may be a little
overbearing, but they are engaged in a basic human endeavor,
elaborating and evangelizing for their very own saving vision,
attempting to create a world in which they can feel safe and
free. They have, in fact, however blindly and ruthlessly, un-
dertaken the task which I recognize is mine as well, and yours.
Discover your vision, give it form, and manifest it in the world
you inhabit. If it enables others, so much the better.

In the manner of all who manage to speak of such matters, I
believe my vision may be, in fact, enabling to others. I believe
that the recognition of a gendered Self provides the most
expansive vessel for the experience of any and all of our
capabilities as women or as men. I believe that the road to the
recovery of the treasure, to the Self and renewed creativity for
men and women and the culture itself, now lies through the
recognition of the feminine and of the masculine as separate
and co-creative powers. When neither masculine nor feminine
is found to be derivative from a more desirable other, when
both men and women are valued for their authenticity rather

than their complementarity, then we will discover not only ourselves, but, perhaps for the first time, the reality of relationship.

So saying, I fell in love with a woman. Eros is the engine that drives our lives, leading us into connections within ourselves and with others that will require and enable further self-discovery; logos follows as best it can, making conscious sense of necessity. Every love in my life has been real and important, an essential part of the journey, this last no more so than the others. What this love of woman gives me, however, is room, a room of my own which can be shared with another without the necessity of playing a gender role or complementing another's. I no longer have the doubtful comfort, the oppressive safety of "fitting" into a role-defined identity, one-half of a human wholeness. Out of our likeness and our authentic difference, not prescribed but discovered, my partner and I create together a home and a way of life that make possible both pleasure and joy, and a vision that enables each of us to manifest most fully what is in us to give to others.

I do not think this is impossible between men and women. I imagined it at twenty, newly married to the man who would become the father of my children. I imagined it then, but I was naive. I had a great deal to discover before it happened, much to learn about myself and the barriers to full partnership my world contained. Above all, I had much to claim of my own powers, along with the responsibilities they entail. Perhaps it is true that the co-creative relationship I describe is less difficult to sustain between same-sex partners, simply because the requirements of gender performance and the blinding projections which must follow do not intrude. But I'm still finding my way, and I can only speculate about what may be possible for others. I am grateful my way has brought me here, into a loving companionship that does not cost me myself.

Notes

1. C. G. Jung, "Woman in Europe" (1927), in *The Collected Works of C. G. Jung* [CW], vol. 10 (Princeton: Princeton University Press, 1970), para. 243.

2. Irene Claremont de Castillejo, "The Animus—Friend or Foe," in *Knowing Woman: A Feminine Psychology* (Boston: Shambhala Publications, 1990), pp. 73–89.

3. Marion Woodman, *Addiction to Perfection: The Still Unravished Bride* (Toronto: Inner City Books, 1982), p. 19.

4. Jung, CW 12 (1968), p. 355n.

5. Ibid., para. 20.

6. Jung, CW 11 (1969), para. 238.

7. Ibid., para. 233.

8. Jung, CW 5 (1967), paras. 128, 129.

9. Ntozuke Shange, *For Colored Girls Who Have Considered Suicide When the Rainbow Is Enuf* (New York: Bantam Books, 1980), p. 67.

10. In one discussion concerning the Self, Jung insisted that the appearance of a hermaphroditic figure "is a pre-stage. But the divine form in a woman is a woman, as in a man it is a man. . . ." C. G. Jung, *The Visions Seminars, Book Two* (Zurich: Spring Publications, 1976), p. 456. See also CW 9/1 (1968), para. 310.

Her Radiance Everywhere
Poems from a Midlife Awakening

MORGAN FARLEY

These poems are addressed to a woman whose love changed my life—all but the first and last, which serve as prologue and epilogue. The first came like a prophetic dream months before I had any conscious notion of ever being intimate with a woman. The last reflects the inner marriage forged when the union in the world dissolved. All the rest were inspired by her and fueled by my need to let her know how deeply she moved me. With these words I wooed her, bared myself to her, celebrated her, challenged her, let her go. I offer them as a faithful account of what I lived with her.

I have called it an awakening because this woman's love and desire for me broke me open and made it impossible for me to live as I had lived. I had to leap from one world into another to meet her: from innocence into extremes of experience, from safety into enormous risk. She danced me down into the deep roots of my body, reached into me and found the selves I had lost. I gave birth to myself between her legs.

The poems give voice to an archetypal and initiatory dimension of the love between women. They locate this love in a sacred, communal ground. When a woman opens her body to another in ecstasy and anguish, she discovers in herself the earth and stars, all the animals, the wellsprings of aliveness.

For such a woman, to claim the embodied self is to embrace
the world.

   More might be said of this rite of passage, but I am reluctant
to make maps of such a personal journey. To me, what is of
value in these poems is inseparable from what is most particular: the voice of one woman speaking to another in love.

A Woman Is Waiting

A woman who comes to draw the boat of tears
out of the silent rushes, is waiting
for me to wake, she is waiting
for my breasts to gush sweet milk
warm with the blood heat of forgotten languages
she waits for the great cry that will
split the world in two
like lightning splitting the oak
that has grown for a thousand years
and as she waits, there is
a smile on her face, a secret smile

she holds up the golden cup, the Grail
brimming with dark wine, and lets it
drop through her fingers
smash and splatter
she grinds the bread under her heel
like the Virgin stamping out the snake
and the snakes under her skirts
hiss and rattle, their tongues
flickering like flames

oh she is waiting
in my body, this woman
who has no mercy, no pity
hair like polished steel
her breath is the wind

that scours the open places
laying them bare, she loves
to pick the bones clean of flesh
and lay them out in rows
for auguries, she whistles
the moon down into her cave
and leaves the sky dark all night
the hills black, the roads hidden

oh my mother who is this
waiting with her
hollow sleeves?
she will burn all my boats
set them blazing on the water
just to see how they
shake and ripple in the darkness
drifting in toward shore

> My child she is your sister
> your lover friend ally anointer
> she will soothe your body with pungent oils
> smoothing them down along your limbs
> entering the secret places with her
> soft fingers, she will press
> on every door in your body
> until the last one opens
> and bats stream out blind and purposeful
> darkening the sky
>
> she will leave you
> empty and full, spent
> and refreshed, she will
> lick up the tears of every pore
> washing you like a cat her kittens
> she will lick you
> alive again, drawing back

the caul from your face
seducing your blood
to flow into new channels
like a river that finds
a small crack in its bank
and probes and probes until solid ground
gives way before its ardor

I am sorry I wrote this down, I am sorry I
let her in
this far, what
will become of me?

What you will become
is something she wrote
on a rock in another time
hacking it deep into the stone
in a hidden place high above the river
where none of the village dwellers dared to go

you are raven to her and ravished
you are rivulets running together
you are the waterfall that veils the cave
and the cave
and the bear that sits
in the back of the cave
her red eyes two
rubies in the blackness

ask her your real name if you dare
she knows you the way your dreams do
put out your hand and touch her fur
and find the end of all trembling
in her rough arms

she is massive and warm
she knows you, go to her

she will feed you blackberries and honey
she will teach you the ways
of the fish who glide against the current
and the flashing paw, the spread claw
the appeasing of hunger

she will teach you to claim
what is yours
to enter the cave of your body
like a queen taking possession of her castle
she will teach you the tread
that presses into the earth
leaving a mark, a signature

Oh I could run with bears and never miss
my mother, and forget
the name she gave me
I could grow brown and juicy, my lips
stained purple with berries, my breasts
ripe and succulent as plums
I could live in the woods as if I
belonged there, but I couldn't
sleep, even in her arms
I couldn't sleep the winter through
endure that dying and that being born
year after year the cold
waking into light
groaning walk into the world again
flesh hanging from me like some discarded garment
my long dream unravelling
behind my dazzled eyes

what then to do
in daylight, after
the hard resurrection?

Threshold

And woman, I am set toward you
like a compass to a star
walking underwater canyons, starry chasms
wading through snow
waist-deep, my eyes fixed
on the light that burns in your window

And I can't get out of bed this morning
needing some touchstone to cling to
some sureness to take with me
into the newness
of your breath, your rosy breasts
into the meeting with your eyes

But I will come
empty-handed, naked
to your touch, I will step
over the threshold
of the door you stand in
bringing nothing but who I am—
hearing the child whimper
the great animals rattle their cages
the angels gathering to sing

Calling You

today I take my whole
life in my hands
hold it up to the light
that pours from your eyes
turn it over and over

it is round and full in my palms
as that creature you found in clear water in Florida

all vulva only softer
the color of woman
with a small juicy mouth

I am listening, holding
this weight up to my ear
like a shell, waiting
for the word spoken underwater
the yes! the now! the bloom, grow, ahhh

I put a finger into that opening
the way I probe deep into you
to find the secret you have never told anyone
the name you have not whispered
even to yourself

it is warm inside
and tender, sensitive
as a wound, wet
as a newborn, rippling
like light on water

> *come, it says, come*
> *come in   come close   closer*
> *touch taste feel O feel*
> *me alive and soft*
> *open to receive you*
>
> *gather me*
> *pierce me*
> *lay me out wide as a prairie*
> *wash me like wind*
> *I want   I want you*

this is the song my life sings to me
like a star in my cupped hands
like a mother with her firstborn

at her breast, like the open
furrow to the rain

hear it, lover, it is
all I have to offer, this
little voice liberated
faint as angels
calling you

Holy Land

to speak of you
as you lie across the bed
in the pale light of a winter afternoon

I would have to summon
white doves
to flutter from my open mouth

so I enter you silent
as a pilgrim approaching the holy land
knees weak with longing

that is your music
the moment
when the pilgrim kneels to kiss the ground

Gold

I leap chasms to come to you
swan dive into canyons
to plumb your depths

you are the gold
winking in the river
washed by summit snows

you are the carp in the still pool
rising
stalling the dipped oar

let me learn you like a new tongue
a word that opens ancient doors
onto gardens drenched in dew

lie with me
where four roads meet
at the empty center

see the ten thousand things
bloom
around us

Two Girls at the River

walking under trees with you
our feet in white sneakers stirring the dust
of the path by the river, two women
strolling like chums, I know you

as a girl beside the St. Joe
brownskinnned tomboy leaning into the depths
I find myself again on the banks of the Ottawa
pressing cups and bowls out of wet grey clay

I said, vessel; you said, wand
twisting a green willow to trail in the water
fishing for mermaids while I threw out my line
for a laugh from Daddy in the rocking boat

this is the walk we promised ourselves
as children: that someone come
who hears the river singing
and calls us by our real names

Uncaging the Animals

now that I have plunged with you
to the bottom of the sea
and found there the fire
that is never extinguished

now that I have curled
inside the moon with you
and heard the singing the mermaids hear
waking from long slumber

now that I have rolled with you
in the great waves
with the seals and flashing dolphins
with the motionless whales

lover, now
I can take my daughter on my lap
and tell her about
uncaging the animals—

the beloved deer, the black-maned lion, the bear—
teach her
when to loose them
and with whom

and how to make a sacred grove
for them to gambol in
speaking with each other
in their soft animal tongues

and now, having touched
your face in the dark
with fingertips ancient as parchment
new as plum blossom

now I can put out my hand
to the terrible blank mask
that stares at me always
and reaching through it with soft fingers

stroke the stubble on my father's cheek

The Mare

You waltz into my bedroom
bringing the morning
chrysanthemums and kisses
cool cheeks, a warm hand
to slip under flannel

I uncurl, waking up
to the dazzle of you
as if the sun had somehow
slipped through the curtains
to fall full-length on the bed

Your mouth seeking me
pierces some membrane
some taut skin I have
held over my waters
and the skinless creatures who live there

With milky eyes, webbed
fingers floating, they huddle away
from your soft knocking
cowering blind in corners
where the light never reaches

Unborn, raw
as a wound, they shiver
before your warmth

They have never been touched, and you
lick them alive the way

the mare licks her stunned foal
nuzzling and nudging
her warm breath sighing
over the spindle legs, the matted hair
her tongue saying, Get up and live

The Grimy Child

This is the place your mouth finds me:
crack in the cellar door
cold breath of autumn sighing through it
a child sobbing in the dark behind the furnace
where no one will ever look

Where I am all alone, where I have
always been alone
you gather me up against your softness
enter loneliness to be with me
falling and falling and not letting go

I open my eyes to the light in yours
dawn rising behind the dark mesa
this house warmed through, the grimy child
carried to the sofa soot and all
and sung to until she sleeps

Birth

you take me down into the dark
where I have been waiting for myself
with a rage more faithful than love

you find me back where I
lost myself
rag doll in a bed of rape

and if I threaten to leave you, it is
her face I am running from, the mask
ripped off, the bloody howl released

birth is crude, the contractions
grab you like a fist, drop you
panting and shaken

I had no choice then and I have
no choice now—
the answer is yes, take everything

Leaving the Garden

Thunder like a grey wolf growls in the north
under a grey cloud, and in the west
lightning flickers a semaphore over the Jemez.
Night falls beyond the window, I fall
like the foetus out of the womb—
such painful release, terrible light.

You come close as my breath and then
recede from me, into the past, into
stories I will tell to friends not yet made
when I have lived my way over this threshold
out of this cramp of fear, when I have
become the woman you saw in me.

In my dream my mother accused me
of giving you money. I rescued
your bags from a thief. Tell
me the meaning of your eyes in the morning

tender as dawn, and your hands
like claws at my throat in the night.

I have come too far to go back. No
safety awaits me. My house
occupied by strangers, my phone disconnected.
You are the one I was going to travel with
right off the map.
I never thought of danger.

Lover, I am killing this innocence with my own hands.

Earthly Light

August 6th, I remember
the shadows at Hiroshima
shadows abandoned by their bodies
stuck to charred ground

Two days ago, we sat on the ground at Santo Domingo
felt the drumbeat in our haunches
my hand stroked the adobe dirt
as if trying to comfort a stricken child

The women pressed their bare feet into the earth
soft as a handclasp, an ancient greeting
under a rain so delicate it touched our skin
like the first rain ever to fall

We were all the women
who have ever patted bread
into round loaves, our breasts flowing
with the milk that ends all thirst

Your eyes under the straw hat
found me, I knew this

dance of love we do
is of the earth and for the earth

wooing the clouds to open
the secret seed to break
the heart to yield its coverings
the corn to swell with sweet milk

Yesterday when the shadow fell on us
and we abandoned our bodies
it was the moment when the drum
pauses in its steady beat

when the foot lifts, suspended
five hundred dancers waiting for the call—
to a new direction, a fresh point of contact
rattles whirring in the air like wings

We are the dancers, our steps decide
whether the rain gathers and falls
whether this earth stays green and giving
or goes under

I watch the stars at night and I see
how little we are, how puny our efforts
I know how bright this earthly light is
how far it shines out into the black abyss

Gassho

strange how one glass of burgundy
will melt my limbs soft as ferns
lay me in a bed of bracken
as one ravished and spent

the way you used to do
smelt me down till I couldn't

stand on my legs or remember wanting to
my blood quicksilver, my bones water

no wine, no wine
could split my body open
whirl me out wild as midnight
spangle me with stars

no one but you
could have found me
the way lightning finds the oak—
sending the white-hot stroke into heartwood

lover, the cup you held to my lips
made me forget my own name
take note of this: I am
drunk no longer, but still bowing

At Christ in the Desert Monastery

red rocks, round moon
come be my witnesses
tonight I marry myself

here in this silence
where three deer stood still for me
I join one hand to the other in simple love

as I place the ring on my finger
moon says, marry your own fullness
rocks say, only that endures

no witnesses
but these
no family in rented formal clothes

midnight, the moon
burgeoning with light
spilling her radiance everywhere

I come home to
myself here
prodigal refugee lost child

I marry
the woman I am
ripe and tender and full of juice

oh I am the one
I have been waiting for
with such patient longing

this bride
cannot be bought
at any price

her hand is given
into the keeping
of her own steadfast heart

Homophobia and Analytical Psychology

ROBERT H. HOPCKE

There has been an outstanding shift in the psychological approach to homosexuality since the advent of the gay liberation political movement in the United States two decades ago. Previously considered a mental disorder and therefore a way of life dysfunctional by definition, homosexuality is now understood as a variation on a continuum of sexual orientation, an ever-present dimension of human relatedness, a nonpathological mode of being in the world which cuts across time and culture. While there are some in the psychoanalytic community, and a few analytical psychologists, who wish to continue the discussion on homosexuality as pathology, the general shift away from such a definition throws into stark relief the psychological dynamic that made homosexuality into a problem in the first place: homophobia. Because the level of discussion about homosexuality is currently so rudimentary in analytical psychology, Jungians have given very little attention to homophobia as a psychological phenomenon, though the concept is widely accepted and has been extensively explored by gay and lesbian clinicians. In this chapter, therefore, I wish to provide the literature of analytical psychology with a foundation for further discussion on homophobia, a discussion that touches upon the personal and the archetypal on both theoretical and clinical levels, with psychological and political ramifications.

HOMOPHOBIA AS A PSYCHOLOGICAL CONCEPT

Whether or not George Weinberg himself actually coined the term *homophobia*, his landmark book, *Society and the Healthy Homosexual* (1972), can be credited with launching the term into psychological discourse. [1] This work, which in many ways represents the culmination of decades of more objective research on the lives and psychological adjustment of homosexuals in the United States, [2] states Weinberg's main point and attitude most succinctly in its title: namely, that the "problem" with homosexuality, in modern Western culture and in psychological theory, is not due to anything inherently unhealthy about homosexuality, since less biased research on the real lives of gay people reveals the possibility of "healthy homosexuals." Rather, there is a set of prejudices—social, political, religious, and psychological in nature—that define homosexuality *a priori* as problematic. Using Gordon Allport's definition of *prejudice* as "an avertive or hostile attitude toward a person who belongs to a group, simply because he belongs to that group and is therefore assumed to have the objectionable qualities ascribed to the group,"[3] Weinberg sees society's prejudice against homosexuality, rather than homosexuality itself, as the actual "problem," and he uses the word *homophobia* to describe this prejudicial attitude. In defining this attitude as a phobia and exploring the social and psychological causes of this fear, Weinberg intentionally employed the very sort of psychological jargon so often used to pathologize homosexuality, and in doing so he turned the tables on the psychiatric establishment's participation in the social and political oppression of gay men and lesbians.

Weinberg's description of homophobia and its various elements has served for twenty years as the foundation for any discussion of the phenomenon. Like other phobias, homophobia usually consists of intense fear and disgust that lead to an unfortunate curtailment of social and emotional life:

> There is a certain cost in suffering from any phobia, and that is that the inhibition spreads to a whole circle of acts related to the feared activity, in reality or symbolically. In this case, acts imagined to be conducive to homosexual feelings, or that are reminiscent of homosexual acts, are shunned. . . . For instance, a great many men refrain from embracing each other or kissing each other. . . . Men do not as a rule express fondness for each other, or longing for each other's company. . . . Men, even lifetime friends, will not sit as close together on a couch as women may . . . ; they will not look into each other's faces as steadily or as fondly. Ramifications of this phobic fear extend even to parent-child relationships. Millions of fathers feel that it would not befit them to kiss their sons affectionately or embrace them. . . .[4]

Thus, Weinberg makes the case that homophobia might rightly be called a "disease," given the impoverishment of emotional life that is the inevitable result of such fear and the social pathology that is its derivative, for instance, the myriad forms of social and economic violence inflicted on gay people.

As for the causes of homophobia, Weinberg adduces at least five. The first, "the religious motive," finds support in the Judeo-Christian prohibition against same-sex sexual behavior, a proscription based on a particular understanding of sexuality, which in turn is derived from a particular tradition of biblical interpretation. To give some balance to this picture of religious intolerance, Weinberg acknowledges the existence of other, nonhomophobic ways of interpreting the Bible with regard to sexual behavior, specifically, the theology of the Reverend Troy Perry of the gay-affirmative Metropolitan Community Church.[5]

A second, more psychological cause of homophobia that Weinberg presents is the "secret fear of being homosexual,"

that is, homophobia as a reaction formation against unconscious or subconscious homosexual feelings and desires. This
theory is obviously derived directly from psychoanalytic
thinking concerning phobias in general and homosexuality in
particular.

Third, Weinberg mentions "repressed envy," the perception
that homosexual men and, to a lesser extent, homosexual
women enjoy a freer, easier, and less burdensome lifestyle
than heterosexuals encumbered with marriage and children.
This envy of homosexuals, like all envy, leads to hatred and a
wish to spoil the advantages that the envied others are perceived to have.

A fourth cause for homophobic responses, clearly related to
religious motives and to the envy of homosexuals, is the threat
to values that homosexuality represents. On this score, Weinberg writes: "Anyone who does not adopt a society's usual
value system runs the risk of being seen as undermining the
society. Because the person does not share the interests and
goals of the majority, there is suspicion of him. This remains
so, even if the person produces as much as others and works as
hard over a lifetime."[6] By framing homophobia and its roots in
this manner, Weinberg throws a spotlight on the fundamental
irrationality of homophobia, based as it is on a set of cultural
values and conventions, rather than on any ontological truths
concerning the nature of sexuality.

Finally, the fifth and perhaps most curious cause for homophobia that Weinberg addresses is the threat posed by the fact
that homosexuals are perceived as living an "existence without
vicarious immortality."[7] This perception, Weinberg suggests,
awakens in the unconscious an identification of homosexuality
with death unredeemed by the continuation of life represented
by one's progeny and constitutes a severe threat to the ego,
which cannot tolerate the idea of complete personal extinction.

However varied these causes of homophobia may seem,
they all reflect the perspective that the pathologization of

homosexuality rests not on purely psychological data but rather on religious, social, and political attitudes—a perspective that came to be a permanent part of the movement to revise psychiatric thought on homosexuality. Homophobia is the natural outgrowth of a society in which heterosexual acts are valued above all other forms of sexual behavior and in which procreation is seen as the most important and valuable consequence of sexual activity. This set of cultural values, termed "heterosexism" by activists subsequent to Weinberg, has in fact come to be identified so closely with homophobia that in much gay and lesbian activism, *homophobia* and *heterosexism* have come to be practically interchangeable terms.[8]

Also obvious from Weinberg's discussion is the way in which *homophobia* denotes not simply a fear of homosexuality but rather something more powerful altogether: a hatred of homosexuality. In this latter sense of the term, Weinberg introduced into psychological thought the concept of internalized homophobia. If one is raised within a homophobic, heterosexist culture, then one will eventually internalize the plethora of negative messages, images, and myths concerning homosexuality propounded daily by the media and by interactions in which homophobic attitudes are expressed. For heterosexuals, this internalized homophobia may be psychologically harmful if it leads to inhibitions and irrational behavior, but, as Weinberg and many others after him point out, for homosexual men and women, this internalization is psychologically devastating. In this way, *homophobia* has come to denote a form of self-hatred that the gay-affirmative psychotherapy movement considers the appropriate focus of treatment for gay men and lesbians in therapy, rather than the individual's sexual orientation. As gay-affirmative psychotherapist Alan K. Malyon writes:

> Gay-affirmative psychotherapy is not an independent system of psychotherapy. Rather, it represents a special range of psychological knowledge which challenges the traditional view that

homosexual desire and fixed homosexual orientations are pathological. . . . This approach regards homophobia, as opposed to
homosexuality, as a major pathological variable in the development of certain symptomatic conditions among gay men. The
special complications and aberrations of identity formation that
have been described in this article are considered to be the result
of social values and attitudes, not as inherent to the issue of
object-choice."[9]

Thus, the various psychological complaints that Malyon presents in his article as typical of gay men's presentation in
psychotherapy—anxiety, despair, conflicts around affects and
sexual impulses, poor self-image, arrested development of
social and interpersonal skills—are seen as consequences of
internalized homophobia, to be resolved through increasing
the patient's self-esteem as gay, not through conversion to
heterosexuality.

In addition to this gay-affirmative psychotherapeutic focus,
however, the concept of homophobia has given rise to a whole
field of social-psychological research concerning the effect
of external and internal homophobia on individuals of all
sexual orientations. Along this line, empirical studies on
such varied phenomena as the social-psychological functions
that homophobia serves in contemporary society, differences
in homophobic attitudes between men and women, and the
effectiveness of various educational approaches in changing
homophobic attitudes, have been added to the literature on
homophobia, most notably and expectably by gay and lesbian
researchers.[10]

HOMOPHOBIA AND ANALYTICAL PSYCHOLOGY

To those involved in analytical psychology, how little discussion of homophobia has been integrated into the various
discussions concerning homosexuality, indeed how little discussion of homosexuality there has even been in analytical

psychology is noteworthy and, for gay men and lesbians, distressing. In some cases, this failure of attention may be put down to Jung's relativization of the importance of sexuality, in reaction to Freud. Nevertheless, my own experience points to a particular style of homophobia among Jungians. While among Freudians homophobia most frequently takes the form of pathologization and condemnation,[11] among Jungians, it typically takes the form of neglect.

At times this Jungian neglect feels like a deliberate act of denial. For example, I was told by two Jungian analysts who reviewed the manuscript of my book *Jung, Jungians, and Homosexuality*,[12] that they saw no reason to publish it since "Jung did not have much to say" on the topic and that my comprehensive review of everything he *had* said on homosexuality (filling more than one hundred pages of typescript, including references to interviews and published letters) was a little "thin." At that point, there had never been a monograph on homosexuality in the literature of analytical psychology.

Other personal examples shed further light on the ways and means of homophobia within analytical psychology. An anonymous reviewer of one of my first submissions to a professional journal took issue with my reference to the APA's 1973 decision to remove homosexuality from the list of mental disorders, claiming that the decision was due to political pressure and not based on science. I wanted to ask at the time whether the other one hundred–odd diagnostic categories were viewed with similar suspicion, but since this reviewer voted in favor of publishing my article, self-interest checked my tongue. However, I subsequently had to argue to retain my use of the word *gay* in the article; the editors wanted to change it throughout to *homosexual*, undoubtedly the more "scientific" term, though I had used *gay* precisely because it is more affirmative. Moreover, I discovered that arguing the point can lead to further resistance. When I have objected to the implicit, unconscious homophobia behind such appeals to "science," my writing has been called contentious. Such incidents demonstrate how analysts can succeed in continuing to pathologize homosexuality in subtle ways, as well as stifling all original contributions to a field of inquiry.

There continues to be a notable dearth of openly gay or lesbian analysts within Jungian psychology who feel safe enough to speak out of their own clinical and personal experience concerning homosexuality. The existence of this volume itself is proof of this point, in that its publication comes more than two decades after the advent of gay liberation in 1969, and some of its contributors are speaking about their homosexuality for the first time ever in a public forum. This situation again might be put down to Jungian introversion, but equally plausible is that the fear of coming out and "speaking the truth in love" (to use the title of the editors' workshop on homosexuality) breaks the silence that grows out of an unanalyzed homophobia that exists in all aspects of analytical psychology, from the editorial policies of publications to analytic training to clinical work with patients.

As far as publications are concerned, one can easily compile a list of judgmental, offensive, and patently questionable statements concerning homosexuality within the literature of analytical psychology, while only very rarely is homophobia acknowledged as a problem worth considering. At the top of the list of such statements are those reflecting a theory that has now become almost cliché: that homosexuality is a form of psychosexual immaturity derived from a problem with the Feminine. Uncritically repeated by two generations of Jungian analysts based on certain statements in Jung's own writings, this theory has been emphasized to the virtual exclusion of all other points of view and stands once again as an example of the homophobic silence that surrounds homosexuality in analytical psychology. Despite the much more positive evaluations of homosexuality that can be found if one takes the trouble to read all of Jung's own writings on the topic,[13] analyst after analyst has added his or her own special elaboration to the basic pathologizing theme: that male homosexuals are puer-identified (Marie-Louise von Franz),[14] that they are dominated by a "matriarchal psychology with the Great Mother in the ascendant" (Erich Neumann),[15] that homosexuality is an "escape for men fearing intimacy with women" (Jerome Bernstein, after Melvin Kettner),[16] and homosexuality as a kind of "phallus-fetishism" derived from castration anxiety (Anthony Storr).[17]

Nor is this stream of consistently negative evaluations confined to the less enlightened past. On the contrary, it seems that there is now *less* consciousness of homophobia as a problem within Jungian circles, along with disquieting attempts to reidentify homosexuality as pathological. Two especially disturbing instances of current Jungian homophobia can be found in the July 1988 issue of *The Journal of Analytical Psychology*, wherein analyst Michael Fordham and philosopher J. O. Wisdom turn back the clock to the era of judgmental descriptions of sexual behavior to reinstitute the use of the word *perversion*. Fordham presents two cases of "perversion" in individuals who exhibit a bisexual or homosexual orientation, and Wisdom, apparently ignorant of nearly fifty years of research, wonders whether or not homosexuality is a perversion and, if so, under what circumstances and due to what causes.[18]

In a similar vein, in a review of Andrew Samuels's book *The Plural Psyche*, analyst Alexander McCurdy evinces a certain amount of discomfort with Samuels's argument for tolerance as a cornerstone of pluralism, mentioning in the same paragraph two instances where the "shadow of inappropriate tolerance" would lead to negative consequences: sexual contact between analyst and patient, and homosexuality. When challenged, McCurdy later defended his statements by saying, "I meant to point out and give some life to the debate on the depathologizing of perversions, particularly of homosexuality and some forms of pedophilia"[19]—as if the debate had been prematurely closed back in 1973, as if homosexuality could be seen as behavior on a par with pedophilia and the sexual exploitation of patients, as if the concern with propriety superseded tolerance. My point in citing these various examples of homophobia among Jungians is to make the case for how relevant and necessary an understanding of homophobia is for analytical psychology, even nowadays in a psychological climate supposedly characterized by more tolerance for diversity and less moral condemnation couched in psychological terms. Homophobia is indeed a problem within analytical psychology, one that is made urgent by the clinical nature of analytical work, for it is real people—gay men and lesbians—who suffer at the hands of ill-informed, biased analysts who, subtly or overtly, see homosexuality not as a normal variation of sexual orientation but rather as a problem, a handicap, an unfortunate detour in the road toward heterosexual normalcy.

The ubiquity of homophobic attitudes and feelings suggests that homophobia is indeed a fairly complicated phenomenon, socially and psychologically, and furthermore suggests that archetypal, and not just personal or social, factors might be at work in the fear and hatred that homosexuality arouses in Western culture. Therefore, two questions of vital importance to Jungians present themselves: first, what might be some of the elements that, both personally and archetypally, support homophobia, and second, what are the clinical implications of these factors for the individuation process of gay men and lesbians within Jungian analysis?

THE PSYCHOLOGICAL ROOTS OF HOMOPHOBIA

As Weinberg and a raft of Freudians have made clear, on the level of what Jungians would call the personal unconscious, homophobia most often appears as a defense against unconscious or subconscious homosexual impulses, feelings, desires, and images. People who are secure in their sexual orientation have no reason to fear or hate homosexuality, since another's difference has no power to threaten something with which one feels comfortable and safe. For heterosexual men and women with no conflicts about their sexuality, another person's homosexuality would be a matter of indifference, while men and women who have accepted their own bisexual or homosexual orientation have already worked through whatever fears or negative feelings they once had. This point is brought home to me again and again in my clinical work when homosexual imagery in dreams comes up for discussion in a therapy session: for heterosexuals conflicted about their sexuality, such imagery is almost always experienced as a frightening, unwanted intrusion. Sometimes this threat is projected out onto me within the therapy relationship; for example, such patients often express the fear that on the basis of these dreams I am going to tell them that they are "really" gay. Sometimes the dream imagery itself gives these patients good reason to feel threatened, for those who have anxiously suppressed all homosexual feelings in order to cling defensively to a heterosexual persona will often be presented with a compensatorily violent backlash in their dreams: homosexual rapes, bondage and domination at the hands of torturers, same-sex authority figures demanding sexual and psychological submission.

With such imagery, we have arrived in the realm of the shadow. Like other phobias, homophobia is without doubt a shadow dynamic, since the fear and hatred of homosexuality are derived directly from cultural values which insist that heterosexual marriage alone is normative and good, all else aberrant and bad. Thus, on a personal and cultural level, homosexuality is thrust into the unconscious and made into a shadow, given the stridently heterosexist framework within which we live. One place where this shadow quality is obvious is in the various negative stereotypes of homosexual relationships, many of which have been proven untrue by subsequent research[20] but which nevertheless persist in personal and cultural consciousness because they preserve the persona of heterosexual normalcy: Homosexuals are incapable of long-term, committed relationship (the heterosexual divorce rate is conveniently ignored). Homosexuals are promiscuous and obsessed with sex (heterosexual infidelity and the commercialization of heterosexuality to sell everything from toothpaste to automobiles, again conveniently ignored). Homosexual men are effeminate and want to be women (the fact that most transvestites are heterosexual, again ignored). The rigid value given to heterosexuality, especially procreative heterosexuality, in Western culture all but determines that homosexuality as a phenomenon and homosexual individuals specifically will become the carriers of all the shadowy aspects of sexuality that do not fit into this heterosexist schema.

The term *homophobia* itself, however, gives us a clue to an even deeper understanding. Strictly speaking, one would expect the term to be "homosexophobia," and yet this conceptual parapraxis, so to speak, is telling. The literal meaning of *homophobia*, "fear of sameness," lays bare how the roots of such fear and hatred are at the core of patriarchy itself. As a psychologically one-sided system, patriarchy, with its gender definitions and concomitant validation of all that is "masculine" to the denigration of all that is "feminine," has awarded men a great deal of social, economic, and political power. However, what is not often seen is how this system requires, on a psychological level, a consistent form of self-alienation from both women and men.

This dynamic is clear when seen in relation to women's roles in the patriarchy. If women's love for women were accepted and validated, this love would lead to a radical revision of social and personal values, which are currently based on women's alienation from themselves, their bodies, and their souls. For men, who are bought off with social and economic privilege to continue such a one-sided way of living, the self-alienation is more subtle. Certainly if men were to love men freely and

openly, much of the competitive edge that keeps the patriarchal system alive would become irrelevant; the economic
and social incentives that fuel men's vision of other men as
potential rivals would be supplanted by another set of experiences and another set of incentives, perhaps more powerful
than money or power: namely, love, intimacy, and acceptance
from other men.

More threatening, however, is the way that homosexuality
calls into question the very one-sided patriarchal definition of
masculinity that undergirds the whole system in the first
place. By encouraging men to identify with a phallic masculinity to the exclusion of all other aspects of masculine
experience, a patriarchal system actually ends up alienating
men from the fullness of masculine experience. Hence, homophobia, a natural outgrowth of patriarchy, is precisely what it
literally denotes: a fear and hatred of the self. For women, the
inferior status of the female within patriarchy inculcates self-
hatred almost from birth, so that the coming-out process for a
lesbian winds up being in large part a reclamation of the self.
By contrast, for gay men, the patriarchal equation of masculinity exclusively with phallicism must be abandoned, and
the gender definition expanded to include aspects of the masculine self that have been denigrated or feared: for instance,
all the values represented symbolically by the quiescent
phallos, such as receptivity, flexibility, and inwardness, or the
qualities inherent in the image of the Earth Father, such as
groundedness, affection, and nurture.

Thus, homophobia, so often appearing as a fear of the same-
sex other, is a pernicious psychological dynamic, not just for
gay men and lesbians, but equally for heterosexual men and
women, because behind the fear of the same-sex other is a
devastating fear of the self. The clinical manifestations
of homophobia in heterosexuals need not be simply a hatred of
gay people but can be all manner of phenomena: a fear of
taking pleasure in one's own body; a lack of intimacy with

other men and women, and a concomitant lack of validation and community; or, as a more extreme example, a near-paranoid sense of competition with and persecution by the very people who might be expected to mirror oneself and one's soul—those who are like ourselves, other men, other women.

If homophobia is indeed a fear of the self, then it is almost certainly also a fear of the Self, particularly the Self in its ambivalence. Gay men and lesbians, by living at odds with the prescribed one-sided, unvarying sexuality propounded as normal, face this culture with the true breadth and variety of human experience, face it with a wholeness that ultimately derives from the Self. Here the lack of Jungian theorizing on homosexuality subsequent to Jung becomes especially disappointing, for Jung himself suggested that homosexuality is an "incomplete detachment from the hermaphroditic archetype, coupled with a distinct resistance to the role of a one-sided sexual being." "Such a disposition," Jung continues, "should not be adjudged negative in all circumstances, in so far as it preserves the archetype of the Original Man, which a one-sided sexual being has, up to a point, lost."[21] Like the androgyne, the homosexual can be seen through the lenses of fear and hatred, seen as monstrous, a freak of nature, the radical Other, and yet Jung's work itself requires that a different attitude be taken altogether. If homosexuality is one place where, in a one-sided patriarchal culture, the values of androgyny live and thrive, then homosexuality is one of the few places where the Self is made manifest and where the wholeness of who we are as men and women can be fully realized.

Anthropological research on homosexuality in other cultures continues to present us with this seemingly archetypal link between homosexuality and the androgynous Self, for it is the "third sex" in native cultures, the "men-women," who perform the shamanistic and ritual functions for so many tribes, the role that mediates between heaven and earth, the other world and this.[22] Thus, one must wonder if the sacred power that such individuals embody for the tribe, the taboo that they guard and represent, does not inform on a deep, archetypal level the homophobia that so many heterosexuals feel in our culture, out of envy or even terror of the sacredness of homosexual love.

CLINICAL IMPLICATIONS OF HOMOPHOBIA

If homophobia is indeed a shadow dynamic based on a fear of self and a fear of the Self, then one should never be so blithe or naive as to dismiss the possibility that homophobia may be playing a part in one's own perceptions. With gay and lesbian patients, homophobic attitudes on the part of the analyst can range from out-and-out denial that a patient is gay to more subtle denigrations of his or her sexual, erotic, or emotional life, from ill-advised attempts at heterosexual conversion to simple ignorance about contemporary gay lifestyles. Gay and lesbian patients, particularly those psychotherapeutically savvy enough to be interested in Jungian analysis, are often on guard against blatant homophobia and attempt, understandably, to ensure a minimum of problems in this area by finding an analyst who is openly gay or lesbian. Yet, if homophobia is a psychological dynamic with archetypal aspects, having an openly gay or lesbian analyst is no iron-clad guarantee that homophobia will not be an issue. As always, self-analysis on the part of the analyst is of paramount importance.

Moreover, homophobia ought to be recognized not just as an issue affecting gay and lesbian patients but also as a dynamic that is present with all clients of the same sex as the therapist. All too often, as an openly gay psychotherapist, I am required to repair with appropriate acceptance and affirmation the lack of same-sex erotic attention that is necessary for men, of whatever sexual orientation, to have in order to blossom and love their masculinity, a lack that has unfortunately been replicated in therapeutic experiences with analysts whose homophobia led to a coldly rigid interpretive stance (rationalized, of course, as "abstinence" or "neutrality") or who have consistently ignored abundant homoerotic material in the transference-countertransference relationship. The conspicuous lack of forthright discussion concerning homoerotic countertransference in the psychological literature, Jungian and otherwise, must be seen, at least in part, as still another example of homophobia at work in determining what is discussed and what is not. With heterosexual male patients, my open identification as gay and my comfort in working with homoerotic material supply them with a true neutrality around issues of sexuality and often provide them with what they have come to analysis to find, a way to love their masculinity as men, as fully, as deeply, as passionately as I love my own masculinity as a gay man.

On the subtler end of the homophobia spectrum is the attitude—popular with analysts for whom appearing nonhomophobic is more important than actually being nonhomophobic—that homosexuality is "merely" another variation in sexual orientation, neither more valuable nor more execrable than heterosexuality or bisexuality. This *belle indifference* typical of self-styled liberals is a particularly insidious form of homophobia, since for homosexually or bisexually oriented individuals, their sexual orientation is in fact one of the primary modes of being in the world, with a host of implications in a heterosexist, patriarchally organized society, and the homosexual impulses of a predominantly heterosexual individual almost always carry important, unique pieces of that person's psychic experience. One who is doing social science research may be free to note dispassionately that homosexuality and bisexuality are merely variations, but a practicing clinician is enjoined through his or her role to give homosexuality more weight, to attempt to see its goodness and value in the individual's life. On this point, I am tempted to go so far as to say that anything less than gay-affirmative psychotherapy with gay patients is homophobic. The fear, as voiced by McCurdy, that gay-affirmative psychotherapy will in some way lead to an inappropriate tolerance and uncritical acceptance of even destructive aspects of homosexuality seems a bit alarmist, given the largely homophobic cultural context within which psychotherapy currently takes place. In a society surfeited with images of the worst aspects of homosexuality, gay-affirmative voices in psychology and in the culture at large are still needed to protest the impoverishment and destruction wrought by homophobia. If heterosexuality itself is not questioned when an analyst in a clinical setting is faced with destructive sexual dynamics between men and women, then the basic rightness of homosexuality for a gay or lesbian patient ought not to be called into question.

A gay-affirmative psychotherapeutic stance, therefore, requires a great deal of the analyst. A tolerance of ambiguity is necessary, as well as considerable experience in dealing nondefensively with his or her own homosexual feelings. However, given the less than gay-affirmative atmosphere in most training institutions, often the only way to acquire such experience is to happen upon a particularly nonhomophobic training analyst. Furthermore, respect for the patient, a paramount value in all forms of psychotherapy, is especially necessary when dealing with gay and lesbian patients, who have often been the recipients of physical, sexual, economic, and social violence, in addition to whatever psychological or emotional harm has been inflicted. These psychotherapeutic values are all classic Jungian analytic attitudes, and yet the forces behind homophobia, particularly the shadowy quality of such hatred, may cause the analyst to inappropriately abandon such values. Psychotherapeutic training unfortunately provides analysts with any number of clever ways to rationalize or hide their homophobic behavior, when not actively reinforcing homophobic attitudes directly.

In addition, however, to holding these classic values, a

truly gay-affirmative analyst must be aware of the social and political context in which gay and lesbian patients grew up and now live, for the oppression and intimidation of gay people—which are often the reason they seek help from a therapist—are all too frighteningly, literally real and not just a symbol or a fantasy, however prone Jungians may be to exploring the symbolic dimension of experience with patients. And finally, analysts ought to be aware of the role they play in the social and political sphere as experts, as arbiters of what is normal and good, as the scientific decision-makers concerning human behavior. Because of the rather introverted stance of analytical psychology, Jungians perhaps more than other areas of psychology have a tendency to shun political controversy and tightly define their vision to the inward, the symbolic, the psychological. For gay men and lesbians, whose very existence is indeed a political issue in a patriarchal, heterosexist society—and, with the advent of AIDS, an urgent issue of life and death—analysts cannot truly heal or aid in the individuation of gay and lesbian clients unless the hermetic container of the consulting room is understood as part of the larger sociopolitical context of healing and transformation.

My hope in confronting homophobia Jungian-style is that equal doses of clear thinking and courageous speaking will cast out fear and make way in analytical psychology for a true appreciation of the diversity of the individuation process. The result will be not only an enrichment of gay and lesbian lives, but the enlargement of consciousness in all aspects and for all human beings.

Notes

1. George Weinberg, *Society and the Healthy Homosexual* (Garden City, N.Y.: Anchor Press Doubleday, 1972).
2. A concise summary of the history of the revision of psychological opinion concerning homosexuality can be found in Ronald Bayer, *Homosexuality and American Psychiatry: The Politics of Diagnosis* (New York: Basic Books, 1981).

3. Weinberg, *Society*, p. 8.

4. Ibid., p. 6.

5. In the last twenty years, nearly every major Christian denomination in the United States has in its midst active organizations of gay and lesbian members seeking both to change church policy and to fight social discrimination. Gay synagogues are working along the same lines from within Judaism.

6. Weinberg, *Society*, p. 15.

7. Ibid., p. 16.

8. See Joseph Nelson, "Heterosexism vs. Homophobia," in the national gay and lesbian quarterly *Outlook*, Fall 1990, for a discussion about the similarities and differences in these two terms.

9. Alan K. Malyon, "Psychotherapeutic Implications of Internalized Homophobia in Gay Men," in John C. Gonsiorek, ed., *A Guide to Psychotherapy with Gay and Lesbian Clients* (New York: Harrington Park Press, 1985), p. 69.

10. For a selection of some of this research, see John P. De Cecco, ed., *Bashers, Baiters and Bigots: Homophobia in American Society* (New York: Harrington Park Press, 1985).

11. For a comprehensive account of the checkered past of Freudian psychoanalysis on this issue, replete with citations of some truly hair-raising homophobic statements on the part of various psychoanalysts, see Kenneth Lewes, *The Psychoanalytic Theory of Male Homosexuality* (New York: Simon and Schuster, 1988).

12. Robert H. Hopcke, *Jung, Jungians, and Homosexuality* (Boston: Shambhala Publications, 1989).

13. See ibid., chap. 3, "Jung's Attitudes and Theories," pp. 30–66.

14. Marie-Louise von Franz, *Puer Aeternus* (Boston: Sigo Press, 1981).

15. Erich Neumann, *The Origins and History of Consciousness* (Princeton: Princeton University Press, 1954), p. 141.

16. Jerome Bernstein, "The Decline of Masculine Rites of Passage in Our Culture: The Impact on Masculine Individuation," in Louise Carus Mahdi, Stephen Foster, and Meredith Little, eds., *Betwixt and Between: Patterns of Masculine and Feminine Initiation* (La Salle, Ill.: Open Court, 1987), p. 147.

17. Anthony Storr, "The Psychopathology of Fetishism and Transvestitism," *Journal of Analytical Psychology*, July 1957, p. 157.

18. Michael Fordham, "The Androgyne: Some Inconclusive Reflections on Sexual Perversions," *Journal of Analytical Psychology* 33, no. 3 (July 1988): 217–28; and J. O. Wisdom, "The Perversions: A Philosopher Reflects," *Journal of Analytical Psychology* 33, no. 3 (July 1988): 229–42.

19. Alexander McCurdy, in response to Gary D. Astrachan, "Correspondence," *Journal of Analytical Psychology* 35, no. 4 (October 1990): 479.

20. David P. McWhirter and Andrew Mattison, *The Male Couple: How Relationships Develop* (Englewood Cliffs, N.J.: Prentice-Hall, 1984).

21. C. G. Jung, *The Collected Works of C. G. Jung*, vol. 9/1 (Princeton: Princeton University Press, 1968), p. 71.

22. For this phenomenon in Native American culture, see Will Roscoe, *The Zuni Man-Woman* (Albuquerque: University of New Mexico Press, 1991); Walter Williams, *The Spirit and the Flesh: Sexual Diversity in American Indian Culture* (Boston: Beacon Press, 1986); and Jonathan Katz, *Gay American History: Lesbians and Gay Men in American History* (New York: Thomas Y. Crowell, 1976); for examples from other cultures, see Mircea Eliade, *Shamanism: Archaic Techniques of Ecstasy* (Princeton: Princeton University Press, 1964).

Women Loving Women
Speaking the Truth in Love

KARIN LOFTHUS CARRINGTON

As a lesbian/feminist, my nerves and my flesh as well as my intellect tell me that the connections between and among women are the most feared, the most problematic and the most potentially transforming force on the planet.

—ADRIENNE RICH

I fell in love with a woman when I was thirty-three. It was a miracle. A homecoming. The fulfillment of an ancient cellular longing. A subtle, intricate, erotic remembering of something lost to me long ago. My love for another woman was also terrifying, outwardly disorienting, overwhelming. And it was unspeakable.

Emotional and sexual love between women has been consistently feared and pathologized. Like so many of the most profound, moving, and transformative experiences of women's lives, the love of one woman for another has remained unspeakable—without a place in the theoretical framework of Western culture and psychological tradition. To name and describe embodied love between women poses a threat to the consensual reality of our culture as well as to the women who dare to speak the truth of their experience in love with another woman. For centuries, women have kept silent, often going mad as we split ourselves between our inner knowing and the expectations of patriarchal culture. The alternative to silence or madness has been ridicule, humiliation, banishment, imprisonment, or death. Perhaps in Jungian terms, keeping silent is thus the true shadow side of our feminine nature. The accepted portrayal of women's shadow as devouring may be a counterphobic response, distracting us from the real threat that the truth of a woman's life and inner knowing poses to androcentric culture. Some years ago Muriel Rukeyser said that if one woman would tell the whole truth about her life, the world would split open. The time has come to boldly tell the truth of our life, our love and our history.

In the Babylonian creation myth, the hero Marduk slays his mother, Tiamat. He then dismembers her and flings her body parts into space. With this act, the myth records, the world is created. Matricide becomes equated with creation, and the consciousness of Western culture begins with an image of a woman mutilated in order to create the hero's world. Individually and collectively, women are called to gather themselves into one body again and to speak the truth of their *whole* experience. Individuation for a woman consists in remembering who she really is, not who she thinks she should be, and then living from that place of remembering. The love of one woman for another evokes a deep cellular remembering of her origins, her darkness, her beauty, her power, her wisdom, and her limitless desire. At the same time, old longings are satisfied and new longings, never before experienced, are created. This has profound implications for both the lives of individual women in love with other women and the lives of all those whom we touch in this culture.

My work is an attempt to begin mapping the feared and forbidden territory of women loving women and to describe the healing images that reside at the core of women's love relationships with one another. For years I have reflected on my experience of love with women; about five years ago, I found these reflections beginning to take a particular focus. I became mildly obsessed with a feeling, somewhat inarticulate initially, that as human beings we all had to expand, destroy, or relinquish many of the boundaries that separate us from others as well as from parts of ourselves. I have often had the experience of "permeable boundaries," described by Heinz Kohut and others. I wondered what keeps us from living with more permeable boundaries in our regular levels of awareness. Why are those peak moments of permeability, of oneness, so typically limited to extraordinary states such as love, ecstasy, or madness. Or, as Catherine Keller has asked, "What would it be like if the original continuum from which we all emerge, call it preoedipal, narcissistic, oceanic or empathic, were neither shattered nor repressed, but extended and transformed? If maturation meant the gradual differentiation and modulation of the empathic continuum?"[1]

It is through a return to this original continuum of empathy that we remember our true nature, our connection to all life, and permeable boundaries rather than separateness become the reality of daily experience. Susan Griffin, feminist poet and philosopher, recognizes the capacity of women to maintain the continuum even in a culture that denies it:

> At the center of the earth there is a mother . . .
> Some of us have decided
> this mother cannot hear all of us
> in our desperate wishes.
> Here, in this time,
> our hearts have been cut into small chambers
> like ration cards
> and we can no longer imagine every
> morsel nor each tiny
> thought at once,
> as she still can.   *This is normal,*
> she tries to tell us,
> but we don't listen.

Sometimes someone has a faint memory
of all this, and
she suffers.
She is wrong to imagine
she suffers alone.
Do you think we are not all hearing and speaking
at the same time?
Our mother is somber.
She is thinking.
She puts her big ear
against the sky
to comfort herself.
Do this, she calls to us,
Do this.[2]

As my thoughts began to crystallize, I had a series of
dreams in which I am released from prison or concentration
camp, and others are freed as well. The dreams were not
heroic; the liberation seemed a grace—simple, humble,
rather straightforward. Then a new genre of dreams began:

> I am sitting with my woman lover under palm trees on a very
> expansive, unobstructed white sand beach near the ocean. It is
> warm and we are having a picnic with our five-year-old daughter.
> She turns to me and asks: "Mommy, what is the secret of life?" I
> look at her with deep affection and tenderness, and without a
> moment's hesitation, I say: "Everything is made up of the same
> tiny, brilliant diamonds."

This dream provided me with the direction and validation I
needed for the oceanic feelings of expansion and bound-
arylessness I continued to experience. It became clear that
through my experiences of loving women and being loved by
them, eros had called me beyond my separativeness, beyond
those constricting separate chambers in my own heart. Eros
has a way of doing that. And the love of women for women does
it in a particular way. For within our deep unconscious knowing, inside the darkness to which so much of our truth and

power have been banished, and from which on our own terms we draw wisdom, creativity, and sensuality, we know that everything is, indeed, made of the same tiny diamonds.

The alchemists knew this truth. In all traditions, alchemists were experimenters, working to expand health and achieve immortality by locating the link among common elements that transform all life. The ultimate goal of alchemy was to regain the original perfection inherent in matter—that tiny diamond-ness. To do this—to redeem what the Buddhists call the diamond body and what alchemists call the philosopher's stone—one must, as Marie-Louise von Franz reminds us, *repeat the whole process of creation*. The individuation process of a woman in love with another woman is clearly an alchemical one: they repeat the whole process of creating themselves, return to the original perfection of their true, instinctive natures, and redeem themselves and their world through reunion. The wounding of premature separation, both archetypally and personally, can then be healed.

Birth stripped our birthright from us,
tore us from a woman, from women, from ourselves
so early on
and the whole chorus throbbing at our ears
like midges, told us nothing, nothing
of origins, nothing we needed
to know, nothing that could re-member us.
Only: that is unnatural,
the homesickness for a woman, for ourselves,
for that acute joy at the shadow her head and arms
cast on a wall, her heavy or slender
thighs on which we lay, flesh against flesh,
eyes steady on the face of love; smell of her milk, her sweat,
terror of her disappearance, all fused in this hunger
for the element they have called most dangerous, to be
lifted breathtaken on her breast, to rock within her
—even if beaten back, stranded again, to apprehend

in a sudden brine-clear thought
trembling like the tiny, orbed, endangered
egg-sac of a new world:
This is what she was to me, and this
is how I can love myself—
as only a woman can love me.[3]

ARCHETYPAL PATTERNS OF LESBIAN LOVE
AND INDIVIDUATION

What, really, is this love between women? It is not simply a
sex-object choice, nor is it an avoidance of men and the
masculine principle because of some early wounding. It is not
an immature sexuality hopelessly fixated on the mother, nor is
it a retreat from the challenge of a mature, differentiated,
conscious life. Yet, in a manner of speaking, all of these
caricatures of lesbian life and relationship contain a seed of
truth: all of the things the love between women is *not*, it also *is*.
Ultimately, to expand and hold this paradox for ourselves, for
our lesbian clients and friends, we must *all* be initiated, at a
mute and cellular level, into the mysteries of the feminine
embodied and celebrated in the erotic love between women.

I have come to recognize four archetypal patterns that
beckon women into love with other women. These patterns are
intimately connected and serve in the healing of different
wounds to both the individual and collective feminine. Each of
the four has an image at its core—an image of two aspects of
women's selves that have been separated by the patriarchal
system and are longing for reunion in an embodied merger.
Women yearn to recollect their dismembered selves and become whole once again, for as Robin Morgan reminds us, "We
have been ourselves before."[4] In each of the four patterns
there is the potential for overidentification with the core images or resistance to their transformative power. This unconscious response is the shadow aspect of each of the patterns.
There is also an opportunity for reconciliation with some

aspect of women's internalized masculine in the reunion of each of the four images. Though the four patterns could be viewed developmentally, I find such a perspective far too linear and limiting. The patterns have a kind of spiraling, interrelated autonomy and tend to echo one another. While a woman may enter into a relationship of love with another woman through one of the images at the center of a particular pattern, *all* of the images resonate throughout the different phases or moments of lesbian relationship.

Return to the Source

In the first of four archetypal patterns for individuation, a woman in love with another woman does not set *out* to imitate the man's heroic separative journey that will dismember the ego first and rebuild a new form later. Women are already dismembered; we set *in*—and back in further—back toward the original source of our wholeness. Beckoned by the erotic and sexually compelling love of another woman, a woman falls into an uroboric union with the lover/mother whom she, in a sense, never really had. I have observed again and again that it is almost impossible to let something go until you have really had it. Adrienne Rich once wrote, "The mother I needed was silenced before I was born."[5] This is more than a writer's personal statement. It implies that all our mothers and our mothers' mothers and our mothers' mothers' mothers have lived divided against themselves—egoless in some sense, with deep feelings of inadequacy, voicelessness, and a longing to have it otherwise. When I first began writing this paper, I misquoted Rich and wrote: "The mother I needed was *dead* before I was born." Perhaps keeping silent about our love, our lives, our dismemberment, is a kind of death. This is part of the legacy we are given to redeem. This first pattern of the individuation experience for a lesbian is in response to some cellular need to merge again and then reemerge more complete, reclaiming her body and her soul from patriarchal imprisonment.

A lesbian woman is drawn to a union and merger with another woman, to a kind of *participation mystique*, which involves a deep identity with the loved one. This union, which is a numinous experience, beyond the personal, also deeply embodies the personal. C. G. Jung describes the archetypal mother in these words: "This is the mother love which is one of the most moving and unforgettable memories of our lives, the mysterious root of all growth and change; the love that means homecoming, shelter, and the long silence from which everything begins and in which everything ends."[6] This reunion is not simply the remembering of the archetypal mother; it is also the reawakening and celebration of our woman's body. A lesbian in her thirties, after having sex with the woman she loved deeply, recalled her earliest memory: she is about ten months old, being bathed by her mother, splashing the water, and feeling completely embodied, joyful, and safe. So often our original memories as women are from a time *after* we have been separated from the original source represented by this mother—after we have been diverted from the original continuum; and we are already feeling uniquely inadequate and disembodied. To varying degrees, the potential exists for a woman to remember this original feeling of being wholly (holy) herself through deep erotic love with another woman and to begin to heal the legacy of inadequacy and silence that has been passed on through generations.

I want to tap into the mythological well for a moment to amplify the archetypal image at the core of this first pattern of relatedness and transformation for same-sex love between women. In ancient Greece, in that space between matrifocal and patrifocal cultures, the Sanctuary of Eleusis, near Athens, was the center of a religious cult that endured for nearly two thousand years and whose initiates came from all parts of the civilized world. Originally the rites of this mystery religion were reserved for women; but, in time, initiates of both sexes were guided to Eleusis from Athens at both the

spring and fall equinoxes and there participated in rituals—
mute, silent, highly secretive—a process not unlike that of
the alchemists.

The mysterious contents of their initiation have fascinated
scholars for centuries. What is indisputable is that the initiation into the mysteries centered on the archetypal image of
mother and daughter as reflected in the myth of Demeter and
Persephone. In the beginning, Demeter and Persephone are
living in harmonious union on the earth. They are suddenly
separated, according to patriarchal tradition, by the rape of
Persephone by Hades, who takes her as his bride into the
underworld and, according to matriarchal tradition, by Persephone's compassion for the lost spirits of the dead who are
wandering about and whom she chooses to serve and initiate
by descending with them into the underworld. Mother and
daughter are eventually reunited; and prosperity and harmony
return to the earth during their reunion, only to disappear
again during the period of their separation for six months each
year. Monique Schneider writes:

> It is important to see that in this myth one is not dealing with a
> relation of power as in the case of the myth of Oedipus. Demeter
> accepts a compromise. Her daughter will disappear in autumn
> and winter and reappear in spring and summer and be reborn in
> every bud that blossoms forth. Kore [Persephone] cannot be
> identified as a precise shape. She cannot be localized. And it is
> this terrifying power that woman experiences in the amorous and
> maternal which allows her to recognize something of herself in
> everything which is in the process of taking shape. [7]

In discussions of the meaning of this myth for women's
psychological development, the central emphasis is often on
the separation of mother and daughter by the heroic masculine. We are told that through the intervention of Hades,
mother and maiden are separated and saved from a hopeless
enmeshment. Nancy Chodorow discusses the complexity of

women's development in terms of object relations and sees that women *maintain* their relation to the mother throughout their lives while developing an attachment to the other/male object as well.[8] This theory applies to heterosexual female development in terms of the transference of amorous affection. This is the *compromise* to which Schneider refers above. In understanding lesbian individuation, the emphasis is not on either the *separation* or the *compromise*, but rather on the original *union* and the *reunion*. Separation and compromise ultimately figure in love relationships between women, although this shift in emphasis to union and reunion is radically important.

Jung and Carl Kerényi write:

> A woman lives earlier as a mother, later as a daughter. The conscious experience of these ties produces the feeling that her life is spread out over generations—the first step towards the immediate experience and conviction of being outside time, which brings with it a feeling of immortality. The individual . . . [woman's] life is elevated into a type, indeed it becomes *the archetype of woman's fate in general.* . . . An experience of this kind gives the individual a place and a meaning in the life of the generations, so that all unnecessary obstacles are cleared out of the way of the life-stream that is to flow through her. At the same time the individual is rescued from her isolation and restored to wholeness. . . .
>
> The Demeter-Kore [Persephone] myth is far too feminine to have been merely the result of an anima-projection. . . . In fact, the psychology of the Demeter cult has all the features of a matriarchal order of society, where the man is an indispensable but on the whole disturbing factor.[9]

It is crucially important to reframe and understand this first pattern of lesbian individuation in the clinical and social context. The element of merger (union and reunion) in same-sex love between women is intensely threatening and often treated as pathological. Yet it is this very fear of merger and loss of ego boundaries that creates the "separate chambers" in our hearts and may be at the core of all homophobia. Christine Downing has aptly written:

> That licit transgression of boundaries relates closely to what I see as Demeter's most important signification with respect to same-sex love among women. For Demeter reminds us of a time when there were no boundaries, when lover and beloved were one. I believe that all close bonds between women inevitably conjure up memories and feelings associated with our first connection to a woman, the all-powerful mother of infancy. They remind us of a time in which one neither required the phallus nor rebelled against its power, when it was merely irrelevant. The *pull* to reexperience that bond of another—*and* the *fear* of reexperiencing that bond of fusion, of being swallowed up by a relationship, of losing one's own hard-won identity—enter powerfully into all woman-woman relationships. This does not mean that in a relationship between two women one partner will play the mother role, the other the daughter role; but rather that it is likely both will experience the profound longing to be *fully* embraced once again as by the mother of infancy—and the imperious need to break away. [10]

Union and reunion between two women are particularly threatening as archetypal images to men who seem to wish to disturb them. I remember how my male friends reacted when, in my thirties, I first fell in love with a woman: they always wanted to walk between us. They shared with me their fantasies of a *ménage à trois*. The response of one male client upon learning that I am a lesbian was: "Of course, I feel rejected. I feel rejected in some sense by all lesbians. Any man who is being honest will admit that he wants to feel he has something unique to offer a woman, which no other woman could even come close to providing." Twelfth-century male monastics, who, in the hierarchy of the church, are the lawgivers, had a more extreme response to nuns who had become lovers. So long as they expressed their love through poetry and intimacy that involved no penetration of each other's bodies, their relationships were condoned; if, however, there was any evidence or admission of penetration, they were subject to a sentence of death.[11] In an attempt to make sense of these strong reactions by men to women loving women, I wrote: "For if women are gazing into mirrors and into one another's eyes as a way of remembering their wholeness, who then will mirror to men *their* souls?"

The shadow side of this archetypal pattern of love between women centers on a potential enmeshment in which individual definition of self may be lost, or in which the transformative power of the merger as a form of sympathy and empathy is not fully embraced and integrated. In this first archetypal pattern, lesbians are challenged to work with their own internalized heroic masculine and to address issues of their own pull toward heroic separativeness and narcissism. In this pattern, as well as in each of the others I am describing, there are opportunities to address many levels of internalized homophobia as well.

Reunion with the Lost Sister Self

In the second pattern, the lesbian experiences a *coniunctio* with the lost sister self through her relationship with her lover. As Sylvia Perera describes it: "This incestuous bonding between women is a way of incorporating the mother's [or sister's] dark powers rather than destroying or escaping them."[12] She adds that "this erotic bond between women allows access to positive shadow qualities a woman could not otherwise access in herself."[13] The creation myth in which Lilith and Eve are separated in the Garden of Eden is one archetypal image at the center of this pattern of individuation for lesbians. In this creation myth, woman is not dismembered but, rather, divided against herself. Lilith—mythic embodiment of the spirited, seductive, instinctive, and aggressive dimension of woman's psyche—is classically portrayed as the snake in the Garden of Eden, in the *Zohar* as the Bride of the Devil; and in Western culture she becomes the whore. In contrast, her sister, Eve, is portrayed as the pure, submissive bride of Adam. Simultaneously, Eve is forever tainted and labeled inferior because of her refusal to let all of her darker side be banished with Lilith to the wilderness. She carries with her some of Lilith's wisdom, for by eating of the apple that Lilith offers her, Eve gains the consciousness that Lilith embodies and thus retains some cellular memory of her sister self. This incorporation of Lilith is what Christianity calls "the bringing of evil into the world." In this second pattern of lesbian individuation, a woman reclaims her lost sister, her shadow self, through the tension of opposites, a sacred, embodied union occurs with a part of herself from which she has been separated by patriarchal myth and culture from time immemorial.

Another image at the center of this second pattern is a Sumerian myth that recalls the descent of the light sister, Innana, into the underworld of her dark sister's realm. In this myth Innana undergoes the death and rebirth as she is initiated by her sister, Ereshkigal, into the fullness of her true nature and reunited with her darkness, her wildness, her sexuality, her nakedness, and her voice. The reunion and *coniunctio* of the sisters ultimately transforms them both.

Judy Grahn's contemporary play *The Queen of Swords* uses a lesbian bar as the underworld setting for Innana's initiation. Ereshkigal is "the Butch of the Realm," and the initiation includes a sexual meeting between the sisters as part of their reunion. Helen, the name given to Innana in this poetic drama, asks her sister of the Realm, "Who are you really?" Ereshkigal's answer—bold, aggressive, disrobing, erotic, and penetrating—ends with:

> Yes, I am the Butch of the Realm, the Lady
> of the great below. It is hard for me
> to let you go.
> When next you say "you bitch"—"wild cherry"
> and "it just happens"—

> you will think of me
> as she who bore you to your new
> and lawful
> place of rising,
> took the time and effort
> just to get you there
> so you could moan Innana
> you could cry
> and everyone you ever were
> could die.[14]

Grahn's use of the term *butch* to identify Ereshkigal's role in relationship to Innana, who in the language of lesbian culture might be considered "femme," points to what I have observed and experienced as a shadowy aspect in this archetypal pattern of love between women. *Butch* implies the more masculine and dominant woman lover, while *femme* implies the more feminine and submissive one. Overidentification with these polarized roles in lesbian relationships can create the same "split" in consciousness that characterizes the patriarchal system in which instinctual/culturally acceptable subject/object, dark/light, mind/body remain forever oppositional. While there is *value* in recognizing the depth of these splits in our psyches as women, there is *danger* in imitating the dysfunctional power imbalances of heterosexual lineage. It is essential for women to reclaim their own dark, sensual, sexually aggressive energy on their own terms, in a relationship of mutuality and expansiveness, so that both women liberate the dark or light sister previously lost to them. The intense passion generated between such opposites can ignite the souls of both and transform each woman, bringing her to another level of her own deepest truth.

The same energy can also pull women into killing envy or violent power struggles and these are major difficulties in this archetypal pattern. In this reunion of dark and light, the aspect of the internalized masculine which is awakened and challenged to transform, is the misogynist, womanizer, and, in many cases, sexual and emotional abuser and tyrant. The numinosity or sacred energy of this second archetypal pattern for women's same-sex relationships is clearly dark, involving the symbolism of death, descent, and reformation. It does not have the light-infused, undifferentiated numinosity of the first pattern—nor the same threat of fusion. Rather, women in this pattern of archetypal reunion are called to a more oppositional kind of transformative remembering of their power, depth, and beauty.

Remembering My Whole Self: Twinning
The third archetypal pattern has at its core the image of the twin. Here women come to their emotional and sexual love of one another through the twinning of the Self by another woman who is very much like them. There is a familiarity in this pattern of loving, a natural flowing of active and passive exchange and a deep intuitive understanding and nurturance between the women in love. Mitch Walker describes this type of love between men, distinguishing "double love" from "anima love," identifying the former as being characterized by "uncanny feelings of unity, strength, and reinforcement of personal identity."[15] His description of double love between men also characterizes this dimension of women's love for one another. Accompanying the strengthening of their personal identities and the experience of merging with the twin self, women frequently have dreams of giving birth—either to a child or to some other creative expression. Walker identifies the energy in the twinning or double archetypal union as having its own procreative reality, quite independent of any sexual or biological procreativity. Downing describes this procreative exchange between women: "Even though women's lovemaking with women is not biologically connected to reproduction, experientially it touches on that mystery through a mutual return to and a mutual departure from the gate of our origin."[16]

A lesbian in this twinning experience had the following dream:

> I am standing at a meadow's edge with my closest friend. I see my lover riding bareback across the meadow. She is about six months pregnant and I know it is our child. I also know the child will be a boy.

The child who comes forth from the twinning merger may be male. He is like the boy Triptolemos, whose name means "the bringer of grain into the world" and who frequently is pictured with Demeter and Persephone after their reunion. He is the soul child, the creative essence of the lesbian woman's life, symbolic of a deep, often joyful recognition of her Self, coming forth in a creative attitude and relationship to her world. The procreated child from the twinning union may also be a girl, as in this woman's dream:

> I am giving birth. My child is a beautiful girl with black hair. I bring her immediately to my breast as she comes from my womb. The cord is not cut, she is not crying, or in distress. Though she is newborn, she feels mature. Holding her I feel a joy and completeness I've never known.

The dreamer experienced the creative birthing, abiding connection, and abundant nurturance that are often a result of the union in the twinning pattern of lesbian love relationships and individuation.

Another lesbian dreams about the procreative manifestation of creative life very differently:

> I am with X [a mentor in her field whom she respects and admires for his creativity and originality] and we have been commissioned to do a theater piece—a new rendition of *The Wizard of Oz*. As we are working, I say to him, "We are not on track. We need to create something that has never been before—something completely original." He agrees and we take a lunch break. As we are sitting eating and resting, I say to him, "I am wildly in love with Y [a

woman whom he knows and who is the dreamer's twin]. He smiles and says, "That's wonderful," and talks about how well we are matched. Then he pauses and says, "But the two of you together are too much earth. Perhaps you need a man." I am touched because I feel he is trying to protect my creativity; but I also feel that he is missing something about women that I know. He just has no idea how much earth women's creativity requires.

The shadow potential in this particular archetypal pattern is that women in love with each other can become mesmerized by their Self reflections and begin imitating each other; this imitation may prevent a deeper exploration of the subtlety and nuances of their sameness, which ultimately leads a woman to that procreative expressive core that twinning makes available. The relationship to the internalized masculine in this pattern involves a new meeting, cooperative though questioning, with the teacher/trickster/mentor aspects of herself.

"World as Lover, World as Self"
The fourth and final archetypal pattern for lesbian individuation and relationship echoes the first pattern I described, in which a woman remembers her wholeness through a uroboric reunion with the lover/mother. The difference is that reunion with the mother in this fourth dimension is not with a personal mother, but with Griffin's "mother at the center of the earth,"[17] and Joanna Macy's metaphoric "world as lover, world as self." Here love is manifest in a partnership that promotes a renewal of the bond of the individual woman with the deep source of all life. The archetypal pattern here is found in Celtic mythology, Native American tradition, and ecofeminist ethics, all of which are subjects too vast for in-depth exploration here. Androcentric culture and patriarchal ethos—with its valuing of separativeness, property, production, order, control, form, unity, visibility, and erection—has all but annihilated our memory of an ethos based on what Paul Gunn Allen has called "gynocentric culture,"[18] which values fluidity, permeability,

interconnectedness, chaos, multiplicity, and differentiation within a network of relatedness. A lesbian in this pattern might say, "Just as this woman and I have returned to each other at no small cost, just as we have been reunited and remembered who we truly are, so I am renewing and remembering my deep original bond to the earth and to all that is forming itself through the changes of life and death." Monique Schneider discusses the myth about Demeter and Persephone (or Kore), suggesting that

> Demeter, who just lost her daughter, feels an antinarcissistic experience; she thinks she heard a cry at the moment when the earth opened and Kore disappeared. And each time she hears a cry, she thinks that her daughter is there, and that is what makes her go all over the world. There is here something beautiful concerning maternity which is not just limited to the womb. It implies in the maternal and in woman a sort of complicity with everything which is not a form, it is the dawn, the beginning of language, and each time that something beyond the word emerges, Demeter has the feeling that it is Kore who reappears, and that makes the mother go all over the earth, in disarray, without adornment, a torch in each hand, looking for her daughter night and day. Looking for her daughter is looking for everything which is in the process of taking form; no mirror, no definite shape, can stop her. [19]

The mother searches for the daughter, the daughter for the mother, both for all that is disappearing and re-forming itself. This process leads women to a new orientation that is spiritual, embodied, earth-focused, and expressed in rituals, both ancient and contemporary, which echo the holographic theory of modern physics. In today's quantum physics, the world is revealed to us not as a collection of separate, discrete physical objects, but rather as a complicated web of interrelations among the various parts of a unified whole. The political events of the world since November of 1989 clearly depict this holographic interrelationship and indicate that people everywhere are being asked to face the chaos out of which the liberation of new forms will naturally emerge. Perhaps what Gregory Bateson referred to as the "epistemological error of Occidental civilization"—the notion that we are all separate—is actually beginning to be corrected. [20] Optimism, courage, and basic trust are required to hold and anchor this new paradigm. Women in love with other women have experienced this paradigm through their remembering of the empathic bonding with the Source to which they have returned at both personal and collective levels. Joanna Macy, a Buddhist scholar, peace activist, and environmentalist, writes,

> This ecological self, like any notion of selfhood, is a metaphoric construct and a dynamic one. It involves choice, choices can be made to identify a different moment, with different dimensions or aspects of our systemically interrelated existence—be they hunted whales or homeless humans or the planet itself. In doing this the extended self brings into play wider resources—courage, endurance, ingenuity—like a nerve cell in a neural net opening to the charge of other neurons. There is a sense of being acted through and sustained by those very beings on whose behalf one acts. [21]

In this fourth pattern of lesbian individuation, the shadow aspect centers around the potential for inflation and loss of grounding by the women in love. Lesbians are called to form a true partnership with their internalized masculine and with the men in their community at this juncture. The boundary between masculine and feminine must now also dissolve, as the paradigm of partnership and mutuality becomes truly universal. Without the interplay of all four patterns, this all-embracing partnership is not possible.

In summary, the first archetypal pattern of same-sex love between women involves the return of the lovers to the Source through a kind of *participation mystique* that echoes the original mother-daughter bond. In the second pattern, a woman experiences a reunion with her lost sister-self and begins to heal the virgin/whore split of the feminine in patriarchal culture. In the third pattern, a woman remembers her deep Self, consummating a procreative union with her twin and bringing forth into the world the creative/spirit child birthed from this deep union. In the fourth archetypal pattern, a woman's bond with the "mother at the center of the earth" and with the world is renewed, and the boundaries that separate her heart into tiny chambers and keep her from seeing the tiny diamonds at the source of all life are dissolved. In all four patterns, a woman in love with another woman is re-creating—re-forming—herself and her world.

Out of the chaos of our modern world, the miracle of love between women emerges as prophetic and visionary: "the edge *is* becoming the center."[22] Redeemed from ignominy and shame, the love of one woman for another can hold transformational potential for all our lives. The time has come to actively create an analytic theory that honors the beauty, courage, consciousness, mystery, and meaning in the experience of emotional and sexual love between women. My deepest hope is that this offering will help to break the silence of women loving women and initiate a deeper speaking of the truth that will inform and inspire a reformation of psychological theory and practice.

ORDINARY, AS LOVE

Love between women,
you don't know this yet!
How can I put it into words?
Think of the face of that singer,
the way her hand went to her temple.
Imagine yourself, you listen
as she sings the highest note.
You have taken in the air of silence
and while this silence leaves your body

you are becoming sound. Now
you are so close to that singer
you rise and fall with her breath.
But this may be too strong.
Think then of a warm wind
so gentle, so subtle you can
scarcely see it as it
holds you, not touching but
hovering so near, so
near you feel the field of gravity
and in the grip of this breeze
you who are transfixed like stone
have become light too, part air,
part color, brushed
by the softest wings
while you taste this
insubstantial substance
that dissolves inside you. But
perhaps this is too pale.
Think then of a longing.
You are afraid to want so much.
Those winds that brushed you
recede into night, this night with
eyes so black they are endless
and you have fallen
fallen as far as you can measure
and are still falling
God help you
pray as you
descend, remember
you are only human
the sun will rise
there will be a day again, though
you don't know this yet,
a day, ordinary as love, a day
familiar as women.

SUSAN GRIFFIN[23]

Notes

1. Catherine Keller, *From a Broken Web: Separation, Sexism, and Self* (Boston: Beacon Press, 1986), p. 153.

2. Susan Griffin, *Unremembered Country: Poems* (Washington, D.C.: Copper Canyon Press, 1987), pp. 61–62. Used by permission of the poet.

3. Adrienne Rich, "Transcendental Etude," in *Dream of a Common Language* (New York: W. W. Norton, 1978), pp. 72–77. Used by permission of the poet.

4. Robin Morgan, "A Country Weekend," in *Going Too Far* (New York: Vintage Books, 1978), p. 142.

5. Adrienne Rich, *Poems: Selected and New, 1950–1974* (New York: W. W. Norton, 1974), p. 221.

6. C. G. Jung, *The Collected Works of C. G. Jung*, vol. 9/1 (Princeton: Princeton University Press, 1968), p. 9.

7. Monique Schneider, in E. H. Baruch and L. J. Serrano, *Women Analyze Women in France, England and the United States* (New York: New York University Press, 1988), p. 187.

8. Nancy Chodorow, *The Reproduction of Mothering: Psychoanalysis and the Sociology of Gender* (Berkeley: University of California Press, 1978).

9. C. G. Jung and C. Kerényi, *Essays on a Science of Mythology* (New York: Pantheon Books, 1950), pp. 225 and 245.

10. Christine Downing, *Myths and Mysteries of Same-Sex Love* (New York: Continuum, 1989), p. 204.

11. E. Ann Matter, "My Sister, My Spouse," in *Weaving Our Visions* (San Francisco: Harper & Row, 1989), pp. 51–62.

12. Sylvia Brinton Perera, *Descent to the Goddess: A Way of Initiation for Women* (Toronto: Inner City Books, 1981), p. 46.

13. Ibid.

14. Judy Grahn, *The Queen of Swords* (Boston: Beacon Press, 1987), p. 56.

15. Mitchell Walker, "The Double: An Archetypal Configuration," in *Spring*, 1976, pp. 165–75.

16. Downing, *Myths and Mysteries*, p. 204.

17. Griffin, *Unremembered Country*, p. 61.

18. Paula Gunn Allen, at an author's luncheon at Artist Proof Bookstore, Larkspur, Calif.

19. Schneider, p. 186.

20. Gregory Bateson, quoted in Joanna Macy, "Greening of the Self," in A. H. Badiner, *Dharma Gaia* (Berkeley, Calif.: Parallax Press, p. 53.

21. Joanna Macy, "Empowerment Beyond Despair—On the Greening of the Self," *Vajradhatu Sun*, April 1989.

22. Rich, *Poems* (emphasis added).

23. Griffin, pp. 118–19.

Dreaming the Myth
An Introduction to Mythology for Gay Men

WILL ROSCOE

Step inside   misses and misfits
Acknowledge your symptoms
Prepare for travesties and profound transvestitures
This is the morality-shaking magician
Androgyne the Great

Behold the unseemly hermaphrodite
as he really seems
Is he the master of your questionable solutions?
Is he the mistress of
your insoluble questions?

Warning
He is addicted to effrontery
He can mess up the neatest arrangements
He can make certain that
your squirmings engulf you

He is a harmless rascal
He is a revolutionary harlot
He offers you nothing less than the risk of everything
He desires all your desires
He prickles with fecundity

Cunningest of cunts
cockadoodle of all cocks

he will dive for treasure in your deep vaginas
he will grasp your testes
and play ball with heaven

What more could you want?
What are you afraid of?
Does no one here wish to embrace the Celestial Totality?
Does no one want to live out
the whole holy story?

—JAMES BROUGHTON, "At the Androgyne Carnival"[1]

Although James Broughton lures and teases us with the delights of the androgyne, between his lines there is a warning: this carnival may not be for you.

To begin with, not every gay man needs a gay "myth to live by." The extent to which one's sexual identity serves as the crucible of growth has to be a matter of personal choice. Individuation is, after all, individual. Beyond this, as Broughton hints, the mythical figures one is likely to encounter on this quest, while always compelling, are not always nice. Myths often lead to strange realms where monstrous hybrids of gender and sexuality and violent transformations of the body are the rule. Even so, many gay men today are ready to answer yes to the call to "live out the whole holy story." They find their sexuality and identity bound up with images and perceptions that can only be described as archetypal. For these gay men, myths and mythology can be a valuable resource.

In what follows, I would like to share some of the reasons I believe mythology can be useful to us, using examples of stories from a variety of traditions that I believe speak to the interests of a gay perspective.

The world's mythology is of value to us in the first place because in our homophobic society with its centuries-long conspiracy of silence the psychological experience of the gay person is rarely represented. On the other hand, the many non-Western cultures in which homosexual and gender-variant individuals occupy recognized social roles and are seen as making distinct contributions to their communities must see something that our culture does not; and these insights are likely to have been incorporated into their religion, mythology, art, and other cultural forms. Myths, therefore, can be valuable evidence of the presence of gay-related roles—like the berdache of native North America, the *mahu* of Polynesia, and the *hijras* of contemporary India—and of the skills, personality traits, and spiritual capacities that these cultures believed to be associated with homosexuality.

For example, in the Navajo origin myth, a figure called Nadle (Nahd-LAY-ee) appears in an episode in which the men and women of the primordial community quarrel and decide to live on opposite sides of a river. Before the men depart, however, they summon Nadle for advice. Although he is male, Nadle is accomplished in all the domestic skills and crafts of women. "So it is, I see," says the leader of the men, "you can make everything, you can do anything, I see, my Grandfather, my Grandmother! Nothing is lacking, I see."[2] Nadle agrees to join the men and, as a result, they fare better than the women. Eventually both sides become lonely, and the men summon Nadle again. Now he advises the men to rejoin the women—which they do, but with a higher awareness of their mutual interdependence.

Nadle is the Navajo word for "berdache," the anthropological term for those individuals, found in most Native American tribes, who combined the activities and temperaments of both men and women. Among the Navajo, the *nadle* were often expert weavers (women's work) as well as healers and religious experts (male roles). Most *nadle* were homosexual or bisexual; some, but not all, cross-dressed or wore clothing that distinguished them from both men and women.

Today Navajo speakers often use the term *nadle* to refer to gay men.[3]

The mythical account of Nadle adds to this social profile further insights into the psychological dimensions of this role. Nadle is a *mediator* and a *catalyst*; his name means, literally, "he changes." He makes the separation between men and women possible, and he is the vehicle of their reunion. By leading the men back and forth across the river of gender difference, he functions as a psychopomp—a conductor of souls across the liminal and uncharted realm between opposites.

The theme of mediation can be found in many myths in which figures like Nadle appear. In one of the world's oldest recorded stories, "The Descent of Ishtar," inscribed in Sumer around 1000 B.C., a being called Asushunamir ("his appearance is brilliant") is created by the god Ea to rescue Ishtar from the underworld. Asushunamir is neither male nor female; and, like Nadle, he is the counterpart of a special class of priests who served in the temples of Ishtar in ancient Sumer (the *assinnu* and *kurgarru*). Because he lacks gender, Asushunamir is able to circumvent the proscriptions that prevent the living from entering the realm of the dead. Ea tells him, "The seven gates of the Land of no Return shall be opened for thee."[4] The mediator of gender becomes a mediator of the living and the dead.

Now, when we read that berdaches in several California Indian tribes often served as burial attendants because their supernatural power protected them from the spirits of the dead, I think it becomes clear that we are dealing here with what Jung called an archetype. That is, all these local instances of mediation are evidence of a common and universal psychic representation, an archetype, whose most prominent characteristic is the ability to bridge cultural and psychological differences that are normally distinct—life/death, male/female, culture/nature, and so forth.

Based on this insight, I have reexamined my own life for ways that being gay has enabled me to cross boundaries, and I have found many examples. Of course, myths are not recipes to be followed literally! Theirs is the language of metaphor and symbol. A woman's dress on a male figure, for example, is a symbol of an inner *psychological* state as well as the trapping of a social role. In my own self-exploration, for example, I found that my ability to communicate well with both men and women has nothing to do with the clothes I wear but is related to my overall attitude toward gender—that of a male who does not identify with heterosexual male role models.

Mediation is not the only social and psychological potential that has been associated with homosexuality, however. Other myths highlight the creative possibilities of such a status. Another Navajo story, for example, credits a berdache god called Bego chidii with the invention of pottery, while Hawaiian legends attribute the origins of the hula dance to mythical *mahu*. The common theme of these myths seems to be that the opportunity to combine men's and women's skills and knowledge can result in useful cultural and social innovations.

Yet other myths suggest that same-sex bonding itself can be an enabling factor. Among the tribes of the Iroquois Confederacy, for example, a legendary male couple is credited with introducing key historical and cultural changes. Dekanawida is the miraculous (i.e., fatherless) offspring of a woman who dreams that she will "bear a son different from all other men." Because Dekanawida hates war and killing, he leaves his home village to find people willing to receive his message of peace. In his travels, he meets Hayontawatha (a.k.a. Hiawatha), a man whose family has been killed by an evil monster called Adodarho. In his grief, Hayontawatha has decided to abandon his former life and devote himself to helping others similarly afflicted. Dekanawida heals Hayontawatha, instituting the Iroquois condolence ceremony. The

two men form "a strong friendship," and together they establish peace among the Iroquois tribes and cure the monster
Adodarho of his evil.[5]

One motif that I have found in both Western and non-
Western folklore is what I refer to as the myth of the triumphant
"queen." In these stories, a protagonist who is powerless in
physical or social terms (that is, in the terms that men define
power) manages to overcome adversity by strength of character
alone. The female movie stars, divas, and femmes fatales
idolized by many gay men are obvious examples of this kind of
figure, as are the personas portrayed by Quentin Crisp, Harvey
Fierstein, and Molina in *Kiss of the Spider Woman*. In the non-
Western versions of this story, however, an added dimension is
revealed, the specifically *spiritual* nature of these protagonists'
inner resources. From the Chuckchi people of Siberia, for
example, we have a story concerning a special class of
shamans called *yirka'-la'ul-va'irgin*, or "soft man being"—
men who, in Chuckchi belief, have been transformed into a
being of a "softer sex":

> In a tale widely circulated among the Chukchee, a "soft man,"
> clad in a woman's dress, takes part, with other members of the
> family, in corralling the reindeer-herd. The wife of his brother
> taunts him, saying, "This one with the woman's breeches does not
> seem to give much help." The "soft man" takes offence, and
> leaves the family camp. He goes away to the border-land of the
> Koryak, who assault him in his travelling-tent. He, however,
> snatches his fire-board implement, and with its small bow of
> antler, shoots the wooden drill at his adversaries. Immediately it
> turns into a fiery shaft and destroys all of them one by one. He
> then takes their herds, and, coming back to his home, shows his
> newly acquired wealth to his relatives, saying, "See now what
> that of woman's breeches was able to procure for you."[6]

Although the myths I have described so far can be read
simply for their confirmation of gay presence in other times

and places, their *archetypal* qualities point to a second value of mythology: the psychological nature of its content and its appeal.

Myths are collective creations. Their form is the result of having passed through many hands and many retellings. Whatever is extraneous, inessential, or individual is weeded out until only the most memorable and universal remains. Furthermore, all this occurs according to rules that are largely unconscious. This is why Jung considered mythology strong evidence for the collective unconscious, a universal repository of archetypal images shared by all individuals—this and the often striking similarities between personal dreams and myths.

If there is such a thing as gay mythology, then it is a potentially valuable source of insight into the unconscious wellsprings of our sexuality and identity. Indeed, the very existence of gay-related figures in mythology is potential proof of an independent archetypal basis for gay personality. For this reason, gay mythology offers much more than confirmation of our presence. One of the challenges we face is to see our lives in terms of an intrinsic cycle of growth and development that does not take a heterosexual model as its point of reference and thereby view gay personality as a variant or derivative. Myths can offer glimpses of such nonheterosexual and non-oedipal individuations.

For example, in Zuni mythology, Kolhamana (*ko-*, supernatural; *lhamana*, berdache) is the firstborn of a brother and sister who commit incest. Initially, Kolhamana goes to live with his mother in the underwater home of the souls of the Zuni dead. Here, the dead become supernatural beings called kachinas and spend their time happily dancing under the patronage of the Kachina Mother and her berdache son. Occasionally, they don masks and travel to Zuni to appear in masked kachina dances.

In the next episode of the myth, however, a war breaks out

between the gods of the Zunis and an enemy god-people.
Kolhamana leaves his mother's home to join the other male
kachinas in the war. He is captured by the enemy along with
two other Zuni kachinas and taken to their stronghold. The
enemy gods hold a dance, in which the captives are required
to appear, to celebrate their victory. But Kolhamana protests
so loudly and vehemently that the leader of the enemies, a
giant female figure called, simply, "Warrior Woman," has him
dressed in female attire, telling him, "Perhaps you will now be
less angry."

This incident can be read as a rite of passage. At the hands
of the Warrior Woman, the berdache god undergoes a transformation that results in a new identity, symbolized by the new
clothes he receives (a common feature of Zuni initiations), and
with it the level of self-control that Zunis expected of adults.
(The other two captives, a warrior kachina and a sacred clown,
are also transformed by symbolic wounds but at the hands of
the male warriors of the enemy gods.) The episode ends when
the Zuni kachinas finally defeat the enemy. The captives,
including Kolhamana, are freed from (maternal) captivity and
return from their "hero journey" with new social capabilities
and a more mature psychological outlook.[7]

What is of particular interest in all this is that the pattern of
individuation for the berdache figure unfolds without the intervention of a father figure. Instead, the progression of the myth
takes Kolhamana from the home of his mother, a benevolent
mother goddess, to a dramatic confrontation with an archetypal Mother Terrible, the Warrior Woman, who is able, by her
own agency, to effect the break between childhood and adulthood that is usually reserved in Western mythology for masculine figures.

Another example of this kind of individuation—although
reflecting a very different social milieu—is provided by the
myth of Attis, the devoted follower of Cybele, whose mystery
cult was among the more popular religions in the Greco-

Roman world. Here is the version of the Attis myth as told by
the Roman poet Ovid:

> Attis, a Phrygian boy of handsome appearance who lived in the
> woods, bound himself with a chaste love to the tower-bearing
> goddess [Cybele]. She wished him to be kept for herself to guard
> her temple, and she said, "Determine that you may wish always
> to be a boy." Having been commanded, he gave his word; "If I
> lie," he said, "may the love for which I may break faith be my
> last." But he broke faith with the nymph Sagaritis and ceased to
> be what he was, and for this the angry goddess exacted penal-
> ties. . . . Attis went mad and, believing the roof above his
> marriage-bed to be falling in, he fled, and running to the top of
> Mount Dindymus, he pleaded at one moment, "Take away the
> torches!," and at another he shouted, "Remove the lashes!" And
> often he swore that he could see the Stygian goddesses [the Furies
> or Moirai] approach him. And so, with a sharp stone, he mangled
> his body and dragged his long hair in the unclean dust and his cry
> was, "The blame! With blood I pay the penalty deserved. Ah!
> Perish the parts that were my ruin! Ah! Let them perish," he kept
> saying. He cut away the burden of his groin, and suddenly none
> of the signs of manhood were remaining. His madness is an
> example, for unmanly ministers [galli, the priest of Cybele] cut
> their virile members while tossing their hair.[8]

Compared to the Zuni myth, the story of Attis is fraught with
tension and violence. Attis is caught between the demands for
loyalty on the part of Cybele and the social requirements of
patriarchal male roles. As this version of the myth hints,
heterosexual marriage is somehow against Attis's nature. (According to other versions, Attis is "safe" only if he remains
"free" of marriage.) All this points to the larger social context
of the myth, a world in which feminine and masculine perspectives were sharply at odds. Like contemporary Western
society, Greek and Roman cultures were thoroughly male-
dominated. But unlike us, the Greeks and Romans continued
to honor and revere images of the archetypal feminine in the

realm of religion. This contradiction between men's idealization of women and their actual behavior toward them was the
source of many conflicts in male psychology in the ancient
world. It shows up in many other myths, like that of Oedipus,
in which violence is directed not only against the self but
against others as well (e.g., Oedipus kills his father and, after
committing incest with his mother, blinds himself). As the
Attis myth underscores, denying the feminine in one's own
psychology carries a heavy price—a violent return of the
repressed, represented here in the form of the feminine deities
of fate.

With this background, I think we can better appreciate the
meaning of Attis's self-castration: first, as an act of aggression
against the phallus as the symbol of masculinism and patriarchy in an era of heightened sexual tensions and, second, as a
radical transformation of the body that, like the more benign
dressing of Kolhamana in the Zuni myth, represents a rite of
passage from one identity to another.

Self-castration may seem alien or irrelevant to us today. But
is it not possible to see in the gay fascination with bodybuild-
ing, costuming, tattooing, and piercing, and with the physical
and psychological extremes of sadomasochism, in particular,
a similar impulse—a radical transformation of the body that
constructs a new identity, the removal of a part in a metaphorical operation of self-birth?[9]

The Attis myth has many features that distinguish it from
the Zuni myth of Kolhamana, but I think it is possible to see in
both stories examples of nonoedipal individuations in which
the protagonist gains independence from the maternal image
without repressing or denying the continuing psychological
significance of the feminine. Consequently, Attis, Kolhamana,
Nadle, and many other figures function as deputies of the
goddess, as beloved and trusted familiars and as her representatives in myth and ritual. Jung considered such figures examples of the divine child archetype, an image that, in the

individuation process, anticipates "the synthesis of conscious and unconscious elements in the personality. It is therefore a symbol which unites the opposites; a mediator, a bringer of healing, that is, one who makes whole." The hermaphrodite is one of its most common incarnations. [10]

So far, we have considered myths in terms of their ability to inform and inspire. A third value of myth that I want to mention goes beyond these functions: it is their power to *transform*.

Working with myths—like dream analysis, free association, active imagination, and creative expression—can open channels between conscious and unconscious. Of course, by "working with myths" I mean something more than collecting and analyzing them, although these are important projects. I mean *living* the myths, something that can only happen after a long period of contemplating, questioning, and imagining them. As Lévi-Strauss points out, if religious ceremonies can be considered "acted myths," then myths can be viewed as "thought rituals"—mental enactments of rituals, with the same potential for fostering psychological transformation and growth. [11]

The technique that I have developed for this involves visualizing the myth not so much as a narrative film but as a series of tableaus or still pictures—mandalas, if you will—that can be held in the mind and minutely examined. Each tableau can be compared and questioned: what has changed and how? what is the point of view of each character? what are the relationships between them? and so forth. Often, I will do this while meditating or as I am falling asleep. And, of course, the converse of this process is to compare actual dreams with myths for insights into their archetypal associations.

As Jung once wrote, "Even the best attempts at explanation are more or less successful translations into another metaphorical language. . . . The most we can do is to *dream the myth onwards* and give it a modern dress." [12] It is the *images* that myths generate, not their words, that finally engage the unconscious. And this is why myths are good for dreaming. When we dream the myth, we speak the language of the unconscious, and we move thereby closer to that alignment of the total psyche that Jung termed the Self.

POSTSCRIPT

It would be somewhat misleading to end without saying something about the obstacles that the gay mythographer faces. Before we can "dream the myth onwards," it is often necessary to break through a veil of exoticism that surrounds it, acquired in the course of its transmission. The sad fact is that the vast majority of myths of value to us today were not recorded by individuals who were able to identify with their protagonists. The deeds of Nadle, Kolhamana, Attis, and others have struck most writers as alien, inexplicable, and abnormal, and they resorted to a variety of inconsistent labels and descriptions to refer to them—like "transvestite," "transsexual," and "hermaphrodite"—which makes it difficult for us to see their relevance to us today. Most of these contemporary Western categories and labels are foreign to the ways that non-Western cultures (and the pagan cultures of the ancient Western world) conceptualize gender and sexuality, and, in any case, they rarely have been applied on the basis of any real knowledge or understanding of the inner motivations of the figures described.

In other words, myths come to us with interpretations and explanations already woven into them. This is often apparent in the choice of language used by the recorder. Observers of North American berdaches have, for centuries, used the passive tense and passive grammatical constructions when describing them. A typical example comes from a member of the Lewis and Clark expedition: "If a boy shows any symptoms of effeminacy or girlish inclinations he *is put* among the girls, *dressed* in their way, *brought up* with them & sometimes *married to* men. They *submit* as women to all the duties of a wife."[13] The repetitive use of the passive voice works like a subliminal message negating the possibility that berdaches might have actively or consciously desired their lifestyles.

In short, few recorders of the mythology of gay-related figures were able to imagine why these figures behaved as they did and what they might have *gained* by doing so. They can only imagine what was *lost*—the status and privileges of the heterosexual male.

Another problem arises when myths are made to fit the expectations of a Western dual gender system. In this system, all individuals must be assigned to one or the other of two sexes; if they do not fit into one category then it must mean that they are trying to fit into the other. Assumptions like this have led many observers to describe mythical figures like Nadle and Attis (as well as their social counterparts) as crossing genders when in fact they occupied recognized *third*-gender roles within their respective cultures. The American Indian berdache, Polynesian *mahu*, Indian *hijra*, and *galli* priests of Attis and Cybele are all examples of alternative gender roles based on a combination of male, female, and/or unique (i.e., third-gender-specific) traits. Their mythical, psychological, and social power derives from their paradoxical state of being *neither* gender, a psychological stance that Harry Hay believes modern gay people can attain as well: "We Gay folk— emotionally, temperamentally, and intellectually . . . or, in a word that subsumes all three, *spiritually*—may be a combination of both hetero-masculine and hetero-feminine, but mostly we are a *combination of neither*."[14]

From this perspective, we can see that many of the androgyne figures we encounter in mythology are a reflection of heterosexual anima/animus projections. Their origin or birth is based on a union of male and female that resolves the tensions typical of individuals identified with only one pole of the gender spectrum (a "one-sided sexual being" in Jung's terms). These heterosexual androgynes do not really challenge or transcend a dual gender system. Examples include Hermaphroditus, who becomes both male and female by merging with the nymph Salmicis, and the Hindu deity Ardhanarisvara, a hybrid of Shiva and Parvati. These figures, I would argue, are of limited value from a gay perspective compared with those discussed here who are *neither* male nor female and who manifest distinct, "third status" characteristics.

In sum, myths often come to us distorted and "otherized," their connection to us and their meaning rarely obvious at first sight. By way of conclusion, then, I would like to offer the "talismans" that I try to keep in mind when reading myths in order to pierce this veil of exoticism and find their gay-related themes.

- Imagine the rewards and inner motives.
- Question single-dimensional labels—"homosexual," "transvestite," "transsexual," "hermaphrodite."
- Imagine gayness as a multidimensional constellation of traits.
- Look for multiple genders and spiritual "neitherness"; look for "nonheterosexual" as well as "homosexual" figures.
- In the battle of the sexes, who stands with the mother?

Notes

1. James Broughton, "At the Androgyne Carnival," in *Ecstasies: Poems 1975–1983* (Mill Valley, Calif.: Zyzygy Press, 1983), pp. 82–83. Used by permission.

2. Bernard Haile, *Women versus Men: A Conflict of Navajo Emergence* (Lincoln: University of Nebraska Press, 1981), p. 20.

3. See Will Roscoe, "We'wha and Klah: The American Indian Berdache as Artist and Priest," in *American Indian Quarterly* 12(2): 127–50.

4. James B. Pritchard, ed., *Ancient Near Eastern Texts Relating to the Old Testament*, 2nd ed. (Princeton: Princeton University Press, 1955), p. 108.

5. Shirley H. Witt, *The Tuscaroras* (New York: Crowell-Collier Press, 1972), pp. 13–19.

6. Waldemar G. Bogoras, "The Chukchee," *Memoirs of the American Museum of Natural History* 11, no. 2 (1907): 449–53.

7. See Will Roscoe, *The Zuni Man-Woman* (Albuquerque: University of New Mexico Press, 1991), chap. 6.

8. Ovid, *Fastí* 4.223–44 (my translation).

9. This reading of castration as a birthing metaphor is suggested by Freud himself, in "The Interpretation of Dreams," in *The Basic Writings of Sigmund Freud*, A. A. Brill; ed. (New York: Modern Library, 1938), p. 388.

10. C. G. Jung, "The Psychology of the Child Archetype," in C. G. Jung and C. Kerényi, *Essays on a Science of Mythology: The Myth of the Divine Child and the Mysteries of Eleusis* (Princeton: Princeton University Press, 1969), p. 83.

11. Claude Lévi-Strauss, *Anthropology and Myth: Lectures 1951–1982* (Oxford: Basil Blackwell, 1987), p. 201.

12. Jung, p. 79.

13. In Donald Jackson, ed., *Letters of the Lewis and Clark Expedition with Related Documents 1783–1854*, 2nd ed. (Urbana: University of Illinois Press, 1978), p. 531 (emphasis added).

14. Harry Hay, "A Separate People Whose Time Has Come," in *Gay Spirit: Myth and Meaning*, Mark Thompson, ed. (New York: St. Martin's Press, 1987), p. 284.

Homo/Aesthetics
or, Romancing the Self

LYN COWAN
for A. D.

> "Beauty is truth, truth beauty,"—that is all
> Ye know on earth, and all ye need to know.
> —JOHN KEATS, from *Ode on a Grecian Urn*

>> Without warning
>> as a whirlwind
>> swoops on an oak
>> love shakes my heart.
>> —SAPPHO

This is a musing, personal and subjective, about love and affinities. I have no inclination to theorize about love. I am an unabashed, anachronistic romantic, reconstructed, it is true, but a romantic nonetheless. And I am a near-insatiable sensualist, constantly craving smooth milky chocolate and blue moonlight, even though I wear the persona of a near-ascetic. While my mind reads books and takes in important data and thinks, it is my fingers, my hands, my mouth, my eyes, my skin that tell me pleasure and speak to me in the language of beauty. The language of beauty that speaks the truth of love is sensate and immediate, conveyed in touch and gesture. All ye need to know.

It has always felt to me rather chilling that Jungian psychology tends to speak of romantic love in terms of "projection," as if the *concept* of projection fully explained all we need to know about what makes the passion, the excitation, the depth and bittersweetness of erotic matings. Projection is, indeed, an inevitable mechanism and invaluable for consciousness; but to speak psychologically and aesthetically of love in such conceptual language reduces experience to concept, the organic thus rendered mechanical, psyche as machine. Conceptual explanatory language gives primacy to "mental insight" and assigns "bodily knowing" to second place, body as reactor to insight rather than as first discoverer of "truth." No mere mind-spawned word can leave such a taste of eloquence and knowledge on my tongue as can the soft skin of my lover's body. To imagine love in conceptual terms, however accurate the terms, is to separate love from body, to separate the beautiful from the sensate.

And then, Jungian psychology tends to speak almost exclusively of romantic love as *heterosexual* projection, not noticing that all the thick emotionality and convolutions of the heart that attend romantic love are not at all different when the "other" is of the same sex. Women and men learn to *interpret* the eroticized aspect of animus or anima, projected onto a literal opposite-sex person, as romantic love. Not only do we so learn to interpret, we learn to *experience* this projection in a culturally predetermined way: finding beauty in what is not like ourselves because we have learned that that is where beauty resides, finding our sexual desire flowing out toward a figure we recognize as Other because we have learned that the "other" must be literally so, finding psychological reassurance in the normalcy of our sexual desire for literal otherness, because we have learned that this is the only *real* kind of love there is.

I remember, at sixteen, having a crush on the captain of the football team. It was 1958, and no doubt my as-yet-unrecognized lesbian self sought safety in convention. To this day, I do not know for certain how much of that crush was genuine, and how much of it I cultivated so that I could have the kind of heterosexual adolescence I was supposed to. But at sixteen, for certain, what made my blood rush was the lovely, enviable luster of my best friend's long black hair. During the day I thought about the football captain, but at night, alone in my bed, my fingers kneaded the air, like a cat's, wanting to touch her breasts. For the sake of normalcy, which to me meant survival, this truth I could not, would not, know.

The dictum that "opposites attract" has been narrowed to mean that *only* opposites can or do attract, as if the opposition of "otherness" is somehow more compelling and numinous than the attraction of "likeness." So what happens when the attraction—sexual, erotic, emotional, physical, mental, spiritual—is not to an "opposite" but to a "like"? What does it suggest that the phallic form, in my beholding eye, is a passionless aesthetic, interesting and admirable, but hardly compelling? How am I, as a woman, to understand over-whelming and wordless numinosity when it comes to me in the form and flesh of a woman like myself?

My male analyst in Zurich in the early 1970s once commented to me that my experience of "the numinous" always seemed to come through a woman. I was immediately struck by the emotional accuracy of his observation. Yes, it was so, had always been so. He had named my feeling, and thus I gained something important: an almost tactile piece of self-knowledge that began to take shape out of the vague emotions of nameless longing and bittersweetness that since childhood had floated uneasily around a veiled female psychic figure. However, we never fully pursued the implications of this truth to see what it would reveal of my deeper sexual self, a more authentic self than the one that was, at the time, having a mad and maddening affair with a black-eyed, handsome, wildly romantic *puer*.

We avoided following, or benignly neglected, the path of that particular truth: I no doubt because I was very afraid, didn't want to know, and the time for me to know was not yet; my analyst perhaps for the same reasons, or because it simply did not occur to him that there was something more to pursue. Now, nearly twenty years later, our "reasons" are irrelevant. What is important is that that essential piece of self-knowledge, the realization that "woman" is the carrier of the numinous for me, has been deepened, from mental insight to psychological reflection to knowledge embedded in the very flesh of my body. That began to happen when I was past forty years old, and so I had to go back to the beginning and start "knowing" all over again, in a different way, from a different source, through a different medium.

The different "way" is my body, the different "source" is my lesbian, rather than heterosexual, self, and the different "medium" is my female lover and mate. Of course, she and I project all kinds of things grandly, wildly, and sometimes painfully onto each other. But we are neither sexually opposite nor in sexual opposition, not agents or representatives of that realm of "the unknown." She is an "other" to me because she is different from me, but she is not my opposite. At first glance, many of our attitudes and approaches to life appear almost identical, informed by the fact and consciousness of our femaleness; yet our differences (not necessarily oppositional) can be dramatic. We are both introverted; but while she engages the world vigorously in corporate boardrooms, I flee to the seclusion of my study. We both want to be scholars and are academically minded, but the land and a farm are her deepest joys, while I dream of libraries and self-filled reams of paper. She wants dog and cat, I am content with cat. She is more maternal with children; I am maternal with her. Our endless making of differences from the same essences requires attention to detail, an ear for nuance, a love of subtlety. When we fail in these, we blur and lose ourselves for the time.

The individuation process requires that we become skilled in differentiation. In female/male romantic relationships, where the attraction of the opposite sex is attractive primarily because it is opposite, initial differentiation is relatively broad-brush. Our culture, and Jungian psychology to the extent that it serves the culture, makes such differentiation fairly easy, by defining for us what *is* female and what *is* male, and by pre-differentiating certain psychic components as abstract principles: "feminine" and "masculine."

A woman whom I love is "like myself" and "like my Self," requiring a differentiation now of the most minute, the most subtle separations of the smallest particulate matter(s), full of nuance. In this subtle likeness there are no broad categories of gender and sex into which to sort and contrast all the ways in which we are different, for in these ways we are not so different—and this is where we are as likely to be afflicted with psychic blindness as blessed with the most acute and penetrating vision. Because of our fundamental female likeness, the individuation process requires the most exact differentiation of the myriad subtle shades of nuance that distinguish our projections. Projections onto a screen must become carefully noticed reflections into a mirror. She turns this way, I turn that. My individuation depends on being able to tell the difference between my projection (*what* I see of myself in her) and reflection (*how* I see my Self in her).

A heterosexual woman or man suffers a loss of soul by not knowing that figure in the psyche who delights in a homoerotic aesthetic. No one is one-sidedly sexually oriented, except those neurotic souls who are completely identified with one sexual polarity or another. The virulent heterosexual, whose homophobic fear of the inner self-lover may appear as Macho Man or Vacant Female, lives at one pole, while at the other pole lives the insistent homosexual, whose heterophobic fear of otherness in her/his own psyche may appear as self-limiting political correctness or thinly disguised contempt for

the opposite sex. Total identification is especially psychologically limiting for heterosexuals because it is defined and
accepted as "normal." They are encouraged, even threatened, to remain unconscious of that imaginal psychic figure
within them who appreciates the beauty of sameness and is
attracted to a sexual likeness.

By remaining unconscious of the homo/sexual aspect of
themselves, exclusively heterosexually identified people leave
a potentially creative and loving aspect of themselves split off
from consciousness. If the self-lover within is banished to the
darkest cavern of repressed fears, then a pathway of differentiation for the sake of individuation, marked by an appreciation of the subtle beauty of affinities, reaches a dead end. The
same-sex-loving figure is forbidden to enter consciousness.
Without loving one's self-lover, can one truly be a whole lover
to anyone, being split at the root?

I believe there are some women whose interior image of the
Self, of woman-as-goddess, woman-as-eminently-worthy-of-
love, an image correlated with individual self-respect, suffers
and deteriorates when that image is not embodied in a romantic sexual relationship with another woman. Romance, after
all, is an aesthetic of the erotic imagination, a *fabula*, to use
one of the Latin words for "romance," or the fabulous telling
of a love story. Because romance celebrates Eros as "firstborn
and fairest of the gods," romance is one of the ways we
worship, and making love is the making of prayer. I think
women, as "idea," are beautiful. I think my woman lover, as a
person, is beautiful. The beauty I see reflected back to me
from the mirror of my lover's soul is my own, and she sees her
own in me. The divine presence of Eros attends such psychic
reflection in the form of physical passion. To be able to recognize this beauty as my own soul is more a redeeming truth I
need to know than a pathological form of narcissism, which
is, sadly, the only way we have been taught or allowed to
"know" this reflection.

The terrible anguish of Narcissus, who cannot touch the face of his own soul, is a psychologically instructive story of projection that cannot be claimed, a lesson about how one's soul may be lost and one's life with it. But the romance in the myth of Narcissus has been severely pathologized, defined in modern terms and times as a personality disorder, as if the appreciation of the beauty of one's image and the longing for a soulmate of one's own and in one's own likeness are symptomatic of disorder. The conventional warnings against narcissistic introspective indulgence are as Murray Stein wrote, evidence for the deeper knowledge of how strong the "reflective instinct" is, that there exists in psyche a "powerful tendency in the direction of Narcissus," and that one "has a profound unconscious love of [her] own soul and of the activity of reflecting upon [herself] for [her] own pleasure." The taboo against self-absorption is intended to protect us from the "fascination and beauty" of one's soul-image. [1]

An equally strident disapprobation of the narcissian way of loving comes through our culture's pervasive and deeply rooted homophobia, the collective dread of self-attentiveness that looks reflectively within and finds one's own image to be stunningly beautiful and desirable.

The psychic image of Narcissus, gazing into the pool with desire and lovesick eyes, does not want an explanation of itself. It wants itself. That sweet, beautiful youth of not-yet-fixed gender is itself an image of wanting, and of wanting denied.

> . . . he saw
> An image in the pool, and fell in love
> With that unbodied hope . . .
> . . . .
> Everything attracts him
> That makes him so attractive. Foolish boy,
> He wants himself; the loved becomes the lover,
> The seeker sought, the kindler burns. [2]

Beautiful, young, and indeterminate, Narcissus is an image of undifferentiated eroticism, knowing only itself and not an "other." Anyone who remains poolside with Narcissus suffers his fate. For one brief moment, though, where perhaps we all begin, in that eternal moment of gazing into one's reflection— just before one reaches for the untouchable, before one begins to waste away with impossible love and unmet desire—in that moment, one may perceive one's beauty as one's true self, and one's truth as a beautiful self. At this moment, the love of affinities, the romantic longing to touch and embrace and caress one's likeness, is born. Even after one leaves the pool's water-mirror, the image remains in one's psyche always, an icon, a thing of beauty that endures forever. But now the beholder must move on and find an "other" who can best embody that image now engraved in the soul, an "other" whose living heart beats with the same rhythm.

No one myth is adequate for a whole human life. The tale of Narcissus is a tragedy in one act. One's life needs at least a second act, conscious action, to move the individuation process to a romantic, satisfying, as close to happy ending as possible. Reflection is not enough. Psyche needs erotic embodiment. Not enough is the distant coolness of fixed image, however lovely. The body wants wetness and heat and throbbing of blood, impact of muscle, particular scent.

Narcissism is a pathology not when it suggests homosexuality, but when it excludes love of an Other, an Other of either sex whose separate reality ought to evoke and excite love rather than preclude it. The merely gazing and mournful self-absorption of pathological narcissism do not belong to an aesthetic of romantic same-sex love, and still the aesthetic of such love is created in the narcissistic passion to embrace one's essential self in its unique, separate, beauty. Put another way, the aesthetic of same-sex romantic love requires not only a narcissistic passion for one's own image, but also a differentiated eroticism that recognizes in an "other" a worthy self-likeness. My love is not only of self; it is requited in the image of my lover's face, and all my senses, feasting on her, draw forth my delighted recognition.

Women who love women sexually have long been accused of (among other things) psychological infantilism, of wanting to regress to the womb, to merge mindlessly with the Mother. (Odd, how little this "pathology" has been theoretically differentiated from the presumed psychology of gay men.) Lesbian sexuality has been seen as childish and immature. Some theorists still judge such sexuality as a "phase" to be outgrown, appropriate only to adolescence. Too many heterosexual men still think that all a lesbian—of any age—needs to help her "grow up" is "a real man." This is as absurd as assuming that the reason women love *men* sexually is because they hate their mothers and are trying to become men by sexual assimilation.

How ungenerous such disembodied theorizing is to a soul in love. Such bald ideas have no truth in them for me because they are not beautiful, have no substance, no body with skin and fine animal fur, are not congruent with what my flesh knows as intimate fact (her rose-petaled lips, the line of her throat, the exquisite symmetry of her eyelashes).

What first captures the heart and desire of Narcissus is beauty, his reflected beauty. There is health in falling in love with another of the same sex who embodies one's own form, in finding it beautiful, even in identifying with it—as in, "this lovely woman, this too is me, for I also am a woman." Homo/ sexuality, or sexuality among sames, is a recognition of homo/ aesthetics and can be affirmed on grounds of beauty, as well as and apart from any other.

Mnemosyne is the Mother of the Muses, whose name means Memory. She is the matrix of all art, poetry, and song, and the Greeks correctly perceived that history, too, is an art. Without Mnemosyne, I could not remember myself as a woman; but when I recall my first, original, archetypal female form, when

I recall the tender and wild Beauty that attends all Love in her first form, then Memory sends a daughter to me, and my Lady Muse leads me back to the memory of beauty and first love. Audre Lord wrote in a love story, ". . . wherever I touched, felt right and completing, as if I had been born to make love to this woman, and was remembering her body rather than learning it deeply for the first time."[3]

So it is true, after all, what those theorists say: "Lesbianism" *is* a way of returning to the womb, but there is a vast difference between "regression" and "return." The desire to return to one's source, an archetypal desire, not a particularly homosexual one, can be construed as "regression" only in a culture like ours, which fears the Mother and elevates the Father as a defense against her. For women, return to the Mother is not necessarily regression; it is a return to what we are intended to become.

There is more going on in lesbian loving than we know. Somewhere far below the cultural accretions, the social prohibitions, the legal obstacles, the psychological confusions, the developmental mistakes, and the religious judgments, somewhere my self is seeking a Self, its own original maternal image writ large and as naturally as sunrise the numinous Self comes to me through a woman and in her form. To feel myself returning to this Mother-Self is like coming home. My body remembers that home; my body is that home, re-created.

The power of Mnemosyne, Mother Memory, is felt in the body. The mother of all art quickens the sensual body, recalling me to remember what has been lost as I have grown up and away from the Mother: self-knowledge, self-love, self-respect, self-pleasure. This is too much loss. The Patriarch is relentless in his destruction of perceived female threats to his high place. He has tried to make the world an arid, cold, dangerous place, as unlike the womb as he can imagine.

If I follow my Muse, she can restore these losses, through whatever art she gives me to embody, as a way of re-creating my first home, my deepest self. My Muse, like my lover, guides my sensate touch to an enduring mystery in my Self. Indeed, she takes me to herself, her own temple. When the Muse is upon me, caressing and arousing me, my body's memory recalls and calls forth yet again all the deep pleasures I have known of woman. Then once more, like a whirlwind, "love shakes my heart."

Notes

1. Murray Stein, "Narcissus," in *Spring*, 1976, p. 39.

2. Ovid, *Metamorphoses*, lines 419–22 and 429–32.

3. Audre Lord, *Zami: A New Spelling of My Name* (Freedom, Calif.: The Crossing Press), quoted in Laura Chester, ed., *Deep Down: The New Sensual Writing by Women* (Boston: Faber and Faber, 1989), p. 237.

Homovision
The Solar/Lunar Twin-Ego

HOWARD TEICH

Homophobia runs so deep in our culture that relationships between men command little or no recognition, let alone acknowledgment. In the videos, films, and literature of popular culture, where nearly eighty percent of stories feature two men and a woman, the emphasis invariably falls on resolving the male-female tension. Relationships between men are so rarely explored in popular culture that they appear not to exist. There have been times in our history when certain male-male configurations have risen to the limelight; for example, the past two world wars brought the innocent young "buddies" motif to American theaters and books, and soon we may see its return. The father-son configuration also emerged early in this century when psychology brought that male-male dynamic to our collective consciousness. But, for the most part, the many revisionist social studies of male-male relationships are hard-pressed for popular material of substance and depth.

Even our standard interpretation of the Oedipus myth revolves almost exclusively around the son's incestuous interest in his mother and murder of his father. Little or no attention is given the impassioned relationship between father and son, initiated by the father's attempted murder of his son. More disturbing is our regular failure to recognize Oedipus's father,

Laius, as the "inventor of pederasty" and the "founder of warrior homosexuality." The original cause of conflict—the initial male-male incest taboo and the infanticidal "love-murder" dialectic that goes on between father and son—is almost entirely unnoticed. Revisioning the myth with an eye toward this powerful male-male dialectic would require our reinterpretation of all the subsequent stages in the myth.

It is critical that we reclaim our "homovision"—our ability to see the same-sex dynamic—at the root of masculine individuation. We need to support men, irrespective of sexual orientation, in focusing on the primary male-male configuration for healing the rifts between men as fathers, sons, brothers, and lovers. Jungian perspectives on men's relationships usually revolve around Jung's contrasexual archetype of the feminine, or anima. But the male-male union emerges as a critical step in all men's individuation processes—and as the final step for some. Jung himself discovered this male-male union to be the secret of alchemy ("the hidden to be revealed"). Having come across this critical step—known as the monocolus, or Union of the Same—in the latter part of his life, Jung did not have the opportunity to fully develop the far-reaching implications this mysterious male union would have for his psychology of the unconscious. [1]

Mitchell Walker was on the right track in 1976 when he explored the possibility of another Jungian archetype of the masculine—of a male-male configuration as opposed to the male-female anima/animus theory—in his provocative essay on "the double." [2] Walker envisioned the male "double" as an archetype of the psyche, of equal importance in masculine individuation as Jung's anima. Historically, Western culture has seen the male-male dynamic as a light/dark duality, an irreconcilable good-versus-evil tension personified in God and the Devil. In Jung's psychology, the light/dark duality is initially manifest in the relationship of the ego and the same-sex shadow archetype.

John P. McIntyre points out a male-male dialectic that is markedly different than the dark-versus-light tension featured in our classical literature. In his homovisionist study of American literature, McIntyre cites Nathaniel Hawthorne, who associates this mysterious male-male dialectic with the "sun-man" and the "moon-man." Hawthorne envisions this male-male dialectic not as being at odds for good or evil intent but rather as two coexistent forces in separate realms, each exercising influence over its separate sphere:

> Generally the sun-man represents the establishment; he has achieved the economic and political resources necessary to consolidate power. Using logic and religion, he maintains his social status usually at the expense of others. . . . The moon-man, however, dissembles by day and creates by night. Because he cultivates a visionary sense, he threatens the power-elite, who either force him underground or into exile.[3]

Hawthorne refers here to a particular stage of our culture's development, wherein sun-man and moon-man emerge as separate symbols of the seemingly insurmountable male-male duality, a split duplicated in nearly all our mythologies and sociopolitical structures. As he suggests, our patriarchal culture regularly identifies the sun-man as the establishment hero and relegates the moon-man to impotence and oblivion.

In Jungian thought, the moon-man is often confused with the anima. Jung built his psychology on the central female-male configuration of anima/animus, equating the moon (Luna) with the anima, or feminine, and labeling the sun (Sol) as animus, or masculine. These gender labels assigned Sol to the unconscious "masculine side" (animus) in women. Similarly, lunar energies in men were tied to their unconscious "feminine side" (anima), making it clear to men that lunar behaviors belonged to the feminine.

But if we dig deep enough in the mythologies of virtually any culture—including our own—we find that at some point the sun-man was almost always born with a lunar twin. The universal theme of solar/lunar male Twins is documented in nearly all cultural histories: it can be easily spotted in the mythologies of African, Mayan, Roman, Greek, and East Indian civilizations. Rivalrous pairs, such as Romulus and Remus and Jacob and Esau, may be most familiar to us, but examples of amicable solar/lunar male Twins abound as well. Many—perhaps most—twin male couples remain buried in the annals of our history. It is, for example, seldom recalled that even our superhero Hercules was born with a twin named Iphicles.[4] The overwhelming evidence of suppressed or murdered male Twins has led mythologist Jaan Puhvel to assert that the Twins may occupy the very deepest layer of our "mythological layer cake."[5]

The Twins are a holistic model of male unity, transcendent of the disproportionate light/dark duality upon which so many male-male configurations are prefigured. Together the Twins represent a balanced, complete energetic principle of the masculine, partaking of both light and dark influences. Perhaps the most succinct and eloquent exposition of the solar/lunar masculine principle is found in Joseph Campbell's insightful commentary accompanying the legend of the Navaho twin heroes:

> The two, Sun-child and Water-child, antagonistic yet cooperative, represent a single cosmic force polarized split and turned against itself in mutual portions. The life-supporting sap-power, mysterious in the lunar rhythm of its tides, growing and decaying at a time, counters and tempers the solar fire of the zenith, life-desiccating in its brilliance, yet by whose heat all lives.[6]

It is the "single cosmic force" of these two principles that represents male wholeness. Up to now, our Western culture has equated only the Solar Twin principle with masculinity. Those qualities associated with solar psychology—clarity, willfulness, competitiveness, endurance, perfection, linear thinking, goal-directed behavior—are labeled masculine, while the lunar qualities—tenderness, receptivity, intuitiveness, compassion, changeability, abandonment, frenzy, emotional availability for dance, song, and prayer—are said to be feminine and homosexual. Lunar masculine attributes, those spontaneously instinctual, reciprocal, and affectionate emotional behaviors, have long been perceived as a potential threat to a patriarchal order based on strict division of masculine and feminine behaviors.

In Western psychology the solar-masculine/lunar-feminine split goes all the way back to Romulus (solar) slaying Remus (lunar). But prior to the ascendancy of Roman and Greek solar traditions, many mythologies considered the solar principle to be feminine and associated lunar qualities with masculinity. Campbell concisely summarized the solarization our mythologies have undergone:

> The new age of the Sun God has dawned, and there is to follow an extremely interesting, mythologically confusing development [known as solarization], whereby the entire symbolic system of the earlier age is to be reversed, with the moon and the lunar bull assigned to the mythic sphere of the female, and the solar principle to the male.[7]

With the sacrifice of the lunar male twin, the lunar principle is carried almost exclusively by women, and the solar principle becomes men's dominion. The solar/lunar dichotomy thus underlies the gender split that has characterized our social order, making balanced heterosexual and homosexual relationships difficult.

The predominant solar-masculine principle is not without value, but the Solar Twin has become notoriously inflated in our society. Regardless of sexual orientation, many men continue to be resistant to alternative styles of manliness that encourage them to become "more like women," with the implication that their masculinity is shameful or suspect. Resolving the "masculinity problem" first requires that men recognize that the style of masculinity embodied in the traditional solar masculine principle represents only half of the full structure of the male psyche.[8] Anthropologist Paul Radin, who proclaimed the legend of the Twin Heroes "the basic myth of Aboriginal America," emphasized that both Twins must work together to achieve a common purpose:

> . . . each twin constitutes only half an individual psychically. It is because the two are only complementary halves that they have always to be forced into action. . . . Each alone can do nothing positively. . . . For constructive and integrated activity . . . the two halves must be united.[9]

Simple recognition of our incomplete "solar" distortion of masculinity will not automatically rid us of its influence. Lunar traits in men have often been regarded with suspicion as "effeminate" or embraced defiantly as "gay." In their youth, many gay men learned that this lunar energy was labeled feminine and that it evoked the wrath and violence of other men. Equating the lunar with the feminine has also carried with it a certain sexual charge that ignites men's homophobia, making it difficult for many men, irrespective of sexuality, to engage their own lunar masculine energies or to accept such attributes unequivocally as masculine. Uniting solar and lunar masculine energies will require much hard work on the part of men, not only collectively but also each within the privacy of his own unique process.

THE THERAPEUTIC VALUE OF THE SOLAR/ LUNAR TWINS ARCHETYPE

Analytical psychologist Edward Edinger has asserted that "the individuated ego is destined to be born a twin."[10] This birth of consciousness of the solar/lunar ego will catapult the ego into a new stage of rapid growth. Without this growth of consciousness, the inflated solar–deflated lunar ego or inflated lunar–deflated solar ego will be "split" off in men.

In Jung's psychology, the split-off same-sex figure has traditionally been seen as the shadow that needs to be acknowledged and incorporated into the ego. Incorporating the shadow means taking responsibility for this "piece" as a part of ego consciousness. However, there is a more substantive masculine issue that needs to be seen in relationship to this same-sex figure. In a study of the Greek god of healing, Asclepius, Jungian analyst C. A. Meier concludes that the same-sex figures are an emergence archetype of wholeness:

> Analytical psychology shows that the appearance of a pair of identical figures, which we call a "doublet," is as a rule associated with the emergence of material into consciousness. Emergence into consciousness is closely related to healing.[11]

Restoring the Twins archetype to men's consciousness is the first step toward healing the solar/lunar split that has characterized the traditional Western male ego. The inflated solar "male ego," split off from the mitigating influence of its lunar twin, continues to incur such disfavor that many critics prefer to minimize the importance of the ego as a notion of Western psychology. Jung, however, was convinced that the ego plays a key role in relating to and accessing the energies of the unconscious.

Jung's alchemy, based on masculine psychology and individuation, shows us an illuminating x-ray into the need for both solar and lunar twin-energies to be at work in the male. The twin solar and lunar aspects of the masculine ego-principle are united in the critical stage of alchemy known as the "monocolus," or Union of the Same, which is a prerequisite to the Union of Opposites.

The twin-ego principle can be seen as the psychological counterpart of the physiological dichotomy of right brain (lunar) and left brain (solar). When an individual or culture is skewed toward either the left or right hemisphere, this imbalance is reflected in its images, language, and behavior. In Western culture, where the lunar male twin has been killed, the solar masculine (left brain) has become the "ego ideal." Its objective, linear, goal-directed, and calculating behaviors are revered, as opposed to the devalued intuitive, emotional, spontaneous, and artistic aspects of lunar masculinity (right brain). Because all men have the capacity for both right- and left-brain behaviors, the dissonance between the solar, left-brain ideal and actual male experience causes neurotic confusion and a lack of self-esteem in many men.

The following dream exemplifies the plight of a heterosexual man who ascribed to the solar-masculine ego ideal as a defense against suppressed homosexual encounters from early childhood. This man was frustrated and alienated even in his most intimate relationships. He had a "trickster" personality that was hard to pin down. He tended to be overinvolved with women and to avoid interactions with men. Although secure in his heterosexuality, he still deeply feared any male attention; for him, contact with men was always unconsciously sexualized as a result of his childhood experiences. He would regularly sabotage his own financial success out of fear that his outstanding work would expose him to male attention. With this dream, he began working toward establishing the internal unity of his solar and lunar sides and diffusing the sexual connection through balancing the twin males in a Union of the Same.

> I'm in an old wooden milk wagon and with me is a gay, happy, laughing, fun person who I feel is also homosexual. He's trying to convince me to make love with him, and I am clear that I don't want to. I'm stern, and he's laughing, joking and kidding me. I am pinned to the side of the cart, but finally I break away. I get on top of my homosexual friend or brother. For some reason I feel he's a twin of mine, and all through the dream I'm struck with the bond I have with this man and how I feel I need to be on top of him. I'm aware that once I'm on top, I'm okay.

The healing of this man's deep-seated homophobia allowed his lunar twin, whom he identified as homosexual, to be brought back into union. He had long been "pinned down" by his suspicion that any male advances, even of a playful nature, were a homosexual threat. Exploring the admirable, spirited qualities of his lunar twin helped him begin to break through his fear of being close to men and brought back his happy, laughing fun side. He also began to realize greater success in his work and in his relationship with his wife.

It is this same spirit of lunar heroism that is sorely lacking in many men's personal and professional lives. However, the resurrection of the lunar hero by itself will not solve the problem. The reconciliation of a man's solar and lunar energies requires that he take part in an initiatory process to ensure an enduring healing of his solar/lunar ego split. His solar/lunar twin-ego consciousness must be repeatedly tested and renewed to assure that its union is solid and secure. Once the energies are united, this renewal will change his attitude in encounters with both men and women.

Consciousness of a balanced twin nature, developed in the safety of a ritual or therapeutic space, will ultimately help men eradicate solar/lunar distortions that complicate many male-male and male-female relationships. Relationships between lovers are not the only ones complicated by solar/lunar projections. Fathers and sons are among the first to get caught in a solar/lunar split. A solar-masculine father, not in touch with his twin nature, cannot support (or may even feel compelled to destroy) his son's lunar attributes. Likewise the overly lunar father, liable to be threatened and intimidated, will unconsciously seek to suppress his son's emerging solar characteristics.

The following dream shows another common side of the masculinity issue, a not infrequent case in which a homosexual man endures an inflated feminine principle. The regular recurrence of idealized or inflated feminine figures in gay counterculture no doubt occurs as a reaction-formation to the unyielding solar-masculine standard set up as a hegemony. In this dream we see Twins emerge to bring an end to the dominance of an overidentified, inflated feminine principle. Without the encumbrance of an overruling anima, this man was able to begin the journey toward reinstituting his sovereignty and balance in his male psyche. His overidentification with the feminine had resulted in a series of somatic complaints and a long dependent relationship on a solar-masculine partner who compensated for his lack of decisiveness and power. He presented this dream in his first therapy session:

> There's a blue shadow king and queen. They live in a circular castle. The queen is inside the castle. The king is on the outside. The queen is evil. The king has to destroy this queen, but when he does, he has to give up his own life force to destroy her. Since he's on the outside of the castle and she's on the inside, he needs some help. The help comes in the form of two blue men. These two blue twins walk to the wall of a castle and open a hole in it. One of them goes to the inside of the castle, one to the outside. The man on the inside throws a beam of light or energy directly at the queen. The one on the outside catches the same beam. The same colored beam is going through the king. As I'm watching, I see the king shaking as if dissolving. This beam of energy is going right through the hole held open by the twins. It is now directed to the queen. She is starting to shake and she is starting to expand. She is about to blow up. The last thing I see is the king twitching on the ground, shriveling up. She explodes into a nova.

Jung saw the King (solar) as the ruling masculine archetype and the Queen (lunar) as the ruling feminine, or anima. Here the Queen appears so inflated that she has become an evil entity, split off from her counterbalance, the King. To liberate his ego identity from the feminine Luna, the twin warriors arrived to establish the psychological conditions for his new beginning.

Jung has said that the ego "mirrors" the unconscious. A solar/lunar twin-ego therefore impacts further upon Jung's theory of the unconscious. From the homovisionist perspective the twin-ego conveys, we can see the bipolarities that define each and every archetype—including the anima—without restrictive cultural and gender distortions. Homovision allows us to see clearly that, beyond gender, all the archetypes are of a bipolar, solar/lunar nature. Thus our ability to take inventory of the anima's energetic potential is dramatically expanded by viewing its "raw material" through this homovisionist solar/lunar lens. Our increased awareness of the anima's fundamental bipolar nature furthers our understanding, not only of how it functions in the Union of Opposites, but also of how the inner dynamics of the archetype work toward generating its own unique energetic charge.

In the first stage of masculine individuation, the Union of the Same, the male ego consciously differentiates between the archetypal twin images Sol and Luna. Then the fully integrated male ego moves into the next stage, the Union of Opposites, by making another differentiation, this time in terms of "masculine" and "feminine" images.

Jung's mature thought shows that the function of the "feminine" image, or anima, is the same for all men in the Union of Opposites, irrespective of sexual orientation. By positing and uniting with a symbolic feminine Other in a Union of Opposites, a man can integrate his bodily energy with his conscious mind, or ego. He now lives through his body, kinetically, the solar/lunar balance he had up to now maintained in his mind, consciously.

Here we can see the anima's "feminine" gender label for what it is: a referent to the unconscious gender-free archetypes, Sol and Luna. Jung has said that the anima is "the life of the body." Jung's symbol of the feminine mediates the solar/lunar energies of the unconscious, directing them to the body and libido, rather than to the intellect and emotions. The anima allows a man to feel this balance in his body and live it in his relationships and life. When the solar/lunar balance is established, the neurological, psychological wiring allows for the integration of mind and body.

When there's an anima problem, it often emerges as psychological or physiological problems, such as moodiness, unhealthy relationships, and somatic complaints. The homosexual client mentioned earlier had complained of feeling "listless," "powerless," and "ineffectual." He also suffered serious intestinal disorders as a result of the "faulty wiring" in his distorted relationship to the anima (his access to bodily energy). The following dream shows that, after several years of working to establish his twin-ego unity, this man has risen to a new psychological "stature" in relationship to the feminine which once dominated his unconscious:

> I'm standing in a room with several people, facing a woman on the far side of the room. She's very tall. I say, "Let's change places," and when we switch positions, now I am the same height as she. I laugh and say how this reminds me of the fun house at Santa Cruz. She wants to change back now, but I think it's better now that she is the same height as me. I think to myself, "Let's just leave it like this."

He was now prepared to enter into a balanced Union of Opposites with his solar/lunar anima and to integrate his bodily energy with his strengthened twin-ego, or conscious mind. The dream continues, showing that he is moving into the hermaphroditic Union of Opposites in the unconscious:

> The dream shifts, and now I'm lying down, having to force myself to get up and do something. A person enters the room, and I realize that it is both male and female. I couldn't see this, I just know it. The person is wrapped in a long snake, and it too is hermaphroditic. Half its body is covered in scales and the other half in feathers. It completely surrounds the person. I get up, thinking to myself that it's important to have self-discipline

enough to get yourself up and moving even when it's difficult to do. The figure does not seem at all strange to me.

Here the Opposites emerge in the psyche as male and female entwined in androgynous union in the image of a hermaphroditic feathered snake. The winged serpent, well known in mythologies as an archetype of united opposites, combines the lunar and solar principles of the unconscious, respectively represented in the body (snake) and the spirit (wings, feathers). The man's ready reception of this potentially alarming figure shows that he appears to have resolved the tension of the male/female Opposites and successfully integrated them in a deeper Union of the essential archetypal opposites, Sol and Luna.

As we noted, among this client's original difficulties were passivity and a lack of self-discipline. Here we see that, coming into contact with the creative ground of the unconscious, his strengthened twin-ego is not eclipsed. No longer identified with the feminine, his male solar/lunar twin-ego enjoys a counterflow of solar/lunar energies along what Jungians would call the ego-Self axis. This man's unconscious energies are now grounded in his actions, where they had previously been blocked or at odds with his conscious intentions. His chronic physical condition has begun to subside as well. With his twin-ego energies intact, he has restored to his conscious life the vital, creative energies of the unconscious. He continues to discover that he has increased stamina to work through all his conscious challenges—intellectual, physical, emotional, and interpersonal.

It is time that we restore our homovision and resurrect the male-male dialectic as a critical psychological positioning step in masculine individuation. Heterosexist theories of male psychology, as we have seen, invariably entail too much focus on the male-female configuration. The feminine, in the form of mother or anima, often takes on ominous proportions, appearing as an entire other "half" of the male psyche.

Reinstituting the solar/lunar twin-ego configuration as a structural principle of the male psyche liberates us from the sexual anxiety attached to lunar-masculine aspects and frees us from the morality implied in an exclusive male-female focus. Moreover, a solar/lunar twin-ego allows men to feel more than "half" masculine inside when they encounter the anima. The man who works toward integrating his solar/lunar energies no longer sees himself as "half" feminine or "less than" masculine. From the homovisionist perspective of a solar/lunar twin-ego, he understands that the "feminine" image, or anima, is a door to the deeper solar/lunar energies of the unconscious. Once he can get beyond the gender barrier to embrace both solar and lunar behavioral principles, he has in a sense defeminized the anima. It is only necessary for him to preserve the masculine/feminine polarity in order to periodically renew his access to the solar/lunar energies of the unconscious.

Jung preferred the masculine/feminine dialectic only because it conveyed an empirical opposition that was readily understood by the intellect. [12] But in light of nearly forty years of additional scholarship, and consistent with the ongoing breakdown of patriarchal thought, masculine and feminine no longer immediately convey a sense of opposition. As we continue to transcend limiting concepts of gender and sex roles, it may well behoove us restore the Twins to the male ego and to embrace the same-sex solar-lunar dialectic—instead of the male-female focus—as the orienting axis for male psychology.

Notes

1. C. G. Jung, *The Collected Works of C. G. Jung*, vol. 14 (*Mysterium Coniunctionis*), 2nd ed. (Princeton: Princeton University Press, 1970), p. 508. "Union of the Same" is my own terminology.

2. Mitchell Walker, "The Double: An Archetypal Configuration," in *Spring*, 1976, pp. 165–75. Walker is also the author of a pre-AIDS gay sex guide (1977).

3. Quoted in John P. McIntyre, "The Brothers," *Semia* 13: 81 (1976). I am indebted to William Doty for having drawn my attention to this reference in his comprehensive study of the Navaho twins. See William G. Doty, "Complementary Twin Sibs in Native American Psychomythology," paper presented at the Society for Values in Higher Education, Annual Meeting, 1989, p. 18.

4. See Philip E. Slater, *The Glory of Hera* (Boston: Beacon Press, 1968), pp. 381–83. While few records illuminate the relationship between Hercules and his brother, Iphicles, it has been suggested that their relationship may have been rivalrous, since Iphicles' existence was essentially suppressed. It is not unlikely that Iphicles, whose name implies strength, was at one time a hero in his own right.

5. Quoted in Paul Radin, "The Basic Myth of North American Indians," *Eranos-Jahrbuch 1949*, Olga Fröbe-Kapteyn, ed. (Zurich: Rhein-Verlag, 1950), pp. 359–419.

6. Joseph Campbell and Maud Oakes, *Where the Two Came to Their Father*, 2nd ed. (Princeton: Princeton University Press, Bollingen Series I, 1969), p. 36.

7. Joseph Campbell, *Occidental Mythology: The Masks of God* (New York: Viking Penguin, 1962). See also Janet McCrickard, *Eclipse of the Sun: An Investigation into Sun and Moon Myths* (Somerset, England: Gothic Images Publications, 1990).

8. See Joseph Campbell, *Oriental Mythology: The Masks of God* (New York: Viking Penguin, 1962), p. 91. Campbell further asserts that "the sun must be conceived to be a manifestation of only one half of the life/death principle, which is more fully symbolized in the moon: in the moon-bull attacked by the solar lion." He describes the solar-masculine spirit as somewhat "boyish" and "comparatively superficial."

9. Radin, "The Basic Myth of North American Indians," pp. 359–419.

10. Edward F. Edinger, *The Bible and the Psyche: Individuation Symbolism in the Old Testament* (Toronto: Inter City Books, 1986), p. 36.

11. C. A. Meier, *Healing Dream and Ritual* (Eiseideln, Switzerland: Daimon Verlag, 1989), p. 57. Mircea Eliade has similarly described an heroic consciousness-raising journey of the Zuni twins, suggesting that it parallels the biological process from conception to birth: "[The Twins'] progression . . . is homologous with the emergence of man. [They] lead embryonic humanity up to the threshold of consciousness." See Mircea Eliade, *Myths, Dreams and Mysteries: The Encounter between Contemporary Faiths and Archaic Realities*, trans. Philip Mairet (New York: Harper & Brothers, 1960), pp. 160–61.

12. C. G. Jung, *Aspects of the Masculine*, trans. R. F. C. Hull, intro. John Beebe (Princeton: Princeton University Press, Bollingen Series XX, 1989). Jung acknowledged that the masculine/feminine polarity of Logos and Eros could not compare in its power to the archetypal images of Sol and Luna: "[Logos and Eros] are coined and negotiable values; [Sol and Luna] are life" (p. 86).

Toward an Image
of Male Partnership

JOHN BEEBE

There is a kind of glib, collective way of talking about gay relationships that can lull us into thinking that the problem of being homosexual has been solved. Appropriating a cheerful adjective, we label someone *gay*, describe his partner as his lover, talk about their struggle with the AIDS crisis, and believe that we have really comprehended their experience with each other. Such talk short-circuits empathy and oversimplifies the true quality of a male partnership. It is not so easy to discover what it means to have a partner of the same sex as the central person in one's life. One must look beyond personal and political issues to a deeper, religious level, where these relationships are experienced as sacred by the people involved. To discuss such relationships is to handle sacred materials, and with such handling comes the enormous risk of blasphemy as well as the outrage that inevitably follows blasphemy.

It is just this sense of the sacredness of experienced homosexual reality that ought to set a Jungian approach to homosexuality apart from other psychologies. Jung's psychology is not just an early progenitor of object relations, nor a Jungian form of psychoanalysis, nor even the foundation for a generic analysis of the future—although one can see it in all these guises. Jungian psychology remains distinct as the one psychology that remembers that *experience is sacred*. And so I begin with a request of the reader to meet me halfway. Where I offer homosexual imagery, try to believe that I am using the symbolic neither to attack nor defend homosexuality. Try to look at the imagery I present as sacred imagery, as material to be respectfully considered. Try to hear through the echo of this material how the deep psyche feels about its homosexual relationships.

Jung never spoke directly about relationships involving two adult males who had decided to cast their lot together, set up housekeeping, and share their life as adults. In his 1922 talk to Zurich students about their love problems, he was not unsympathetic to the fact of erotic relationships between young people of the same sex, and he spoke with real feeling about relationships between older and younger men, where the close erotic bond facilitates mentoring and initiation. However, aside from these images of homosexual bonding in youth as an essentially normal part of initiation into full manhood, Jung generally asserted that any permanent choice or experience of homosexuality indicated fixation at an immature stage of psychosexual development. According to classical Jungian psychology, the homosexual man has given too much psychic power to his mother. He does not feel an erotic need for any other woman, and he cannot find the anima within, separate from the mother archetype. Since he lacks the feminine soul to connect him to his depths and to urge him toward a developed life, he does not individuate.

Jung developed and refined his psychology in the context of a series of psychological and sexual relationships with women. Out of these experiences, he concluded that some form of heterosexual relationship was essential for individuation; the withdrawal of projections in the course of the relationship would fuel the development of an inner contrasexuality. This mature contrasexuality, experienced as the anima in a man and the animus in a woman, was the bridge to the deep core of the personality Jung called the Self. For this reason, like many psychiatrists of his time, Jung tried hard to help his male patients overcome their youthful homosexuality. Neither his own experience nor the vicarious experience of his patients' inner lives gave him any reason to think that the homosexual relationship could foster a developed contrasexuality within a man's psyche.

My own quite different personal and clinical experience has led me to an opposing view: the man who takes his homosexuality seriously enough to work on finding a relationship with a male partner and making it prosper also develops a relationship to the anima within and, like his heterosexual counterpart, finds "her" of inestimable value in strengthening his ability to contain the tensions of the partnership while sustaining contact with himself. Indeed, the inner material of a man who has confronted his own internalized prejudices against making so unconventional a commitment will show clear signs of an anima function separate from the mother archetype. This anima will then undergo a developmental process that deepens and secures his inner relation to his homosexuality as well as his lived relationships in the outer world with other homosexual men. Such development clearly parallels the anima's function of deepening the object relations of a heterosexual man and, just as in the heterosexual situation, to the degree that the homosexual man loves convention and his parents' values more than the relationship at hand, the anima will not develop. The homosexual's inner material, like the heterosexual's, will reveal a psyche stuck at some infantile, preadolescent or adolescent stage of development in a classic mother or father complex.

The individuating homosexual man who has had the psychological experiences I describe can easily feel himself to be some kind of freak; neither analysts nor gay psychologists seem to know what to do with the developing feminine figures of his inner life. Recently, various gay writers have echoed Mitch Walker's suggestion that Jung's insistence upon the development of inner contrasexuality is not appropriate to gay individuation. [1] They view the anima as a category derived from heterosexual experience that has been wrongly applied to the psychology of gay men, where a figure of the same sex would more logically seem to hold the central position as the basis of relation to the Self. I do not share this view and believe it too easily confirms the common prejudice that the homosexual psyche must be structured differently from the heterosexual, simply because the outer choice of love object is different. I can only report what I have witnessed: in analytic work I have repeatedly observed the emergence of the anima symbol in the dreams of developing homosexual men. Nevertheless, it is certainly true than an inner figure of the same sex can play an important role in the psychological development of homosexual men, especially in securing the ego-Self relationship in the early stages of deep psychological work. Like his immature heterosexual counterpart, however, the immature homosexual man who has not been able to experience the anima apart from the mother archetype will continue to experience internal moods and outer relationships that convey the pain and pressure of the unliberated archetypal energies.

Although the idea that the anima remains necessary to the mature development of a homosexual man is important, it should not be turned into dogma. The proof is always in the actual material of the individual patient. I stress the anima not as the archetype of love, but as the archetype of *life*. I think the analyst needs to be sensitive to the homosexual man's search for an alive, internal relationship to his homosexuality—an aliveness that the anima is uniquely qualified to bring him. The analyst supporting such discovery of the anima by a homosexual male client will have to overcome the prejudice that love is based on projection of the anima and that, because the anima is not projected and sexualized, she is absent or too undeveloped to be of any help. This prejudice, which has confused the understanding of heterosexual love as well, is an analytic enemy of real individuation. As I have indicated, the job of the anima is better conceived as one of opening up the man's inner depths to himself, and if these depths are homosexual, the anima engagement will make him more homosexual, *not* less.

MALE PARTNERSHIPS IN THE MOVIES

What can two men do to, and for, each other psychologically? What is the pattern of their union, their *coniunctio*? As our culture has begun to take same-sex relationships seriously, its own sources of imagery have spontaneously offered attempts to formulate symbolically what is transpiring in the psychic depths of these unions. I have been particularly helped by movies, which can be a reliable mirror for reflecting incipient cultural and psychological patterns. In the second half of the 1980s, after much collective dialogue about the emergence of the gay male couple as an explicit social entity, several movies depicting male partnership were made. A few provided images of male *coniunctio* that were original enough to shed light on the hard-to-formulate psychological characteristics of male-male relationships. An exploration of three such films—*Kiss of the Spider Woman*, *Prick Up Your Ears*, and *Maurice*—can offer a potent stimulus for psychological reflection, providing images that evoke in us what we already know, making it possible to *see* what we actually think. These images formulate the male partnership with an indirectness appropriate to the sacred nature of an essentially private experience.

Kiss of the Spider Woman
The film that is by far the best known of the three is *Kiss of the Spider Woman*, directed by Hector Babenco from the novel by Manuel Puig. William Hurt won the Academy Award for his performance as Luis Molina, the São Paulo window dresser jailed for corrupting a minor. Molina, a transvestite, is sharing

a cell with Valentin, a macho revolutionary, whose girlfriend has left him because she can no longer tolerate his all-consuming participation in the dangerous leftist cause. As the movie opens, Molina is attempting to entertain Valentin with a bizarre performance: he tries to act like a woman, but he has a soccer player's body. Sadly, Molina never achieves the femininity to which he aspires. Nevertheless, trying for a camp effect, he hits on the idea of telling the story of a movie to his cellmate. This movie is presumably based on a 1940s German film that he once viewed. In Molina's retelling, however, it becomes an outrageous, farcical Nazi *Casablanca* in which a female café singer, acting as an undercover agent for the Free French, falls in love with one of Hitler's blondest army lieutenants. Both this movie within a movie (we see what Valentin imagines the film to look like while Molina is telling it to him) and *Kiss of the Spider Woman* itself mock the roles society prescribes for men and women. What interests me most about *Kiss of the Spider Woman* is the role Molina plays in Valentin's psychological life. By creating a hero figure in his narrated movie with whom Valentin cannot identify (because the hero is a Nazi), Molina subtly rearranges Valentin's fantasy life, which has been built around uncritical acceptance of the heroic. In changing his cellmate's experience of himself, Molina is performing an anima function for Valentin. Here we have the peculiar fascination of the film: watching a man performing an anima function for another man.

It becomes necessary for us to distinguish between anima *function* and anima *figure*. The figures who personify the anima or trigger her projection (whether or not that projection is sexualized) are usually female, even for homosexual men. Greta Garbo was probably the ultimate embodiment of the type of mysterious, nonmaternal woman we think of as symbolizing or manifesting the anima—and, appropriately, there is an image of her on Molina's part of the cell wall. In *Kiss of the Spider Woman*, Sonia Braga enacts the role of the anima figure who appears in Valentin's visualization of the film Molina relates, and who personifies the vital *function* Molina is catalyzing for Valentin. This function is the domain of the anima archetype: to connect the man to his depths through fantasy that catches the reflection of his lived experience; in essence, to put him in touch with himself.

Kiss of the Spider Woman takes place in a Latin culture where women have traditionally performed the anima function for men, to the point of actually preempting the archetype's internal function. Indeed, in many cultures around the world, the control of the unconscious has been assigned to women, just as control of conscious power in the world has been assigned to men. One particular outrageousness of *Kiss of the Spider Woman* is to depict a man assuming this feminine prerogative.

Molina's seductions have a nurturing and cheering effect and, at the same time, manage to catalyze Valentin into examining the myth he has been living. The movie that Molina narrates gives Valentin a way to disidentify with the hero myth by helping him to see that it is based on an absurd, outmoded propaganda. Yet, in deconstructing Valentin's heroic stance as leftist revolutionary, Molina is also a double agent engaged in a subtle sort of brainwashing. He is working (at least in the beginning) for the prison authorities, who have bribed him to extract information from Valentin that would expose his revolutionary group. Here, Molina is enacting another side of the anima: the duplicitous trickster, engineer of betrayal. Yet he emerges from this phase to finally achieve an authentic tenderness and love for Valentin, manifested in a heroic act: Molina also knows that the authorities are poisoning Valentin—and he, now in love, begins to take the poison himself.

The heterosexual Valentin then allows the homosexual Molina to nurse him through the effects of the poison and begins to return Molina's love. Out of the relationship that develops, both men are transformed. Molina agrees to act for Valentin within the revolutionary group when he gets outside. To seal their bond, there is a single, ritual lovemaking, giving the viewer a true *coniunctio* image, humanized by the fact of both men's mortified awkwardness at anal intercourse. This unstable bonding is followed by a difficult, heartfelt kiss in which the men consciously express their love for each other. After these symbolic exchanges, they change roles in the world. Reborn as a revolutionary, Molina is able to enter the hero myth that his previous identity had kept closed to him. Valentin, meanwhile, is able to accept his loss of power in prison (where he will likely die) and allow the anima to bring him peace from within; his fantasy functions for him now without Molina's mediation and is based in the healing presence of an internalized anima figure.

The tired look of Sonia Braga as Valentin's real-life girlfriend at the beginning of this film conveys the burden women experience at what they have been forced to carry. Perhaps that is why women viewers I have spoken with express being moved by this film at a very deep level. Women are touched by signs that men are beginning to understand the feminine principle of eros; that they are using their male relationships as a place to incubate a consciousness of their capacity for relatedness. *Kiss of the Spider Woman* has helped to catalyze recognition and understanding among women that there may be something of ultimate benefit to *them* in the male homosexual relationship.

Prick Up Your Ears
A less optimistic pattern of male *coniunctio* is presented in the British film, *Prick Up Your Ears*, which, like its harsh and punning title, is a movie on the edge of obscenity—hard to watch, harder still to ignore. Based on John Lahr's 1987 biography by the same title,[2] Stephen Frears's film tells the real-life story of Joe Orton, who wrote some of the best farces in the English language: *Entertaining Mr. Sloan, Loot,* and *What the Butler Saw,* which was produced posthumously because, just at

the height of his success, the young playwright was hammered to death in his bed by his lover of sixteen years.

Prick Up Your Ears is the story of the relationship between Orton and this lover, Kenneth Halliwell. Joe (originally John) Orton came from drab Leicester in central England, growing up in the kind of lower-middle-class family from which so many young homosexual men seek escape by coming to a big city. His father was depressed and a very poor provider; his mother was irritable and erratic and hated sex, but she had a good singing voice and maintained an interest in opera, despite her lack of education. She supported her son's interest in reading and even got him into a private school, but was appalled when he became serious about pursuing a dramatic career. She wanted him to go to typing school and qualify for a job as a typist.

Instead, Joe Orton stayed with the Leicester Dramatic Society and got a scholarship to the Royal Academy of Dramatic Art in London. There, at the age of eighteen, he met a somewhat dandified and poisonously witty older student, Kenneth Halliwell, who was the most literate person Orton had ever encountered. Halliwell introduced Orton to the writings of T. S. Eliot, Samuel Pepys, and the rest. The two quickly began living together. This was Joe's first homosexual relationship, yet he was to live with Kenneth the rest of his life.

The man Joe Orton chose to be his mentor was much more wounded than himself. Kenneth Halliwell's mother had died at a young age, and his father had gassed himself; the orphaned child left behind grew terribly brittle. In the manner of many homosexual men who adapt oppositionally to a world that seems unsafe, a rigid, campy facade replaced whatever natural persona might once have existed. Halliwell had a horror-movie hero's schizoid look, no match at animation for the boyish, vibrant charm of Orton. Unlike Orton, however, Halliwell was capable of maternal devotion. He saw to the education of his young man, offering an access to culture that Joe's family in Leicester had been unable to provide.

Joe and Kenneth began to write together. Among other efforts, they produced a farcical satire in modern verse called *The Boy Hairdresser*, which in 1956 was both uncommercial and too far ahead of its time; yet they harbored the absurd ambition of having it published by Faber and Faber, T. S. Eliot's publishing house. Their rejection at the hands of the establishment led them to seek revenge as literary terrorists, writing obscene satirical copy on the jackets of book after book in the public library. This scampery got them six-month sentences in jail. Halliwell never recovered from the shame of incarceration. By contrast, jail was somehow energizing for Orton, who emerged like a liberated hero *maudit*, having discovered his true vocation: being outrageous. Shortly thereafter a play based on *The Boy Hairdresser* was produced for the BBC radio; the success of that effort led Orton to write *Entertaining Mr. Sloan*, in which, as Lahr tells us, he perfected the "macabre outrageousness" that became his "Ortonesque" trademark.

As Orton became more successful, he also became more roguish—although he confined his rebellion to a defiant homosexual cruising. He never left Halliwell, but he became increasingly sexually uninterested in his partner. Halliwell was forced into the role of morose sidekick while Orton, with a perpetual boyish grin, pursued the most promiscuous homosexual life possible, frequenting men's rooms in the London underground and even taking Halliwell on a long jaunt to Morocco, where he hired boy prostitutes to service his sex-deprived partner. Their life became one long gay party to which Halliwell was diffidently invited. Toward the end of the 1960s Orton wrote explicit descriptions of this life in his diaries; to read these passages is to realize the godlike intensity of the trickster Orton was when cruising.

More and more, the perversely animated Orton delights in degrading his partner. He makes Halliwell wear a wig to cover his baldness, and in various ways vaunts his outstanding success and vigorous good looks in the doleful face of his unsuccessful lover. Finally, Halliwell cannot stand it. One night after Orton has gone to sleep—easily, as he has always done, while Halliwell, overstimulated by Orton's provocations and lack of nurturance, lies awake to brood through insomnia—Kenneth beats Joe's brains out with a hammer and takes an overdose of Nembutal, ending his own life.

Both men were cremated. At the end of the movie, in a scene drawn from a real-life event, their ashes are mixed by members of the two families. In his book Lahr explains that the suggestion originally came from a member of Halliwell's remaining family, and that Joe Orton's brother Douglas agreed, "as long as nobody hears about it in Leicester." Perhaps it was finally English to concede that there had been a relationship, and to sanctify it at last by this posthumous *conjunctio*.

The value of *Prick Up Your Ears* is its candid illumination of a troubling pattern of male partnership with a minimum of moralizing; the film, like the families, seemed to understand how the two men belonged to each other. What the film presents with such empathy—the morally sadomasochistic tone of the male partnership—is the pattern of male homosexual relationships that has troubled psychoanalysts the most. Twenty-five years ago it was fashionable to consider homosexuality as a love form founded on mutual contempt. It had not yet dawned upon the profession that such contempt could be the product of internalized homophobia, as most psychologists today would acknowledge. The explanation then proffered by Karl Menninger and others was that homosexual men suffered from an inadequately neutralized pre-oedipal aggressive drive, which was responsible not only for the mutually undermining behaviors of male partners but for the homosexuality itself. Even today, with more enlightened attitudes prevailing, the Joe-Kenneth pattern discourages many psychotherapists who genuinely want to believe in healthy, enduring male-male partnerships.

As a Jungian analyst, I, too, have tried to facilitate balance in male relationships that seemed to swing between the opposites of creativity and destructiveness—relationships that evidenced the frightening homicidal potential of the Orton-Halliwell tragedy. *Prick Up Your Ears* made me realize that these difficult relationships also belong to a form of sacred *coniunctio*. One possible outcome of such relationships is the transformation of aggression. Another is a recognition of the depth of the wounding that the culture's rejection of male *coniunctio* has inflicted upon the male psyche in general. In his groundbreaking book, *Being Homosexual*,[3] psychoanalyst Richard Isay suggests that the homosexual male is especially prone to wounding during the oedipal period when his desires are turned toward a heterosexual father who is likely to be sexually indifferent to him, if not homophobically rejecting. When such crushing rejection constitutes the child's initial experience of genital love, the developing homosexual adolescent and young adult will almost certainly take revenge on his first sexual partners, turning upon them the narcissistic, frustrated rage engendered by the unempathic oedipal father.

Beyond the oedipal origin of aggression between men who become erotically involved, there also seems to be an archetypal ambivalence that gets constellated in the early relationships between men, whether or not these relationships are explicitly sexualized. This unconscious antagonism is depicted in Thomas Gainsborough's painting, *Two Shepherd Boys with Dogs Fighting*. The young shepherds stand side by side, watching as dogs who carry their own contrasting coloring get into a fight at their feet. One of the boys, red-haired and wearing a sensitive, concerned expression, is high-mindedly brandishing a stick at the dogs; the other, dark-haired, puckish, and fascinated, is restraining his friend with a seductive embrace that scarcely conceals his delight: he wants his friend to let the dogs continue fighting. The dogs themselves, wearing vicious expressions, are starting to tear into each other.

Two Shepherd Boys with Dogs Fighting by Thomas Gainsborough. Reproduced courtesy of the Iveagh Bequest, Kenwood (English Heritage).

This painting reveals the shadow side of passionate friendships between boys, but I think its dynamics apply to the
relationships between immature men of any age.

Maurice

A movie that depicts development beyond this ambivalent
stage is *Maurice*, the film most disregarded by critics of those I
have chosen to discuss, but the one that has helped me the
most to organize my feelings about a healthy orientation to
male partnership. This understated film is directed by James
Ivory, who earlier directed *A Room with a View*, a more extraverted film about a heterosexual courtship.

Like *A Room with a View*, *Maurice* is based on a novel by
E. M. Forster. It was written in the mature period of his fiction
(between *Howards End* and *A Passage to India*) but published
posthumously because of its subject matter. (His short stories
with overtly homosexual themes were also compiled and published posthumously in 1972 as *The Life to Come*.) After *A
Passage to India*, Forster stopped writing novels altogether,
because he felt he couldn't deal with homosexual topics as
explicitly as he wanted and still be taken seriously as a
novelist.

Maurice details the maturation of homosexual identity in an
upper-middle-class young man from the suburbs of London.
Except for a few changes that emphasize the repressive tenor
of the Edwardian period, the film is quite faithful to the novel.
Because James Ivory grounds *Maurice* in the introverted sen-
sibility of its central character, a consciousness that lacks any
intuition but takes every sensory detail of the environment into
itself for further study, the movie has a bland, scanning,
uncomprehending surface that is off-putting to many viewers.

This handling of Forster's material serves the function of
getting the audience to experience the world from the inner
perspective of a homosexual person. Maurice (his name is
pronounced like the American "Morris") is solid and obser-

vant but without a clue as to where or with whom he belongs. He must silently bear the tension of knowing within his being that he is destined to place his life in the hands of a person of his own sex; the tension of not knowing how to go about finding or even recognizing that friend; and the overriding global tension of living with the dawning intuition that this deepest pattern of completion for himself has absolutely nothing to do with the culture, the society, and the religion by which others around him live. Nevertheless, he is stubborn and comes to feel in the depths of his being that his is a valid pattern, one with meaning and value, one that has a right to unfold in the world.

Carrying the opposites of Self and Society within creates for the homosexual man a peculiar consciousness that is central to his experience of himself in the world. Moving through society, he does a kind of psychological double-take: with his first glance, he carefully perceives the rules of the social field in which he is moving; with his second look, he scans that same field for any sign that it could also be nurturing to him. Only symptomatically does this testing take the form of cruising for actual sex partners; more subtly, and more continuously, the homosexual man cruises for acceptance of his feeling-style. We see this anxiety not only through the continuous scanning of Ivory's camera but also in Maurice's careful face, eager to please and afraid to relax into the tenderness it would like to express.

One of the pleasures of Maurice as a character is that it does not occur to him to adopt a stylized persona to make himself recognizable, or to dramatize his plight in society. A camp persona, like Halliwell's or Molina's, often functions as a defense and a form of protest against the world. The homosexual person who, like Maurice, opts for his freedom to move in a less stylized way through society pays the price of knowing deep within that he is outside the possibility of fulfilling his society's deepest expectations of him. The experience of finding even the slightest hint of validation for his inner nature is numinous, and the validating person is likely to become too important. Maurice, decent and dull, takes us through such an experience, emerging whole and intact in the end.

Forster was an expert on the topic of friends seducing and betraying each other. The effort to achieve a friendship based on integrity, despite the complications that stand in the way, forms the underlying theme of all his novels. In *Maurice*, Forster is explicit about the most highly charged complication of all—the sexual component of friendship. As Maurice encounters Clive, the first person who can accept his feeling, he also encounters Clive's manipulation and his own vulnerability. The aristocratic Clive is a fellow student of Maurice's at Cambridge. They find themselves in a world where homosexual feeling is covertly encouraged even as its explicit physical expression is condemned. The young men listen to the *Symphonie Pathétique* and learn that Tchaikovsky was in love with his nephew at the time that he wrote it. They read Greek with a vigilant tutor who will not let them translate the homosexual passages in *The Symposium*. What can't be named is called "the unspeakable vice of the Greeks"; Plato's work on the "higher love" is the part to which they should attend.

The shy, athletic Maurice falls in love with Clive but is too bound by Church of England strictures to admit in words what he feels. Clive is the first to speak of love, but Maurice rejects the possibility as "rubbish." By withdrawing in pain and apparent humiliation, Clive has Maurice hooked. Maurice tells Clive he loves him, but the manipulative Clive says he is just being kind. Maurice is forced to pursue Clive, and, climbing through Clive's window at night, kisses his friend firmly on the lips. From this point they are committed lovers, but Clive won't go farther than his Byronic definition of a Platonic relationship, insisting that the only way to justify their intimacy is to eschew the sexual and confine themselves to kisses and caresses. Maurice accepts this frustrating arrangement for the next three years.

After college they develop a life together in London as bachelor housemates at the center of a socially ambitious heterosexual crowd. Since Maurice is athletic and Clive is socially adroit, no one suspects the true nature of their relationship. They make limited love behind closed doors, until the arrest of one of their more Oscar Wilde-ish friends from Cambridge (a liberty the film takes with Forster's original) makes Clive realize that even their lifestyle is dangerous. Clive decides that he has to end the relationship and flees to Greece to mourn. There he meets an Englishwoman who becomes his wife. Maurice is relegated to the role of house guest at Clive's estate, where a gamekeeper develops a crush on him and finally offers him the possibility of a consummated love. There is a manly integrity to the servant's courtship of Maurice, and Maurice responds with an empathy which makes us believe the connection can be made permanent. Both Forster and Ivory are engaging in a sort of irony here: they know that homosexual men do not always treat each other so well. On the more introverted level where the film really comes alive, the young gamekeeper represents a healthy homosexual physicality, and Maurice's acceptance of this partner signals that he has finally outgrown Clive's limitations.

Ivory presents Clive as a callow man who has an overriding love of social norms. If the frustration Maurice feels when Clive withholds sex in the midst of the relationship looks like a problem our less inhibited society has outgrown, we should reflect on who the "Clives" of our culture are today. Had Maurice entered, not Cambridge University in 1909, but a gay bar in San Francisco in 1979, he would still have encountered a "Clive" in some respects. This latter-day Clive probably would have asked for an "open" relationship that provided ample sex but still disallowed any need for committed relationship.

Working with individual homosexual men over the past

twenty years has often pushed me to challenge values prevailing in the gay collective. I have attempted to help clients get past the Clive in themselves, which puts peer solidarity above all else, and connect with the Maurice, who has the courage to find a solution that really satisfies the Self. This solution requires that they recover the introverted meaning of their homosexuality and find the outer forms of relationship that honor it.

CONIUNCTIO AND CONSCIOUSNESS

What significance do the images of male *coniunctio* in *Kiss of the Spider Woman*, *Prick Up Your Ears*, and *Maurice* hold for the development of collective consciousness about homosexuality, as well as for homosexuality's own consciousness of itself? We have been privileged to witness an evolution of attitudes about homosexuality in our time, mirrored in images as well as language. The label *queer* has been replaced by *gay* in public thinking and usage. *Gay* will almost certainly be replaced in turn by something else. The present return to "queer" by many activists is their witty (and angry) insistence that gay is not really a progressive term. Yet as our image of male partnership evolves, we should not be confused by a fantasy of progress. Progress in social and political consciousness is not the same as progress at the psychological level. Revaluing what has seemed "queer," reexamining what we have too easily accepted as "gay," and discovering the true nature of male partnership are part of the inner work involved in integrating homosexuality.

This work has already begun in our films. The potential strength of a "queer" exchange is shown in *Kiss of the Spider Woman*; *Prick Up Your Ears* reveals the still unsolved subtext of lethal ambivalence in many "gay" relationships; and *Maurice* looks with Forster toward a life to come for which we do not yet have a name.

Notes

1. Mitchell Walker, "The Double: An Archetypal Configuration," in *Spring*, 1976, pp. 165–74.

2. John Lahr, *Prick Up Your Ears* (New York: Vintage Books, 1987).

3. Richard Isay, *Being Homosexual* (New York: Farrar, Straus & Giroux, 1989).

Brother Longing and Love
The Example of Henry James

SUZI NAIBURG

In the spring of 1899 Henry James traveled to his beloved Italy and met a man who would change his life. Hendrik Andersen was a handsome Norwegian-born American sculptor living in Rome with dreams of creating monumental art. When they met, the famous American author was instantly attracted and invited Andersen to visit him in his English home in Rye. James's biographer Leon Edel observes that Andersen awakened for the first time in James "feelings . . . akin to love."[1] James was fifty-six and his new friend, twenty-seven.

Although James's relation to Andersen was painfully disappointing, it allowed him to feel—as John Marcher does in James's short story, "The Beast in the Jungle" (1903)—how incomplete life is without love. Marcher's realization came too late, but James's paved the way for the novels of his major phase, *The Wings of the Dove* (1902), *The Ambassadors* (1903), and *The Golden Bowl* (1904), and influenced his relations with a number of younger men. Because James was so reticent about sex, we have no evidence that any of his relationships were ever sexually consummated. Hugh Walpole, a journalist and fellow novelist, told Stephen Spender that James refused him when he "offered himself to the Master."[2] Although the example of James's life does not provide a model of sexual intimacy, the poignant quality of his longing and the extraordinary sensitivity and achievement of his art can serve us well. As we continue to explore the story of James's life, let us look briefly at four literary examples that reflect different patterns of relationships between men.

The first comes from James's autobiography and illustrates Henry's ambivalence toward his older brother, William, the famous American psychologist and philosopher of pragmatism. Henry's relation to William bears many of the marks of twinship. Feelings of intimacy, attachment, and identification are mixed with ambivalence, rivalry, and jealousy. In his autobiography Henry refers to himself and William as "a defeated Romulus, a prematurely sacrificed Remus."[3] While traveling together in Europe, William writes of Henry as "my in many respects twin brother."[4]

Henry's desire to live "by the imagination in William's so adaptive skin"[5] is frustrated by the seemingly unbridgeable distance that separates them. William, fifteen months older, occupied "a place in the world to which I couldn't at all aspire," Henry writes. "I never for all the time of childhood and youth in the least caught up with him or overtook him. He was always round the corner and out of sight. . . ."[6] William was "vividly bright" while Henry pictured himself as "quite blankly innocuous."[7] "W. J. was lost again on upper floors, in high classes, in real pursuits. . . ."[8] Henry was left behind, but he also hung back.

> How far . . . [William] had really at any moment dashed forward is not for me now to attempt to say: what comes to me is that I at least hung inveterately and woefully back, and that this relation alike to our interests and to each other seemed proper and preappointed.[9]

Henry describes himself as always "dawdling" and "gaping,"[10] feeding on so much less than William—"the mere crumbs of [his] feast and the echoes of his life."[11] "So thoroughly I seemed to feel a sort of quickening savory meal in any

cold scrap of his own experience that he might pass on to my
palate."[12] The young gaper "was to go without many things,
ever so many—as all persons do in whom contemplation takes
so much the place of action."[13] Henry felt the "otherness" of
the more assertive and extraverted types beyond his ability to
emulate. "They were so *other*—that was what I felt; and to *be*
other, other almost anyhow, seemed as good as the probable
taste of the bright compound wistfully watched in the confec-
tioner's window: unattainable, impossible."[14]

James employs a similar metaphor when describing his six-
year-old heroine in *What Maisie Knew* (1897):

> So the sharpened sense of spectatorship was the child's main
> support, the long habit, from the first, of seeing herself in dis-
> cussion and finding in the fury of it . . . a sort of compensation
> for the doom of a peculiar passivity. It gave her often an odd air
> of being present at her history in as separate a manner as if she
> could only get at experience by flattening her nose against a
> pane of glass.[15]

Edel picks up the same image to describe his subject. Before
Hendrik Andersen enters James's life, he "had hitherto tended
to look at the world as through plate glass."[16]

In his autobiography Henry clearly separates himself from
William by idealizing his older brother and minimizing himself. He adopts the observer's role, emphasizes the distance
and differences that separate them, and imaginatively and
psychologically erects a barrier between himself and the unattainable yet desirable other—a dynamic not uncommon for
homosexual men when dealing with feelings toward other men
who almost certainly cannot reciprocate those feelings on a
homoerotic level. Several of James's early short stories—"De
Grey: A Romance" (1868), "The Romance of Certain Old
Clothes" (1868), and "A Light Man" (1869)—reveal, in the
words of William's biographer Howard Feinstein, "a strong
homosexual strand linking Henry to William."[17] Edel has

found evidence in William's unpublished letters that he "sensed and feared" Henry's homoerotic feelings for him.[18]

For whatever reason, William would not provide the intimacy Henry craved, albeit unconsciously, for so many years. When William finally married at age thirty-six, Henry was already living abroad as a confirmed bachelor. Yet he was still so enmeshed with his brother that news of William's marriage precipitated an emotionally charged response in which Henry describes himself as "divorced" from William by his marriage.

> I have just heard from mother that you had decided to be married on the 10th ult: and as I was divorced from you by an untimely fate on this unique occasion, let me at least repair the injury by giving you, in the most earnest words that my clumsy pen can shape, a tender bridal benediction.[19]

Due in large part to his relation to William, the image of intimacy between men as brothers and lovers is a particularly poignant one for Henry. When Andersen's brother died in 1902, Henry James wrote his friend offering "to put my arm around you and *make* you lean on me as on a brother and a lover."[20] In 1907 the bisexual Morton Fullerton wrote James when he was anxious about being blackmailed by a former mistress and exposed in his illicit affair with Edith Wharton. James responded by asking rhetorically if he, by the tenderness of his attachment, didn't count as the brother for whom each man yearns:

> *Can* one man be as mortally, as tenderly attached to another as I am to you, and be, at the same time a force, as it were, of some value, without its counting effectively at some right and preappointed moment for the brother over whom he yearns?[21]

A second example of male relationship is revealed in "The Great Good Place" (1900), a story in which James creates an ideal puer fantasy complete with maternal nurture, Apollonian satisfaction, empathic mirroring between men, and symbiotic bliss. In this story a successful and world-weary writer named George Dane falls asleep and dreams of a Brotherhood in which one Brother mirrors the other. Understanding is achieved without effort, even without words. Each Brother feels a comforting identity with the other in an all-male retreat. While sexual intimacy is absent from Dane's dreamscape, as it is from James's life, Dane's brotherhood presents a fantasy fulfillment of Henry's life-long brother longing. The "general charm" of the Great Good Place, which is also called the "Great Want Met,"[22] is difficult to define but has a great deal to do with "the reflection of his own very image" and "the absence of what he didn't want."

> The oddity was that after a minute he was struck as by the reflection of his own very image in this first converser seated with him, on the easy bench. . . . The absence of everything was . . . but the absence of what he didn't want. He didn't want, for the time, anything but just to *be* there, to steep in the bath. He was in the bath yet, the broad deep bath of stillness. . . . *This* was a current so slow and so tepid that one floated practically without motion and without chill. The break of silence was not immediate, though Dane seemed indeed to feel it begin before a sound passed. It could pass quite sufficiently without words that he and his mate were Brothers, and what that meant.[23]

Wanting to escape the "endless press and stress" of life[24] in the world of "mere maniacal extension and motion,"[25] Dane finds himself in a place of softness and stillness where "there was nothing now to time."[26] The Brothers talk of being "babes at the breast . . . of some great mild invisible mother who stretches away into space and whose lap's the whole valley . . . and her bosom . . . the noble eminence of our hill."[27] In this image both Brothers are held by an invisible mother who supports them, an image echoed by James in 1902 when he writes Andersen of the "*most* unfolding and never disowning mighty Mother." Shortly after the death of the sculptor's brother and James's own bout with illness, James writes:

> Infinitely, deeply, as deeply as you will have felt, for yourself, was I touched by your second letter. I respond to every throb of it, I participate in every pang. I've gone through Death, and Death, enough in my long life, to know how all that we *are*, all that we *have*, all that is best of us within, our genius, our imagination, our passion, our whole personal being, become then but aides and channels and open gates to suffering, to being flooded. But, it is better so. Let yourself go and *live*, even as a lacerated, mutilated lover, with your grief, your loss, your sore, unforgettable consciousness. *Possess* them and let them possess you, and life, so, will still hold you in her arms, and press you to her breast, and keep you, like the great merciless but still *most* unfolding and never disowning mighty Mother, on and on for things to come.[28]

While the archetype of the Great Mother, so evocatively imaged in James's letter, is carried by the landscape in James's story, women are conspicuously absent. Dane and the Brothers declare that their retreat from the world into their exclusively male haven—in which the "blest act of consciousness seemed the greatest thing of all"[29]—allowed them to find their soul again. Their retreat is not a "putting off of one's self" but a getting it back.[30] In ordinary reality "surrounded only with the affairs of other people, smothered in mere irrelevant importunity,"[31] Dane had lost possession of his soul. Success became a burden even greater than trouble, sorrow, or doubt.[32] In the Great Good Place "the deep spell had worked and he had got his soul again."[33] "By the simple fact of finding room and time,"[34] "the inner life woke up again."[35]

A Gnostic belief holds that at our birth our twin is born apart from us and that we spend our lives searching for our other half. This image of longing for one's twin to complete oneself is suggestive in light of Henry's homoerotic pull toward William and the mirroring between brothers in Dane's dream.

A contemporary version of this Gnostic belief can be found in the work of psychoanalyst Heinz Kohut, who recognized the need "to experience the presence of essential alikeness" as fundamental to "the sustenance of the self" along with the need "to experience mirroring and acceptance" and "the need to experience merger with greatness, strength, and calmness."[36] In therapy these needs are activated respectively through the twinship or alter-ego transference, the mirror transference, and the idealizing transference. Henry's relation with William in its depth and multidimensionality provides abundant evidence of the needs for idealization, mirroring, and twinship.

At the end of "The Great Good Place," Dane awakens from his dream to find that a young admiring writer has cleared his cluttered desk while he rested. "Dane rose and looked around the room, which seemed disencumbered, different, twice as large. It *was* all right."[37] During Dane's nap, work in the outer world had been accomplished by Dane's younger double. But change had also occurred in Dane's inner world. His room seemed "twice as large." While Dane's dream and the restoration it provides draw on the soothing identity of one Brother with another, an example of what Kohut calls the twinship transference, the frame James creates around the dream pairs a younger man with an older master and allows the younger to assume the duties, if not the identity, of the older for the duration of Dane's dream. In this case the younger man imaginatively merges with his older and idealized brother writer, fulfilling a wish Henry James seems to have had himself.

James creates another pairing of a younger man and older master in "The Middle Years" (1893), a story in which a young doctor's admiration helps a dying writer appreciate his own artistic achievement and accept his life as it is. The terminally ill Dencombe is acutely aware of "the sense of ebbing times, of shrinking opportunity: and now he felt not so much that his last chance was going as that it was gone indeed. He had done all he could ever do, and yet he hadn't done what he wanted."[38] His illness and the fear it engenders cause Dencombe to forget how "extraordinarily good" his previous year's work had been. In rereading his own tale, also entitled "The Middle Years" as is the third and unfinished volume of James's autobiography, Dencombe

> dived once more into his story and was drawn down, as by a siren's hand, to where, in the dim underworld of fiction, the great glazed tank of art, strange silent subjects float. He recognized his motive and surrendered to his talent. Never before had that talent, such as it was, been so fine.[39]

In reconnecting himself to the sacred creative process that is so intimately connected to the unconscious, Dencombe is rejuvenated enough to wish for an "extension." "Illness and age rose before him like specters with pitiless eyes: how was he to bribe such fates to give him the second chance? He had had the one chance that all men have—he had had the chance of life."[40] The second chance, Doctor Hugh assures him, had come, only it had been the public's—"the chance to find the point of view, to pick up the pearl,"[41] to appreciate the artist's work, which is like James's own. As Richard A. Hocks points out, "Dencombe's aim at a 'rare compression' in his fiction and his being a 'passionate corrector' and 'fingerer of style' are all unmistakable characteristics of James himself. . . ."[42]

As Doctor Hugh carries his devotion to Dencombe's bedside, he reawakens Dencombe's own deep appreciation of who he is and what he has created. In this capacity Doctor Hugh functions as an anima figure for Dencombe. Although the anima has traditionally appeared as a female figure in service of the male psyche, a number of contemporary Jungians have argued for the necessity of freeing the anima from gender restrictions. Men—in both inner and outer worlds—may function as anima figures for other men, as for example, "Enkidu functions as the anima might for Gilgamesh."[43] In its feminine guise the anima may also function for women as a guide to soul, thus sometimes wearing "a same-sex face"[44] for both men and women.

Doctor Hugh helps Dencombe appreciate how the mortality of his life and the necessity of his art are inexorably bound. "A second chance—*that's* the delusion," Dencombe concludes. "There never was to be but one. We work in the dark—we do what we can—we give what we have, our doubt is our passion and our passion is our task. The rest is the madness of art."[45] Doctor Hugh can't restore Dencombe's health, but he can and does help him accept the integrity of his life.

We find a fourth example of male-male relationship in James's story of Morgan Moreen and his tutor, Pemberton. In "The Pupil" (1891), this precocious eleven-year-old with a serious heart condition warns his tutor that his parents will play on the poor tutor's affection to keep him on without pay. The Moreens are "a band of adventures,"[46] "a houseful of Bohemians who wanted tremendously to be Philistines."[47] Living abroad on "maccaroni and coffee"[48] and pretension to class while dodging bills and creditors, Mr. and Mrs. Moreen, along with their two daughters and older son, care only "to make an appearance and to pass for something or other."[49] Morgan, their youngest child, cares instead for Pemberton. Idealized by Morgan as "a hero,"[50] Pemberton is far from perfect. Yet he offers the empathic mirroring and love Morgan craves.

James sensitively portrays the "understanding that broadened" between Morgan and Pemberton, beginning with a "clumsy moment at the beach at Nice" when pupil and master each turned red while exchanging "a longish glance in which there was a consciousness of many more things than are usually touched upon, even tacitly, in such a relation."[51] Morgan and Pemberton walk arm in arm that evening in Nice and later dream of "going off to live somewhere together."[52] But Pemberton would go off first and alone three years later when a paying job materializes in England. As the Brothers' communication in the Great Good Place is often made without speech, so Pemberton's decision to go is made with Morgan without words. "It was really by wise looks" that Morgan and Pemberton "knew each other so well."[53] Pemberton then explained himself. "I'll make a tremendous change; I'll earn a lot of money in a short time, and we'll live on it."[54]

Because of the tender bond between them, Mrs. Moreen is able to trick Pemberton into returning to his charge in France. Six months after his return to work again without pay, "the storm had come."[55] Finally exposed in their deceptions and financial failures, the Moreens are thrown out of their rooms and turn to Pemberton "to take their delightful child temporarily under his protection" and off their hands.[56] A "moment of boyish joy"[57] that Morgan enjoys at the prospect of living with Pemberton is followed quickly by his fatal collapse. With characteristic ambiguity, James leaves us wondering about the meaning of Morgan's having a heart attack at this particular moment. Is the fulfillment of his desire to go away with his tutor too much for him to bear? Is he crushed by his parents' public exposure and rejection of him? Or does he sense his tutor's hesitation and intuit Pemberton's own failure of heart to take him in? Yet despite this ambiguity, the story's tragic ending, and the suspicion that Pemberton, like the Moreens, has failed his devoted friend, "The Pupil" poignantly depicts Morgan's longing for Pemberton and the possibility of love— tasted in the first years of their relationship—that has the potential to teach each the way to a wholeness only glimpsed before Morgan and Pemberton had met.

Because James dared not imagine Morgan's flight from his fraudulent family into a lasting and fully intimate relation with his tutor, the quality of understanding, tenderness, and love that initially develops between Morgan and Pemberton stands as a muted testimony to a longing James—at some level— must have known but could not at that moment fully allow.

James's own greatest fulfillment would come through his art, which constituted his primary relationship. When James wrote the preface to *The American* for the New York Edition of his works (published 1907–1909), he forged a telling analogy. James pictures himself "clinging to my hero as to a tall, protective, good-natured elder brother in a rough place."[58] In a notebook entry written in California in 1905, James describes his muse as one might a lover.

> He is here with me in front of this green Pacific—he sits close and I feel his soft breath, which cools and steadies and inspires, on my cheek. Everything sinks in; nothing is lost; everything abides and fertilizes and renews its golden promise. . . .[59]

Meeting Andersen in 1899 opened a floodgate of emotions for James even though (or perhaps in part because) the two men met only a scant six times and letters became the mainstay of their friendship. Edel observes that the letters James wrote after meeting Andersen reveal

> a considerable alteration in his personality. He is looser, less formal, less distant, he writes with greater candor and with more emotional freedom. He has at least opened himself up to the physical things of life—and has fallen in love. We perceive an artist who grows less rigid and more experimental in spite of his aging.[60]

James's letters to the sculptor—"the saddest and strangest perhaps in his entire *epistolarium*"—were filled with unusually "physical, tactile language" and "the reiterated cry for the absent one."[61] James signed a letter to Andersen in 1904 as "your poor helpless far-off but all devoted H.J. who seems condemned almost and never to be near you, yet who, if he were, would lay upon you a pair of hands soothing, sustaining, positively *healing* in the quality of their pressure."[62]

No longer reticent about exposing and valuing his own emotional permeability, James writes his younger friend Morton Fullerton in 1907: "You stir my tenderness even to anguish: a fig for any tenderness (for that matter) that isn't so stirrable."[63] In 1913 James wrote Hugh Walpole:

> We must know, as much as possible, in our beautiful art, yours and mine, what we are talking about—and the only way to know is to have lived and loved and cursed and floundered and enjoyed and suffered. I think I don't regret a single "excess" of my responsive youth—I only regret, in my chilled age, certain occasions and possibilities I *didn't* embrace.[64]

To Dudley Jocelyn Persse, with whom James developed a close and lasting relation, he wrote: "I rejoice greatly in your breezy, healthy, grousy—and housely, I suppose—adventures, and envy you, as always, your exquisite possession of the Art of Life which beats any Art of mine hollow."[65]

Reflecting the essential pattern of "The Middle Years," almost all of the relationships in which James dared a greater measure of intimacy were struck with younger men. Edel identifies James's attraction to Andersen's youth and underscores the idealizing projections at play.

> From the first James treated Andersen as if he were his *alter ego*. The old Henry and the young—it was as if Andersen had been fashioned out of James's old memories and old passions. A warm nostalgia filled their hours together during the sculptor's first visit to Lamb House. James bestowed on Andersen his own taste, his own high standards, his own feeling for beauty. He looked into the mirror and saw smiling and healthy youth instead of his obese and aging self. The image charmed—one might say it enchanted.[66]

It wasn't just Andersen's youth and beauty that attracted James, but also, as Edel observes, the sense of possibility, of beginnings, of artistic aspirations and dreams that James had held for himself as a young man. The puer/senex polarity that is constellated between Andersen and James is not, however, simply of "two halves of life," as James Hillman argues in another context, but two halves of "a single archetype"[67] that seek unification.

> Our other half is not only of another sex. The union of opposites—male and female—is not the only union for which we long and is not the only union which redeems. There is also the union of sames, the reunion of the vertical axis which would heal the split spirit.[68]

The split between the puer and senex calls for a particular type of restoration: of the union of possibility with discipline, of aspiration with perspective, of imagination with realization, of divine child with Saturn, of son with father.

James became deeply disturbed by Andersen's grandiosity, the puer's soaring flights of fancy that Andersen never learned to ground. In 1912 Andersen circulated plans for a world city on a grand scale adorned with his own monumental sculptures. In a letter to Andersen, James criticized his friend's

> working so in the colossal and in the void and in the air! . . . Your mania for the colossal, the swelling and the huge, the monotonously and repeatedly huge, breaks the heart of me for you. . . . this culmination of your madness, to the tune of five hundred millions of tons of weight, simply squeezes it out of me. For that, dearest boy, is the dread Delusion to warn you against—what is called in Medical Science MEGALOMANIA (look it up in the Dictionary!) in French *la folie des grandeurs*, the infatuated and disproportionate love and pursuit of, and attempt at, the Big, the Bigger, the Biggest, the Immensest Immensity, with all sense of proportion, application, relation and possibility madly *submerged.*[69]

Edel reports that Andersen's "sculptured utopia was never built, but some of his unsold statues were used after his death in [Mussolini's] Rome."[70]

Unlike Andersen, James learned to ground his own aspirations. He struck a balance intrapsychically between the puer and senex while at the same time risking greater intimacy and vulnerability in the carefully guarded arena of interpersonal relations into which Andersen had introduced a new imperative. James's life and work depict a variety of patterns of relationships between men in which homoerotic longing and love play a part. Henry's relation to William, the young writer's to Dane, the Brothers in the Great Good Place, Doctor Hugh and Dencombe, Morgan and Pemberton, James's younger friends and James himself are but a few.[71] Other male pairs who are almost or actual brothers appear, for example, in *Confidence*, *Roderick Hudson*, *The American*, and *The Princess Casamassima*. Studying such pairs and the patterns of intimacy between men in James's art and life sheds light not only on this personally reticent master of fiction but also on the myriad forms that desire takes.

Notes

1. Leon Edel, *Henry James: A Life* (New York: Harper, 1985), p. 498.
2. Ibid., p. 652. See pp. 437–39, also note for p. 494 on p. 724.
3. Henry James, *Autobiography* (Princeton, N.J.: Princeton University Press, 1983), p. 127.
4. Howard Feinstein, *Becoming William James* (Ithaca, N.Y.: Cornell University Press, 1984), p. 324.
5. James, *Autobiography*, p. 247.
6. Ibid., pp. 7–8.
7. Ibid., p. 11.
8. Ibid., pp. 121–22.
9. Ibid., p. 8.
10. Ibid., p. 20.
11. Ibid., p. 246.
12. Ibid., p. 418.
13. Ibid., p. 16.
14. Ibid., p. 101.
15. Henry James, *What Maisie Knew* (London: Penguin, 1966), p. 83.
16. Edel, *A Life*, p. 498.
17. Feinstein, *Becoming William James*, p. 233.
18. Edel, *A Life*, p. 82.

19. Leon Edel, ed., *Henry James: Letters*, vol. 2 (Cambridge, Mass.: Harvard University Press, 1975), p. 177. *See also* Edel, *A Life*, pp. 244–246.

20. Leon Edel, ed., *Henry James: Letters*, vol. 4 (Cambridge, Mass.: Harvard University Press, 1984), p. 226.

21. Ibid., p. 473.

22. Leon Edel, ed., *Henry James: Stories of the Supernatural* (New York: Taplinger, 1970), p. 580.

23. Ibid., pp. 576–77.

24. Ibid., p. 583.

25. Ibid., p. 588.

26. Ibid., p. 578.

27. Ibid., p. 593.

28. Edel, *Letters*, vol. 4, p. 228.

29. Edel, *Stories*, p. 577.

30. Ibid., p. 581.

31. Ibid., p. 583.

32. Ibid., p. 582.

33. Ibid., p. 591.

34. Ibid.

35. Ibid., p. 588.

36. Heinz Kohut, *How Does Analysis Cure?* Arnold Goldberg, ed. (Chicago: University of Chicago Press, 1984), p. 194.

37. Edel, *Stories*, p. 597.

38. Henry James, *The Novels and Tales of Henry James*, vol. 16 (New York: Scribner's, 1909), p. 88.

39. Ibid., p. 81.

40. Ibid., p. 93.

41. Ibid., p. 103.

42. Richard A. Hocks, *Henry James: A Study of the Short Fiction* (Boston: Twayne, 1990), p. 55.

43. Robert H. Hopcke, *Jung, Jungians, and Homosexuality* (Boston: Shambhala Publications, 1989), p. 117.

44. Ibid., p. 118. See also *Gender and Soul in Psychotherapy*, Nathan Schwartz-Salant and Murray Stein eds.(Wilmette, Ill.: Chiron Publications, 1991).

45. James, *Novels*, vol. 16, p. 105.

46. Henry James, *The Novels and Tales of Henry James*, vol. 9 (New York: Scribner's, 1909), p. 534.

47. Ibid., p. 521.

48. Ibid., p. 520.

49. Ibid., p. 549.

50. Ibid., pp. 545, 546.

51. Ibid., p. 526.

52. Ibid., p. 545.

53. Ibid., p. 560.

54. Ibid.

55. Ibid., p. 544.

56. Ibid., p. 575.

57. Ibid., p. 576.

58. Henry James, *The Art of the Novel* (New York: Scribner's, 1962), p. 39.

59. Henry James, *The Complete Notebooks of Henry James*, Leon Edel and Lyall Powers, eds. (New York: Oxford, 1987), p. 237.

60. Edel, *Letters*, vol. 4, p. xiii.

61. Edel, *Life*, p. 497.

62. Ibid.

63. Edel, *Letters*, vol. 4, p. 473.

64. Ibid., p. 680.

65. Edel, *Life*, p. 574.

66. Ibid., p. 495.

67. James Hillman, "Senex and Puer," in James Hillman et al., eds., *Puer Papers* (Dallas: Spring Publications, 1979), p. 30.

68. Ibid., p. 34.

69. Edel, *Letters*, vol. 4, pp. 611–12.

70. Edel, *Life*, p. 676.

71. A volume of James's letters to his male friends is now being prepared and edited by Leon Edel and Lyall H. Powers.

Not "A One-Sided Sexual Being"

Clinical Work with Gay Men from a Jungian Perspective

SCOTT WIRTH

> In view of the recognized frequency of this phenomenon [homosexuality] its interpretation as a pathological perversion is very dubious. The psychological findings show that it is rather a matter of incomplete detachment from the hermaphroditic archetype, coupled with a distinct resistance to identify with the role of a one-sided sexual being. Such a disposition should not be adjudged negative in all circumstances, in so far as it preserves the archetype of the Original Man, which a one-sided sexual being has, up to a point, lost.
>
> —C. G. Jung[1]

GAY TERMINOLOGY AND GAY MALE SUBCULTURAL CONSIDERATIONS

Let us imagine the four principal relational orientations (woman with man, man with woman, woman with woman, man with man) as corresponding to the four cardinal directions of a compass—north, south, east, and west. As a compass has 360 degrees, so we might imagine corresponding individual sexual and relational angles and mid-angles, with each person orienting themselves to their particular affectional nature. At times people may consciously navigate their way along their sexual path, but very often a person follows or is shown the way of their intimate nature.

This paper focuses on the general quadrant representing gay male identity or orientation. Within the categorization of male-male erotic and emotional life are complex and varied experiences, as each man's life course is unlike any other's. Yet some common elements run through and unify the erotic, emotional, and psychic realities of gay men. That is, there are archetypal bases for this human pattern of loving.

Acknowledging all the problems and ambiguities of the term *gay*, historian John Boswell concludes that, "like 'democracy,' it is broad and diachronic, but still useful to most speakers and writers."[2] In a remarkable interview with Lawrence Mass, Boswell distinguishes *gay* in this way:

> "Gay" means to me that without constraint, with free and open choice, you *prefer* your own gender. And I *think*—I'm not certain—that there is a variable proportion of people in all the societies I've studied who, regardless of constraints, prefer their own gender. . . .[3]
>
> I'm not including everyone who engages in homosexual behavior under the rubric "gay"—only those who prefer sexual interaction with their own gender (not, for example, prisoners who have no other choice, or children or slaves forced into it). . . .[4]

If we take seriously the psychoanalytic precepts of universal human bisexuality (Freud) and contrasexuality (Jung) then we might more fruitfully speak about the homosexual or gay *aspect* of any given person, rather than "the homosexual" or "the gay person." Kinsey, too, with his findings of a homosexual-heterosexual spectrum, emphasized the variable shadings and vicissitudes of human sexuality. Although sexual orientation, behavior, or identity does not *typically* alter substantially in a lifetime, neither is it so very rare for it to do so (in either direction and at any life stage after early childhood). Behaviorally, the sexual psyche is somewhat fluid and diverse.

Intrapsychically, the psyche is considerably *more* fluid and "plural."[5] Put simply, everyone possesses a common collection of intrapsychic sexual and gender ingredients or elements. Individuals vary in the concentration of these ingredients and in how these sexual and gender elements configure, interact, and jell. When these individual archetypal chemistries join up with sociological realities, the inner/outer meeting produces psychological/cultural identities, one of which is "gay man." Although such a static term restricts imaginative inquiry in some ways, it is nonetheless a meaningful unit that, as Boswell says, is "useful to most speakers and writers."

The majority of patients who call me for psychotherapy identify themselves as gay men. They call me because they have heard that I am experienced, or well trained, or that I helped someone they know, or that I work deeply, or work from a Jungian orientation. They may have heard my name, read something I wrote, heard me lecture. But they also call me, it seems, because they have heard I am gay or "gay-sensitive," a "gay Jungian," sometimes simply because my office is located at an address in a gay neighborhood. They feel or *hope* they will feel safer and better understood by someone who knows this gay world—both the outer sociology and the inward psychological reality of it. At a minimum they want some assurance that they will *not* encounter any significant unexamined homophobia or heterosexual bias in their psychotherapist or analyst—whether this bias is conscious or not, greater or lesser in extent.

In my analytic work with patients, I don't as a rule disclose much about my life story nor about my personal views or private life. Yet, at those times when it seems to me appropriate, I will tell patients that I am gay. On one level being "gay-identified" is a demographic status comparable to gender, age, ethnicity, professional training, theoretical orientation, and other such variables that new patients sometimes need or want to know about their prospective therapist or analyst. When I do disclose my gay orientation, I generally leave it there *relatively* neutrally.

The disclosure of my gay orientation may be of minor or major significance to my patient. It may be a freeing element, facilitating growth, or it may be a countertherapeutic "mistake," an intrusion or a narcissistic wounding. Depending on the individual patient, we will work with it or leave it alone; he will scrutinize or inquire into my gayness or "forget" that he had asked or that I answered.

The analytic psychotherapy of a gay man mostly proceeds in ways comparable to the analytic psychotherapy of any man or woman. The general analytic attitude, theory, technique, and methodology supersede any other particular considerations. Exceptions and adaptations are essentially made on an individual basis. All this notwithstanding, I find that there are certain therapeutic advantages to the professional dyad of a well-analyzed gay male psychotherapist working analytically with a gay male patient. For example, having worked with many gay male patients, I have come to know the characteristic syndromes and presenting problems. From my past and current clinical cases I have compiled the following informal A to Z list of problems I see in gay male patients. The list is by no means exhaustive. Quite a few of the items might appear on *any* thoughtful clinician's survey of any sort of practice. Yet, as an interwoven gestalt, I think that this list reflects some qualitative cultural and intrapsychic differences in a predominantly gay male analytic private practice:

a. splitting of different gender-associated personality components one away from the other;

b. gay stylized "anima possession": e.g., the diva, the bitch, the smothering mother, the sexual toy;

c. an inflated, grandiose and/or narcissistic sense of self as "everything"—this may be exhibitionistically shown off in various bold gay liberationist stances or perhaps kept as a fairly private fantasy of quasi-shamanistic healing powers, artistic grandeur, etc.;

d. intimate relationship problems, especially involving (i) the disappearance of desire, (ii) the separation of desire from emotional closeness, (iii) the inability to stay in a committed monogamous relationship, (iv) age disparity or racial difference in relationship;

e. puer problems of (i) overidealizing, (ii) compulsive rebellion against authority figures, (iii) superficiality or flightiness;

f. sexual promiscuity or compulsive sexuality;

g. social isolation and loneliness;

h. grief and feelings of being overwhelmed by the HIV epidemic;

i. gay ghettoization and social "ethnocentrism";

j. chemical dependencies and/or eating disorders;

k. inability in adult life to leave behind the position of child vis-à-vis mother and/or father;

l. masochistic allowing of the gay or some other aspect of the self to be exploited by others;

m. psychotic delusions of belonging to another (gay) "species";

n. gay stylized forms of paranoia, hysteria, depression, and anxiety;

o. post-traumatic stress syndrome stemming from abuse.

p. getting stuck in various gay roles, personae, stereotypes;

q. spiritual malaise or an overspiritual, disembodied religiosity or "goodness";

r. a tawdry, depersonalized, self-destructive underworld sexual slinking around (sometimes including unsafe sexual practices);

s. an overpreciousness, oversensitivity, or delicateness, including hypochondriasis;

t. fetishization of certain body parts and surfaces, especially the penis, testicles, anus, chest, body hair;

u. hatred of men, keeping only the company of women, or hatred of women, keeping only the company of men;

v. heterophobia, including envious hostility toward procreativity, marriage, and nuclear family life;

w. homophobia (internalized and/or externalized);

x. destructive sadomasochistic sexual rituals and fixations;

y. fixation on youth and beauty, untoward fear of aging;

z. an overstudied, false masculine posing and posturing.

Many of these presenting problems are recognizable to
anyone living in or around the gay male subculture. Speaking
a common language or being "in the know" about these characteristic problematic manifestations of a gay man's psychology may provide a basic sense of safety to get analytic work
started. Before long, however, an overreliance on knowledge
of typical subcultural morays and social patterns can actually
undermine the depth of psychotherapeutic or analytic work.

To go farther analytically it is necessary to have some
understanding of the intrapsychic structures and archetypal
foundations of a gay man's psyche. I would like to turn my
focus now in these directions.

THE MALE AND FEMALE ELEMENTS
TO BE FOUND IN GAY MEN

In an intriguing and little read paper, D. W. Winnicott postulates the existence within each human of distinct male and
female elements, either of which can be discerned as "pure,"
"unalloyed," "distilled," or "uncontaminated."[6] Winnicott
portrays the inner object relating of these gender elements in
a manner easily comprehensible to Jungians, who would
likely describe comparable psychological phenomena as the
operations in the psyche of archetypal masculine and feminine principles. Here I will use these terms more or less
equivalently, referring at certain times to "male or female
elements" and at other points to the operation of "masculine
or feminine principles."

Objections will certainly be raised to *any* given character-
ization of what is masculine or feminine, and it is well that such

challenges should be made, whether from feminist, gay liberationist, anthropological, social constructionist, or various psychoanalytic perspectives. With all due respect, I shall not
attempt to give fair play here to the valid controversies and
complex considerations involved in the study of gender.

As a clinician, what most interests and concerns me are the
personal or subjective associations and meanings that each
individual patient brings to "masculine" and "feminine." Doing psychotherapeutic work with gay men has shown me that
most eventually use the analytic process to define a *personal*
sense of "feminine" and "masculine" for themselves and to
differentiate how these gender qualities show up in their relationships, dreams, memories, and sense of self. The subjective clarification of one's true inner gender qualities will
invariably be hindered (or at least colored) by sex-role and
gay-male-role stereotypes, by what one has been told he "is" or
should be, and by familial distortions. Consequently, it is
helpful to know that there *are*, at least in theory, "unalloyed,"
"uncontaminated," and, following Jung, unseen and unknow-
able yet objectively real archetypes of masculine and feminine. Whatever the objective definitions of *masculine* and
feminine may ultimately be, it seems clear to me that such
impersonal male and female elements do indeed exist and
operate in the human psyche.

Winnicott and others point out that *apart from* environmental factors, individuals vary in their innate endowments of
intrapsychic female elements and male elements: ". . . in
health, there is a variable amount of girl element in a girl, and
in a boy. Also hereditary-factor elements enter in, so that it
would easily be possible to find a boy with a stronger girl
element than the girl standing next to him, who may have less
pure-female-element potential."[7]

The British philosopher and utopian thinker Edward Carpenter, a contemporary and friend of Walt Whitman, articulated a perspective not unlike Winnicott's in his 1906 study of

"intermediates" or "Uranians"—his pre-psychoanalytic terms for homosexuals or gay people: "There are distinctions and gradations of soul-material in relation to sex; the inner psychical affections and affinities shade off and graduate most subtly from male to female and not always in correspondence with the outer bodily form."[8]

As Carpenter and Winnicott suggest—in their writings separated by sixty years—the proportionate strength of "inner psychical affections from male to female" or of intrapsychic "male and female elements" not only may vary from one individual to another, but also does not necessarily correlate with biological gender. As James Hillman wrote, "Persons come in genders, even if psychic persons do indeed transgress this naturalism."[9]

In my personal and clinical experience, nearly all boys who go on to become gay men are psychologically endowed with a concentration of what Winnicott calls "pure-female-element potential." This inner feminine aptitude is a strong dimension of his being about which he becomes precociously aware, generally before the advent of erotic attractions to other males. Male homosexuality itself might even be considered as a secondary offshoot to the primacy of intrapsychic femininity in the gay boy.

Depending on his age, environment, and temperament, the gay boy may or may not have language or symbols for expressing and honoring his feminine True Self. Almost always, from early childhood through adolescence, primary caretakers (and later his peer group and the wider culture) empathically fail to receive, hold, protect, nurture, and stimulate the development of his feminine self.

Of course, along with each gay boy's pronounced female elements are varying strengths of inner male elements. Even if he is endowed with sufficient innate masculine resources *in potentia*, he may very well have problems with integrating these male elements. As Joseph Henderson put it, "In many cases that I've seen in gay men, the anima has developed before his masculine identity. He knows himself more through the anima than he does through his masculinity. That gives him insight into the workings of the anima. This has both value and disadvantages. The danger is that he becomes imprisoned in the anima and can't find his way to his masculine identity."[10]

In other words, in a gay male the anima develops *precociously*; his innate feminine giftedness makes generally for a lagging and usually more difficult assimilation of male elements. But it is not just the lag of masculine development behind feminine development that may be problematic for a gay boy. Nor do integrative difficulties stem simply from imbalances in the proportions between inner female and male elements, with the psychic female elements predominating. Besides these factors of development, timing, and constitutional endowment, the dynamic interplay (or lack thereof) between feminine and masculine lines of ego development plays a crucial role in the emotional health (or illness) of a gay male.

For a gay boy becoming a gay man, psychological masculinity best develops either *alongside* his femininity (in certain periods) or *in alternation with* his femininity (in other phases). In the healthy gay male development of masculinity, there may be, usually *needs* to be, periods of *separation* from the feminine, but this does not mean a drastic *severance* from the feminine. With this assertion I wish to draw a distinction between the characteristic patterns of masculine development in gay as compared to heterosexual men, with awareness of middle-ground bisexual forms (following from Kinsey's findings of a *spectrum* of sexual orientation). Classical Jungian psychology, with an eye to various cross-cultural "primitive" initiation rites, postulates a normal heterosexual theory of masculine development that at crucial moments *does* involve a radical and nearly total break with the mother.

In his classic work *The Origins and History of Consciousness*, Erich Neumann emphasizes the imagery of masculine

ego consciousness struggling to develop against the regressive, confining, and bloodthirsty pull of the Great Mother. Her
primordial matriarchal realm is the retrograde world of vegeta-
tion, animal instinct, infantile dependence, and weak ego or
non-ego. In the original uroboric sphere, passivity and subor-
dination to the Great Mother are required.

In his description of the stage of the Great Mother's dominance over the son-lover, Neumann writes:

> All lovers of Mother Goddesses . . . are youths whose beauty and
> loveliness are as striking as their narcissism. . . ."[11]
>
> Those flower-like boys are not sufficiently strong to resist and
> break the power of the Great Mother. They are more pets than
> lovers. . . . All these youths with their weak egos and no per-
> sonality [have no] fate of their own. . . . The initiative never
> comes from them; they are always the victims, dying like ador-
> able flowers. . . .[12]
>
> The youths who personify the spring belong to the Great
> Mother. They are her bondslaves, her property, because they are
> the sons she has borne.[13]

One can feel the equation made in Neumann's mind between
these statements and pejorative psychoanalytic characteriza-
tions of male homosexuality vis-à-vis the dominant castrating
mother. So it comes as no surprise that in his sole reference to
the subject of male homosexuality, in a footnote, he writes,
"Even today we almost always find in cases of male homosexuality, a matriarchal psychology where the Great Mother is
unconsciously in the ascendent."[14]

Neumann's brilliantly explicated schema seems to illuminate well the psychological development of many heterosexual
men. However, I take issue with it in several respects as a
theory for gay men's evolution of consciousness.

It seems to me that throughout all life stages beyond infancy,[15] gay men's relationship to the primordial feminine
realm is far less threatening and adversarial than Neumann

represents it universally and inevitably to be. I conjecture that in the untraumatized primal self of gay males, we typically find an inner psychic space characterized by an indwelling balance of masculine and feminine elements. I believe that for gay males, throughout most of the life cycle, ego development follows a feminine line as much as a masculine one. The feminine does not evolve exclusively in the anima as classical Jungian theory stipulates it normally should for a man. Indeed, as Donald Sandner has articulated, the anima itself need not appear only in feminine form.[16]

Neumann states that "man experiences the 'masculine' structure of his conscious as peculiarly his own and the 'feminine' unconscious as something alien to him."[17] For a gay man, masculine and feminine are *both* felt as his own and can be *either* conscious or unconscious. It is the untoward separation of the two that is alien to him and unfavorable for him.

Neumann's language and imagery are often militaristic, dramatic, and one-sided. The hero first battles, kills, subjugates, defeats, and overcomes the terrible-mother dragon. In doing so he thus extricates and delivers the captive princess:

> What the hero kills is only the terrible side of the female, and this he does in order to set free the fruitful and joyous side with which she joins herself to him. . . .[18]
>
> The feminine image extricates itself from the grip of the Terrible Mother, a process known in analytical psychology as the crystallization of the anima from the mother archetype.[19]

According to traditional Jungian theory of heterosexual male development, the full "crystallization of the anima" generally comes quite late in life, and this maturation is considered rare. Non-Jungian theoreticians often echo this presumption, for example this statement from Nicolosi: "The true integration of femininity—if it is ever to be accomplished in a man's lifetime—occurs later in life after full assimilation of his primary masculinity, and evolves through intimacy with the opposite sex."[20]

Perhaps for many heterosexual men, reaching maturation or wisdom is accompanied by a late-stage deep integration of femininity, a "crystallization of the anima." For gay men, in contradistinction, the hallmark of maturation or wisdom has more to do with what Jung called a "detachment from the hermaphroditic archetype,"[21] which I will discuss later. But before shifting to archetypal considerations, I would like to discuss gay men's analytical work on the Oedipus complex, on issues of mother and father, on integrating feminine and masculine elements of personality.

THE OEDIPUS COMPLEX VIS-À-VIS GAY MEN

This short article does not permit a detailed theoretical review of the Oedipal complex, those dramatic triangular psychological dynamics which play such a crucial role in personality development and the orientation of desire. In brief, Freud said that this complex potentially presents itself in two chief forms: the simple or "positive" version, based on the story told in Sophocles' tragedy *Oedipus Rex*: "a desire for the death of the rival parent of the same sex and a sexual [and, I would add, *emotional*] desire for the parent of the opposite sex", and the "negative" version, basically the reverse: "love for the parent of the same sex and jealous hatred for the parent of the opposite sex." But "In fact, the two versions are to be found in varying degrees in what is known as the *complete* form of the complex."[22] Freud writes:

> The more complete Oedipus complex . . . is twofold, positive and negative . . . that is to say a boy has not merely an ambivalent attitude towards his father and an affectionate object-choice towards his mother, but at the same time he also behaves like a girl and displays an affectionate feminine attitude to his father and a corresponding jealousy and hostility towards his mother.

. . . it is advisable in general . . . to assume the existence of the complete Oedipus complex.[23]

As Kenneth Lewes writes in *The Psychoanalytic Theory of Male Homosexuality*:

"Fully elaborated forms of the Oedipus complex . . . are extremely complex and ambiguous. Their mechanisms are not straightforward and unidirectional, and the relevant component forces undergo a bewildering variety of transformations, repressions and conversions into their opposites."[24]

Even the presented "great divide" between two chief possible outcomes for the resolution of the Oedipus complex is not necessarily clear-cut. According to Lewes, "Freud posited one of two possible outcomes: an identification with the mother or an intensification of the primary identification with the father. . . ."[25] Freud believed that "the relative strength of the masculine and feminine sexual dispositions is what determines whether the outcome of the Oedipus situation shall be an identification with the father or with the mother."[26] These identifications generally correspond in psychoanalytic theory to the formation of homosexual or "normal" heterosexual identity, respectively. However, "as [psychiatrist Otto] Fenichel observed, one identification does not preclude another; simultaneous identifications are possible and indeed ubiquitous. . . . Rather than speaking of a certain figure as the nucleus for an identification, it is more accurate to specify what aspect of that figure is being internalized."[27] In his analysis of these complexities, Lewes posited *twelve* possible resolutions of the Oedipus complex, six of these in homosexual males.[28]

Whether or not one concurs with Lewes's formulation of six male homosexual outcomes, suffice it to say that there are many vicissitudes of the oedipal complex in gay men. Let us now turn to some of the clinical issues of gay men working through their mother and father complexes.

GAY MEN AND THE MOTHER

As is well known, traditional Freud-based theory on the etiology of male homosexuality gives primary importance to the pathogenic mother-son relationship. Charles Socarides sums up this perspective: "It cannot be sufficiently emphasized that the determinant of homosexuality is, in the last analysis, intimately related to the degree of primary identification with the mother. All other identifications are secondary and are accretions to this basic problem of identification."[29] Irving Bieber and his colleagues, authors of a well-known research study, state: "Our findings are replete with evidence of a close mother-son relationship and confirm the observations of Freud and other investigators that 'mother fixation' is related to homosexuality."[30]

Certainly most gay men have had closer relationships with their mothers than with their fathers. Let us put aside the defensive argument that this claim might be made generally about almost all people, since clinical experience with gay men does often confirm what appears to be "too much" mother in the mother-son relationship and also alienation in the father-son relationship.

Rather than making a simple *causal* link between the development of male homosexuality and a mother who was, for example, close-binding or controlling, seductively overstimulating, possessive, or overprotective, let us consider another possibility in light of one thesis of this paper. Perhaps because of his feminine giftedness (and thus his precocious anima development), the gay boy both consciously and unconsciously draws himself to and actively prefers his mother. In her he finds a much-needed source of narcissistic mirroring for his abundant femininity.

The strong maternal or feminine complex that often forms in the gay male psyche may be produced from the inside (i.e., deriving from innate female elements) as much as (or more than) it is induced from the outside (mother's "too much" mothering). In most cases an *interplay* of inner qualities with outer mothering influences gets the mother complex going. In any case, as Jung pointed out, this development is not without significant value:

> Since a mother complex is a concept borrowed from psychopathology, it is always associated with the idea of injury and illness. But if we take the concept out of its narrow psychopathological setting and give it wider connotation, we can see that it has its positive effects as well.
>
> A man with a mother complex may have a finely differentiated Eros instead of, or in addition to, homosexuality. This gives him a great capacity for friendship, which often creates ties of astonishing tenderness between men and may even rescue friendship between the sexes from the limbo of the impossible. He may have good taste and an aesthetic streak which are fostered by the presence of a feminine streak. Then he may be supremely gifted as a teacher because of his almost feminine insight and tact . . . often he is endowed with a wealth of religious feelings . . . and a spiritual receptivity which makes him responsive to revelation.[31]

Even more glowingly, Edward Carpenter writes:

> The Uranian temperament . . . is exceedingly sensitive and emotional; and there is no doubt that, going with this, a large number of the artist class—musical, literary or pictorial—belong to this description.[32]

> . . . Above all the Uranian temperament has specially fitted its possessors for distinction and service in affairs of the heart.[33]

> . . . I believe it is true that the Uranian men are superior to the normal men in respect for their love feeling which is gentler, more sympathetic, more considerate, more a matter of heart and less one of mere physical satisfaction than that of ordinary men. All this flows naturally from the presence of the feminine element in them and its blending with the rest of their nature.[34]

These passages bring to mind the pantheon of prominent gay male artists, writers, performers, diplomats, and other important figures of the past, more of whom are being "discovered" as gay with time. They also bring to mind all the sensitive "feminine" gay men who are *not* famous but who entertain, smooth human relations, and heal the human condition in so many ways—the musicians, visual artists, nurses, teachers, therapists, decorators, hairdressers, gardeners, animal trainers, cooks, clowns, clerics, theater people, and so on. Although the men in this category are often known to be gay, or "suspected" of being so, even in modern times their gay aspect is too often ignored, exploited, or degraded.

My consultation room fills with stories upon stories of gay men who tried in various ways not to be gay, or not to act, sound, or look gay. Some were "successful" in their subterfuge (even to themselves); many others "failed" and couldn't hide. In a majority of cases, the "give-away" was something positively feminine—a love of home; a flowing movement; a patient or caring gesture; a passionate defense of vulnerability; some inclusiveness or acceptingness of the "other"; a creative, playful, exuberant spirit; a reconciling, peacemaking quality; a loyal "bearing with" slow or painful processes of change; a lyrical vocal tonality; a softer touch; a love of plant life, of the cycles of nature; a healing talent; a response from the body, from feeling or intuition; some feminine stamina or staying power; an affinity with the world of women; a joy in personal sharing; a love of decoration and color, grooming and adorning; an appreciation for the rounds and cycles of daily living; an attraction to service; a diffuse eros in the whole sensuous body; an ecological concern for the web of life.

The mother or feminine complex can also have its negative side when it shows up in a gay man. For example, he may be too nice, too sweet, too self-effacing, too "spiritual" in his persona. He inhibits or represses his aggression, splitting off his dark side in ways that deprive him of the rich energy that shadow elements (whether masculine or feminine) might offer him. He may masochistically sacrifice, defer, and inhibit himself to serve others and in so doing undermine his full vitality. He is "gentle" and doesn't "like" conflict, competition, or intense negativity—he actually fears these. The world is arranged by him to avoid or minimize these encounters with shadow. His is a world of fantasy, illusion, laughter, and "emotion." He may be well liked but not intimately known and is often lonely. In his chosen expressive niche he may go far and deep, but his overall personality lacks roundness and inner diversity. His sexuality may shrivel altogether or project into the "other" man.

For some gay men the negative feminine complex does, indeed, inundate their psyche. In very extreme cases, where a gay man has identified with the feminine archetype, it hysterically dominates his personality, like a sorcerer's apprentice whose powers have gone awry. Here are those cases where a man may be said to be "anima possessed" in a gay male False-feminine Self syndrome. D. W. Winnicott, who formalized the idea of the "False Self," gives a clear description of the psychological subterfuge utilized by the False Self on behalf of the True Self: "The defensive function of the False Self is to hide and protect the True Self. . . . The False Self defends the True Self. The True Self is, however, acknowledged as a potential and is allowed a secret life. The False Self preserves the individual in spite of abnormal environmental conditions. . . ."[35]

The "abnormal environmental conditions" relevant to our discourse are the "not good enough" relating by primary caretakers to the female elements of a gay boy. When a gay boy's femininity has met with extreme neglect or actual violence and abuse, he may defensively produce a False-Self set of protective mechanisms. These various self-protective responses may join up and elaborate into a stylized effeminate presentation, either in an introverted (depressed, masochistic) "sissy" form or an extraverted (hysterical, sadistic) bitchy queen syndrome. A whole set of mannerisms (movements, intonations, speech patterns, idiosyncratic rituals, etc.) embed themselves in the boy's behavior, thereby securing some measure of expression and protection for the True-feminine Self.

A gay man's femininity may take refuge in his effeminacy, but this is a contradictory phenomenon. On one hand, the effeminate part holds and protects the rejected feminine, staking out a territory for its life to be sustained. On the other hand, the effeminacy, especially when exaggerated, exposes a gay male to further outer abuse and humiliation, and also may be inwardly constricting to his masculine development. In general, I have noticed that the greater the neglect and abuse his True-feminine Self has sustained, the "queenier" the false and hysterical presentation a gay man makes. Although the queen can be very funny, at times when she mixes herself up with chemical dependency or other intoxications, the results can be quite unfunny, even lethal.

Winnicott writes:

> The False Self has as its main concern a search for conditions which will make it possible for the True Self to come into its own. If conditions cannot be found then there must be reorganized a new defense against exploitation of the True Self, and if there be doubt then the clinical result is suicide. Suicide in this context is the destruction of the total self in avoidance of annihilation of the True Self. When suicide is the only defense left against betrayal of the True Self, then it becomes the lot of the False Self to organize the suicide.[36]

When a gay man's False-feminine Self (queenly or otherwise) fails, he may actually suicide. A gay man's self-destruction may carry this deep meaning: that his true feminine soul never found safe conditions in which to thrive.

GAY MEN AND THE FATHER

If we read traditional psychoanalytic accounts of the father's role in the production of male homosexuality, we find statements like these, made by Charles Socarides:

> In male homosexuality one finds . . . a search for love from the
> father or father surrogate and a concomitant wish to wreak ven-
> geance upon him which lies beneath the male homosexual's
> apparent devotion to men. The son's wish for masculine identi-
> fication [has] been frustrated earlier by the father's absence,
> coldness, apathy or disdain. [37]

> [To redress these injuries] . . . the homosexual makes an identi-
> fication with the masculinity of his partner in the sexual act. . . . [38]

And, from Anna Freud, writing about "passive" homosexuals:

> . . . the active male partners, whom these men are seeking,
> represent to them their lost masculinity, which they enjoy in
> identification with him. . . . [39]
>
> [These identifications with lost masculinity also entail a] nar-
> cissistic overvaluation of the phallus, a position in which most of
> their libido was not available for the formation of true emotional
> relationships. [40]

In surveying the psychoanalytic literature from which these
excerpts are drawn, I find the Freud-influenced formulations
partially illuminating and apt. There is much to be learned
from the overall psychoanalytic opus on male homosexuality.
At least, to the credit of Freud-based thinkers, a large and
significant body of literature *exists* to relate to, depart from,
agree with, or challenge. Jung and Jungians have, in contrast,
largely left a theoretical vacuum in the clinical literature about
homosexuality, even if the neglect often had a benign motiva-
tion: that is, to do no harm. [41] The long-standing vacuum in the
Jungian literature seems particularly unfortunate because
many gay men are attracted to a Jungian analytic approach.
Whereas disaster stories abound about gay men's experiences
of Freudian analysis, more often than not gay men have had
positive experiences with Jungian analysis.

Too often, Freud-centered writers show a counteranalytic
homophobic bias in their writings about male homosexuality.
In this negative legacy of the psychoanalytic fathers we find a

recapitulation of the failures of personal fathers vis-à-vis their gay male patients (sons). For example, if one reads Joseph Nicolosi's *Reparative Therapy of Male Homosexuality* (the jacket of which includes endorsements by prominent psychoanalytic authorities Irving Bieber, Althea Horner, and Charles Socarides), we find a dogmatic bias, as in this passage: "I do not believe that the gay life-style can ever be healthy, nor that the homosexual identity can ever be completely ego syntonic."[42] About those men who seek his "reparative therapy," Nicolosi states: "They refuse to relinquish their heterosexual social identity. Rather than wage war against the natural order of society, they instead take up the sword of an interior struggle."[43] Such blatant and oppressive negative bias constitutes a betrayal of the analytic ideals of neutrality and respect for individuation. The patriarchal "father knows best" tenor of these and *many* other comparable passages in the psychoanalytic literature aggravates an already problematic relationship of gay men to the Father.

Heterosexist bias in psychiatry constitutes an abusive soul murder[44] of gay men who come for healing and self-discovery and meet with manipulation, deception, and assault. Such "treatment" is destructive, homophobic, and, as Joyce McDougall eloquently articulates, near-perverse:

> . . . should an analyst maintain heterosexual goals for homosexual patients that the patients do not have for themselves, or maintain that analysis is not for the homosexual, it is probable that these countertransference attitudes are linked to unconscious homosexual fears and wishes in the analyst, giving rise to values of a normative and, in view of the analytic ideal, near perverse kind. The analytic couch must not become a procrustean bed.[45]

Analyst Leonard Shengold uses the term *soul murder* to designate "the deliberate attempt to eradicate or compromise the separate identity of another person."[46] If this definition is accepted, then the official annals of psychoanalysis (and much more the unrecorded clinical abuses) are replete with soul murder. On the Jungian side, Robert H. Hopcke (echoing Shengold's ideas about soul murder) points out that if Freudian psychoanalysis in its negative excesses has *abused* gay people while purporting to heal, Jungian analysis in its damaging forms has *neglected* the souls of gay people.[47]

Such problems in the collective psychoanalytic patriarchal structure reverberate at the individual level: most gay men have had poor relationships with their fathers; clinical case histories abound of gay sons whose fathers rejected, abused, ignored, or failed to harmonize with them. These case accounts of failed father-son relating often attain truly tragic proportions, laced with intense affects: grief, bitterness, hatred, fear, intimidation, and desire for revenge.

The failure, however, is not one-sidedly due to the son's inability to identify with and appropriate inner resources from the father's masculine repositories. The father's failure to impart masculine energy to his son may be a significant problem for that proportion of gay men who are deficient in their inner male elements. But, in my observation, most gay men are *not* lacking reserves of male energy. In the Greek legends and myths, virtually all the male homosexual pairs are soldiers-in-arms. Michelangelo completed the Sistine Chapel in an agony of discipline and stamina. Walt Whitman conveyed a great sense of masculine strength, freedom, and sexual virility, "the body electric." UN Secretary General Dag Hammerskjöld waged peace out of a commanding sense of authority. In the AIDS epidemic, thousands of gay men have fought courageously for their own and one another's lives. Yet the masculine potency and strength of these gay men is and was accompanied by an equal or superior grounding in the feminine principle within each of their psychic dispositions.

The father problem of gay men does not consist simply of

the gay son's inability to identify with, metabolize, and absorb the father's stores of masculinity. Nor, to use alternate language, has the heterosexual father simply denied his gay son the masculine initiation which that heterosexual father presumably received from *his* own father. Rather, I would propose that the father problem of gay sons is a problem of *fit* (or misfit) between the two. In general, male elements predominate in the father's psyche. The father's feminine side either tends not to develop appreciably at all, or develops only late in life, long after the gay son is grown and formed. The gay son needs a father figure with well-developed femininity in childhood and adolescence, and this is exactly when his heterosexual father is least likely to meet him in his crucial developmental tasks or initiatory thresholds.

As Jung expressed so insightfully in the epigraph to this essay, male homosexuality involves "a distinct resistance to identify with the role of a one-sided sexual being. Such a disposition should not be adjudged negative in all circumstances, in so far as it preserves the archetype of the Original Man, which a one-sided sexual being has, up to a point, lost."[48] In our present discussion of fathers of gay sons, we might paraphrase Jung to say that gay sons resist identifying with their one-sidedly masculine fathers. In one common scenario of the heterosexual father–gay son relationship, the son may actually spurn, upstage, and even (in a childlike way) harass or humiliate his father, driving him further and further away from any satisfying connection between them. The son lets on that he doesn't need the brutish, hopelessly insensitive father. He writes his father off and burns every bridge in a series of critical and rageful judgments.

In another characteristic pattern, the gay son masochistically carries the burden of gestating and incubating his father's unborn feminine consciousness. Unconsciously and almost instinctively, the gay son takes up the task of living out father's unrealized anima. The son usually carries this burden in grief and imploded rage, some of which may manifest in an exaggerated false-feminine style. The gay son unconsciously presses father to awaken him to the gift of his own anima. The gay son does this partly as a reparation for his fantasy wish of destroying father for disappointing and failing him. But also the son attempts to awaken father so that the latter may in turn more effectively mirror the son's vivid femininity. When the gay son's unconscious efforts to enliven father's femininity are thwarted—and they usually are—the son may then experience feelings of unaccountable depression. Unconsciously, he may feel he has miscarried his father's anima, a loss for them both.

Gay men often resist even the hypothetical *possibility* of tenderly loving or preferring father (although at times some gay men can frankly admit erotic fantasies about their fathers). The son's door is closed to father, but this impermeability and defensive antipathy naturally point to powerful unconscious longings for intimacy with him. Because the son is convinced (often realistically) of the doomed prospects for intimate connection with his actual father, the father-son transference in analysis has a particularly volatile, sensitive character and tonality. To manage such powerful transference requires qualities of equanimity, fortitude, and clarity in the therapist or analyst.

Often in the negative transference the son must freely rage at, criticize, vent guilt-inducing disappointment at, show "insatiable" dissatisfaction with, attack, berate, freeze out, and not speak to the analyst-father without meeting the analyst-father's response of retaliation against or humiliation of the son. Neither, however, should the analyst-father humiliate himself, capitulating into obsequiousness or guilt not belonging to him. The ravenous father-hunger of bitterly disappointed gay sons often shows itself in the transference as an overt demandingness or in the analysand's testing the authority of the analyst, especially the limits and boundaries set by him. When the son's intense father-hunger is unconsciously denied, it may show up in various passive resistant forms, including undermining analytic progress as a punishment of the bad father. To these transference tests, a tolerating acceptance, quiet strength, feelingful understanding, and some form of givingness (including, if necessary, setting limits on the son's rampage) are typically called for on the part of the analyst.

In the positive transference, passionate loving feelings for the father-analyst invariably emerge. These affectionate feelings often include varying degrees of erotic longing: in some cases, strong desires for tender holding on father's lap or in his arms or against his chest. Less often, but not uncommonly, the "daddy-analyst" becomes incestuously desired in various fantasy wishes for direct sexual contact. At times these sexual desires further elaborate, joining with stylized sadistic/masochistic scenarios involving punishment, humiliation, forgiveness, reconciliation, etc.

The son wants yet fears having the father all to himself. The analytic arrangement heightens such exclusivity wishes as the analyst pays close attention to the analysand hour after hour. Images of father and son together in the wild (hiking, camping, fishing, wandering, etc.) may arise. The analyst may become in the patient's mind a symbolic elder, uncle, or big brother helping the boy-analysand over some masculine initiatory barriers (taking him into the sweat lodge, into the brotherhood, on a vision quest, to the altar, etc.). Such themes can show up in either fantasy or dream material. When these positive transferential experiences are acknowledged and received by the male analyst, the gay male patient often feels intense inner affects, bondedness, excitement, relief, even ecstatic or sacred emotional qualities.

The father-analyst needs to perceive, accept, and evenhandedly value these various images and emotions that flow through the son- or initiate-analysand. Especially the feminine aspects (or the mixed boy/girl elements) need a haven in the father's accepting, holding response. The father-analyst needs to convey a recognition and appreciation of these feminine elements that are qualitatively *different* (and somehow not "less than") the father's love for the femininity in his wife or in a daughter. The father-analyst must handle erotic longings from the son-analysand with particular care, neither rejecting these desires nor stimulating them (and most assuredly not "acting in" with the patient, that is, physically contacting him). The son needs to allow himself to feel symbolically (and to a degree "really") seen and cherished by his analyst-father for whichever aspect of himself arises at a given time—the inner boy, the inner girl, the boy-becoming-a-youth, the youth-becoming-a-man. Assuming that the analyst has well enough integrated his own feminine and masculine elements, he will then be able well enough to carry the son's father or mother projections until the son can integrate them as his own.

Different parts of the analysand's personality may be more and less developed. Particularly in gay males, as already discussed, feminine elements may have developed earlier than masculine ones. As Winnicott writes, "the truly imaginative figures of the person's inner psychic reality mature, interrelate, grow old and die. . . ." But "the split-off . . . part of the personality tends to remain of one age, or to grow but slowly."[49] The analyst working with gay men must be particularly adept at recognizing, holding, and managing these unevenly developed inner gender objects, including the problems of those part-objects which have become split off or fixated in their development.

GAY MEN AND DETACHMENT FROM THE ARCHETYPE OF THE HERMAPHRODITE

As we have just seen, a Jungian analytical approach to clinical work entails thoroughly taking up Oedipal dynamics (including mother and father complexes) and working these through in the transference. In addition, in-depth analytical work takes place at the level of the impersonal or archetypal psyche. One particularly relevant psychological and archetypal problem of gay men is their detachment or disidentification from the archetype of the hermaphrodite.

Holding in mind Jung's general dictum that "if one can possibly avoid it, one ought never to identify with an archetype,"[50] (i.e., not with *any* archetype), we might then ask what Jung might have meant in reference to homosexuality by the phrase "incomplete detachment from the hermaphroditic archetype." First of all, what is the "hermaphroditic psychic condition"? Freud wrote this about the hermaphrodite:

> Mythology can teach us that an androgynous structure, a combination of male and female sex characters, was an attribute not only of Mut but also of other deities like Isis and Hathor. . . . It teaches us further that other Egyptian deities . . . were originally conceived of as androgynous, i.e., as hermaphrodite, and that the same was true of many of the *Greek* gods, especially those associated with Dionysus, but also of Aphrodite. Mythology may then offer the explanation that . . . all these hermaphrodite divinities are expressions of the idea that only a combination of male and female elements can give a worthy representation of divine perfection.[51]

About the hermaphroditic psychic condition, Jung said:

> The *Rosarium* remarks . . . that "the body is Venus and feminine, the spirit is Mercurius and masculine"; hence the anima as the . . . link between body and spirit would be hermaphroditic, i.e., a *coniunctio Solis et Lunae*. Mercurius is the hermaphrodite par excellence. From all this it may be gathered that the queen stands for the body and the king for the spirit, but that both are unrelated without the soul . . . which holds them together. If no bond of love exists, they have no soul. . . . Thus the underlying idea of the psyche proves it to be a half bodily, half spiritual substance, . . . an hermaphroditic being capable of uniting the opposites, but who is never complete in the individual unless related to another individual. The unrelated human being lacks wholeness, for he

can achieve wholeness only through the soul, and the soul cannot exist without its other side, which is always found in a "You." Wholeness is a combination of I and You. . . .[52]

In applying this alchemical material to gay men, we might in general reverse the Rosarium's remarks; that is, a gay man might commonly experience his body as mostly masculine (phallic) and the spirit in him (his psychic elements) as primarily feminine. Either *instead* of this or as an alternate "parallel track" in the body/spirit conjunction, a gay man may find in himself a homosexual version of the Rosarium's original comment. That is, he may feel his male body as suffused with feminine qualities (especially his breasts, anus, mouth, or eyes), whereas his spirit (psychic elements) may well have a masculine character.

Whether one or both of these body/spirit conjunctions run through a given gay man's psyche, he may experience himself as peculiarly self-contained, hermaphroditically virginal: that is, "unto himself." The hermaphrodite represents a *fusion* of male and female components, creating an inseparable unity and wholeness. The multivarious possibilities of male-male sexuality (for example, of penetrating or being penetrated, orally or anally; or the emphasis some gay men place on nipple stimulation) heighten the possibilities of allowing the fantasy body to enter either masculine or feminine states. As I have already discussed extensively, the profusion of female elements, alongside "ordinary" quantities of male elements adds to the subjective hermaphroditic brew. Gay men commonly enter altered mind (spirit) / body (sexual) states associated with subjectively experienced psychological unions of masculine and feminine, and erotic exchanges both penetrative and receptive. While these inner unions may bring ecstatic or transcendent qualities, they can also produce narcissistically mesmerizing or autoerotically fixated psychological conditions. As Joseph Henderson says:

. . . the image of the cross, . . . which represents the union of the opposites . . . is great to experience. The person can experience himself as bisexual, but that can become a stalemate. It can become something upon which he is crucified, if he doesn't separate the opposites. Otherwise he stays in the hermaphroditic state and that is not healthy. . . . [The hermaphroditic state] can be a very meaningful experience, but you must detach from it and not live it.[53]

In many people you find this hermaphroditic situation . . . it is really all in the myth of Narcissus. Narcissus saw himself as beautiful; when he looked at himself in the water, he saw what Echo had seen in him. He saw this beautiful face. He thought it was a nymph—a beautiful nymph. He was in love with a man who was somehow also a woman. It seems to me right there you get the idea of the joining union of the masculine and feminine. This can be very powerful and very attractive because it seems to represent a wholeness—a sort of unity—that would solve all problems of relationship. But it doesn't go anywhere. It stays in the same place. It merely repeats.

That's why analysts talk so much today about the narcissistic personality disorder, because people can't get away from feeling that the world owes them everything, that the world should come to them rather than their going out to it. This is based on that essential belief in a psychic wholeness that doesn't really get born into life.

In the alchemical studies we often see where the hermaphrodite is featured as a goal, as an end in itself. But that is not the end of the road—after that there is a reparation of the two, and then a new polarity is formed between the masculine and the feminine. This also appears in the alchemical study *Splendor Solis*. The goal is not this union of the male and female but the making of the gold which transcends either one. [The hermaphrodite] defeats the idea of individuation. It has within it the promise of individuation but it defeats it if it repeats.[54]

In other words, the masculine/feminine opposites can become fused, merged, too close. Perhaps this is what Jung meant by "an incomplete detachment from the hermaphroditic arche-type"[55] in male homosexuality.

The frequent foundering of sexuality in intimate relation-ships between gay men might partially be explained by this problem of identification with the hermaphroditic archetype. If a gay man remains unconscious of the proportions and intentions of his constituent male and female elements, these elements will blur together into an undifferentiated amalgam, making impossible a mature and viable relationship with an-other man. If, on the other hand, a gay man becomes highly tuned to his individual intrapsychic gender makeup—to ac-curately know his true-feminine and true-masculine self-elements and how they operate—then he may be able to enter with satisfaction into close relationship with another similarly conscious man.

Becoming conscious in this way means acknowledging the gifts as well as the deficits in one's masculinity or femininity. It means separating and defining *masculine* and *feminine* indi-vidually and truthfully out of one's personal encounter with the unconscious. As I have indicated, a great deal of work invari-ably must be done on one's own Oedipus complex, on one's childhood drama, on the inevitable love and hate of one's mother and father.

Besides this personal work on the Oedipus complex, a conscious gay man must also allow himself to be touched by the archetype of initiation in a process consonant with his "not one-sided sexual being." As I discussed earlier, in general I conjecture a gay man's experience of initiation to follow a qualitatively different course than that of a heterosexual male.

In *Thresholds of Initiation*, Joseph Henderson distinguishes two patterns of initiation: one, a more linear pattern of "initia-tion as a series of levels or stages,"[56] a "stepladder or evolu-tionary view," and, two, a pattern that shows "a distinctly *cyclic* character in which a return to old patterns is of no less significance than a sense of progression to new ones."[57]

I intuit that heterosexual male development tends to follow the more linear pattern of initiation stages, with greater emphasis placed on leaving behind earlier phases. In contrast, gay male maturation and individuation are better illuminated by the more cyclic model of initiation. Substantiating this intuitive hypothesis will have to wait for another time. However, I will recapitulate an earlier point in this connection.

In the more cyclic model of gay male psychological maturation, the severance or obliteration of the feminine (in the manner which Neumann, for example, describes) would not, could not take place. Rather, in a uniquely individual way a gay man would tend to pass through alternating cycle-phases; during one period focusing more on refining his feminine aspect, during another period being more concerned with strengthening masculine identity (with overlapping integrative transitions between the cycle-phases). Like the two entwined snakes of the caduceus, the dual paths of masculine and feminine development relate back and forth throughout the life cycle of a gay man. It is essential, however, that he *separate* the masculine and feminine strands of his makeup, to differentiate these and individuate himself out of the unconscious hermaphroditic blur into which all too many gay men lapse. As Joseph Henderson has commented:

> If the homosexual patient in analysis successfully meets the conflict of the opposites and works with them by separating them so that he or she feels the tension between them, acknowledging both sides, and experiences that as a kind of initiation, then the person becomes mature.[58]

Notes

1. C. G. Jung, *The Collected Works of C. G. Jung* [CW], vol. 9/1 (Princeton: Princeton University Press, 1968), p. 71.
2. John Boswell, quoted in Lawrence Mass, "Sexual Categories, Sexual Universals: A Conversation with John Boswell," in *Homosexuality as Behavior and*

Identity: Dialogues of the Sexual Revolution, vol. 2 (New York: Harrington Park Press, 1990), pp. 202–233.

3. Boswell, "Sexual," pp. 24–25.

4. Ibid., p. 29.

5. Andrew Samuels, *The Plural Psyche: Personality, Morality and the Father* (New York: Routledge & Kegan Paul, 1989).

6. D. W. Winnicott, "The Split-off Male and Female Elements to Be Found in Men and Women," in *Psychoanalytic Explorations*, ed. Clare Winnicott, Ray Shepard, and Madeline Davis (Cambridge, Mass.: Harvard University Press, 1989), pp. 168–92.

7. Winnicott, "Elements," p. 180.

8. Edward Carpenter, *Edward Carpenter: Selected Writings*, vol. 1: *Sex* (London: GMP Publishers, 1984), p. 186.

9. James Hillman, *Anima: An Anatomy of a Personified Notion* (Dallas: Spring Publications, 1985), p. 173.

10. See "Reflections on Homosexuality and Individuation: An Interview with Joseph Henderson" by Scott Wirth, pp. 231 of the present volume.

11. Erich Neumann, *The Origins and History of Consciousness* (Princeton, N.J.: Princeton University Press, 1954), p. 50.

12. Ibid., p. 51.

13. Ibid., p. 53.

14. Ibid., p. 141n.

15. I concur with Anna Freud when she writes, "Infants, at the beginning of life, choose their objects on the basis of function, not of sex. . . . Although in the strict sense of the term the infant is neither heterosexual nor homosexual, he can also be described as being both." Anna Freud, *The Writings of Anna Freud*, vol. 6: "Homosexuality" (Madison, Conn.: International Universities Press, 1981), p. 186.

16. Donald Sandner, "The Role of the Anima in Same-Sex Love between Men," pp. 219ff of the present volume.

17. Neumann, *Origins*, p. 125, n. 13.

18. Ibid., p. 125.

19. Ibid., p. 198.

20. Joseph Nicolosi, *Reparative Therapy of Male Homosexuality: A New Clinical Approach* (Northvale, N.J.: Jason Aronson, 1991), p. 156.

21. Jung, CW 9/1, p. 71.

22. J. Laplanche and J. B. Pontalis, *The Language of Psychoanalysis* (New York: W. W. Norton , 1973), p. 283.

23. Sigmund Freud, *The Standard Edition of the Complete Psychological Works of Sigmund Freud*, vol. 19 (London: Hogarth Press, 1961), p. 33.

24. Kenneth Lewes, *The Psychoanalytic Theory of Male Homosexuality* (New York: Simon and Schuster, 1988), p. 78.

25. Ibid.

26. Freud, *Standard Edition*, vol. 19, p. 38.

27. Lewes, *Theory*, p. 85.

28. Ibid., p. 82.

29. Charles W. Socarides, *Homosexuality: Psychoanalytic Therapy* (Northvale, N.J.: Jason Aronson, 1978), pp. 146–47.

30. Irving Bieber et al., *Homosexuality: A Psychoanalytic Study* (Northvale, N.J.: Jason Aronson, 1988), p. 308.

31. Jung, CW 9/1, p. 86.

32. Carpenter, *Selected Writings*, vol. 1., p. 234.

33. Ibid., p. 140.

34. Ibid., p. 244.

35. D. W. Winnicott, "Ego Distortion in Terms of True and False Self" (1960), in *The Maturational Processes and the Facilitating Environment: Studies in the Theory of Emotional Development* (Madison, Conn.: International Universities Press, 1965), p. 142.

36. Ibid., p. 143.

37. Socarides, *Homosexuality*, p. 84.

38. Ibid., p. 71.

39. Anna Freud, *The Writings of Anna Freud*, vol. 4: *Studies in Passivity* (Madison, Conn.: International Universities Press, 1981), p. 251.

40. Ibid., pp. 255–56.

41. See Robert H. Hopcke, *Jung, Jungians, and Homosexuality* (Boston: Shambhala Publications, 1989), and Robert H. Hopcke, "Homophobia and Analytical Psychology," pp. 68–87 of the present volume.

42. Nicolosi, *Reparative*, p. 13.

43. Ibid., p. 5.

44. Leonard Shengold, *Soul Murder: The Effects of Childhood Abuse and Deprivation* (New Haven: Yale University Press, 1989).

45. Joyce McDougall, "Perversions and Deviations in the Psychoanalytic Attitude: Their Effect on Theory and Practice," in *Perversions and Near-Perversions in Clinical Practice: New Psychoanalytic Perspectives*, eds. Gerald I. Fogel and Wayne A. Myers (New Haven: Yale University Press, 1991), pp. 190–191.

46. Shengold, *Soul Murder*, p. 2.

47. Hopcke, "Homophobia."

48. Jung, CW 9/1, p. 71.

49. Winnicott, "Elements," p. 175.

50. Jung, CW 9/1, p. 103.

51. Freud, *Standard Edition*, vol. 11, p. 94.

52. Jung, CW 16 pp. 244–45.

53. Joseph Henderson, personal communication, 1991.

54. Ibid.

55. Jung, CW 9/1, p. 71.

56. Joseph Henderson, *Thresholds of Initiation* (Middletown, Conn.: Wesleyan University Press, 1967), p. 181.

57. Ibid., p. 176.

58. See "Reflections on Homosexuality," pages 231–245 of the present volume.

The Role of the Anima in Same-Sex Love between Men

DONALD SANDNER

The restrictions of a short paper, especially one about the anima, make it necessary to declare one's theoretical position quickly and leave the review of differing ideas for another time. Certainly Jung contradicted himself sometimes, not to mention the radical contradictions that exist among his followers.[1] I'm with Jung when he says: "Anima means soul and should designate something very wonderful and immortal,"[2] and "Being that has soul is living being. Soul is the living thing in man, that which of itself lives and causes life. . . . With her cunning play of illusions the soul lives into life the inertness of matter that does not want to live. She makes us believe incredible things that life may be lived. She is full of snares and traps, in order that man should fall, should reach the earth, entangle himself there, and stay caught so that life should be lived."[3]

This idea of the anima-soul is not the same dogmatic notion of soul found in sermons and religious texts. It is rather "life behind consciousness that cannot be entirely integrated with it but from which, on the contrary, consciousness arises."[4] This consciousness occurs by means of projection because unless one is a mystic or a madman, one does not encounter the anima only inside of one's psyche. One unconsciously projects it onto other persons, perceives it there, and imagines (in the most powerful sense of that word) that such persons carry one's soul. This is true anima projection and is commonly known as falling in love.

Jung also said: "When projected, the anima always has feminine form with definite characteristics."[5] Here, with due regard for his pioneering effort, I part company with Jung. His statement is certainly true for a predominantly heterosexual male, but years of clinical work persuade me that it is not entirely true for homosexual, bisexual, or even psychically bisexual men (those who have internalized their love of other men and have not developed outer sexual pathways for it). Every shade of variation exists along the heterosexual-homosexual continuum, and we have only the vaguest notions why things turn out as they do. But for these men the anima, encountered inwardly in dreams and outwardly in projected forms, often appears in the image of another man.

Because this view differs from accepted Jungian theory, it needs some explanation. In my work with men in analysis, I have observed in dreams, in emotional behavior, and in the formation of complexes that, although the anima may, in its deepest form, be as one, it has many aspects and many different faces. In noting whom a man falls in love with, whom he marries, whom he dreams about, and whom he identifies with, I find a natural diversity that has led me in the past to speak of the "split anima."[6]

Although there are many images of the anima in a man's dreams and visions, in clinical situations they tend to group themselves around two poles, which I call the *dominant anima* and the *wounded anima*. Viewed within a more inclusive conceptualization, these two may be seen as two sides of a single condition, a bipolar complex; nevertheless, in practice they are often experienced as separate from and even in conflict with each other.

I will illustrate this inner condition by means of a dream from a young professional man in the midst of his analytic work. Both the dominant and the wounded anima appear in this dream and play parts that are characteristic of their nature:

> I am living in an orphanage with my woman friend. We are both orphans, and the place is run by an older woman with a cruel face, a lipstick gash across her mouth, and dressed in old-fashioned clothes from the twenties.
>
> The orphanage is a dreary place. Every night the older woman chains my woman friend and me to separate cots in the basement far enough apart so we cannot reach each other. During the day the older woman makes me push a piano up and down the corridor in the basement between the cots. It is humiliating work. My fury begins to rise.

In the associations to this dream, the older woman and her old-fashioned clothes were linked with the dreamer's mother and the piano to hated piano lessons as a child. The younger woman was a contemporary woman friend.

This dream—and I could produce more like it from my cases—shows the dominant anima as the older woman who runs the orphanage, associated with the dreamer's mother. It also shows the weak and helpless anima in the person of the young woman, who was at the time of the dream a love interest of the dreamer's. These two personages of the dream represent the split or bipolar nature of the anima. The two poles are distinguished by their qualities. The dominant pole may be represented by a range of qualities—from harshness, rudeness, sadism, and maliciousness or even murderous intent to strong, positive, assertive leadership. The wounded anima is represented by weakness, disability, and illness, but also lovingness, sensitivity, and soulfulness. The heroines of nineteenth-century novels and operas—fragile, soulful, and tubercular—were examples of just such an attractive but weak anima. It is noteworthy that the two anima elements interact in this dream, as they often do: the older woman, representing the dreamer's mother, ties up the younger woman and the dreamer so that they cannot touch. From this dream and others like it, the basic internal pattern of the patient's psyche can be intuited. The mother personage inhibits the two young people and prevents her son (the dreamer) from having an erotic relationship with the young woman. If we take into account the last part of the dream, in which the dreamer feels his fury rising, we might foresee that he will use that fury to break his mother bonds and claim his masculine instinctual heritage. All in all, this is a typical example of the split or bipolar anima, and it accords perfectly with the dreamer's outer situation in relation to his woman friend and his mother.

As I have mentioned, it is possible for one side of the anima to be a young man. An actively homosexual man in his thirties brought me a picture drawn from a dream of a beautiful young man standing against a blue sky surrounded by a rainbow and wearing a crown of stars. This was an idealized picture of his current lover. The younger man was passive and very sensitive, and the dreamer said that the picture was an expression of his soul, and the younger man a carrier of it. If the picture had been of a woman, and the man straight, it would without hesitation be regarded as an anima figure, and that is exactly what it is—an anima representation in masculine form.

But where is the other pole, the dominant anima? A short time later this same man had another dream.

I had appendicitis or a tumor, and I needed an operation. I was very hesitant, but a large woman doctor pushed her way in and announced that she was ready to do the operation. I smelled ether, and I knew I was going under. The operation was painful, but I didn't die or anything.

Here the dominant anima (in feminine form) takes charge, renders the dreamer unconscious, and prepares for an operation, a transformation that does not bode well. This is one of several dreams I have encountered in which the dominant

anima, who is usually related to the mother, operates sur-
gically on a young male dreamer or on the weaker anima.

Here we see the anima functioning on one side of the split as
the bearer of the soul (the young man) and on the other side as
a dominant surgeon intent on subduing the dreamer. As this
case demonstrates, the anima can function on the highest
level, making soul visible, or as a destructive, controlling
sadist, or anyplace in between. To what degree this occurs
depends on many factors, both genetic and environmental.
One important factor is the man's relationship with his father.

This patient had another dream shortly afterward that rather
clearly describes his relationship with his father, again
through the symbolism of a surgical operation.

> I had my appendix removed and afterward I was told I needed
> something else removed—my intestines or something. My father
> made the arrangements, and the doctor turned out to be an
> employee of the sewer treatment plant. I was enraged and
> stamped out of the hospital even though everyone protested.

The important point here, supported by the dreamer's history,
was that this patient could not trust his father either. Without a
father in his young life a man cannot develop his masculine
side and form a counterpoint to the potentially destructive/
constructive mother-anima. Such a relationship with a father
figure, of course, can occur later with an older man (possibly
an older lover), a mentor, or a therapist. When it is a therapist
who plays such a role, if all goes well, the masculine side of
the patient is strengthened and the balance with the anima
gradually becomes positive.

In cases of a split anima, the sexual libido may be projected
and attached from either side of the split. In both cases cited
above, the sexual feeling was attracted by the wounded or
soulful side of the anima, fueling an intense desire to project
this out onto another person and heal oneself by taking care of
it there. This dynamic constitutes one of the greatest pitfalls

for the analyst and the patient: the analyst may project his own wounded side upon the patient. The patient may welcome and promote such a projection, bringing about an entanglement that could halt therapeutic progress and create a false relationship, endangering not only the therapeutic progress of the patient but also the deeper well-being of both the patient and the therapist.

In another variation on this basic pattern, the sexual libido may be attached to the other side of the split—the dominant anima. Then the man may fall in love with a dominant woman or man and enter into a dominant/submissive or even sadomasochistic relationship that can be very strong. The dominance may be expressed psychologically in the relationship itself or acted out in some sadomasochistic sexual ritual. Once one or the other side of the split is projected and sexualized, it becomes compulsive and very resistant to change.

This anima split occurs in all possible variations. Each side of the split may then be projected out onto other persons. I am using *projection* here, following Jung, as the unconscious (that is, unperceived and unintentional) transfer of subjective psychic elements onto an outer object. Each side of the split or bipolar complex, whether envisioned inwardly or projected, contains strong feeling and a rather specific image. The image may be a person of a very particular physical type: a tall, lanky blond man, for instance, or a brunette with prominent breasts; or it may be a narrower image of a body part, such as a large phallus, large breasts, or well-rounded buttocks; or it may be specific sexual ritual acts: certain sexual positions or acts of foreplay, being bound or beaten or entered sexually in a particular way. This particular image then becomes the focus of the most intense sexual excitement.

No matter what the exact nature of the split, there are always two counterforces that keep it in equilibrium. The splitting force itself derives its energy from the emotional pain of the original childhood family situation that made the split necessary in the first place. In such a condition of emotional pain or abuse during childhood, only dissociation of the psyche makes the pain tolerable, giving such splitting considerable survival value. The other force is the integrating force, usually activated by positive life experiences or psychotherapy, that works toward reintegration of the split parts, reduction of the tension between opposing polarities, and attainment of a greater degree of original wholeness.

The split anima, which I have described clinically as the wounded anima and the dominant anima, can contain many different opposing qualities, but one side of the split usually represents earthly instincts of the body (the sexual and aggressive instincts emphasized by Freud) and the other side more spiritual strivings. Long before Jung, this split was specifically described by Plato (in *The Phaedrus*) in the image of two horses and a charioteer:

> The right horse is upright and cleanly made, he has a lofty neck and an aquiline nose; his color is white, and his eyes dark; he is a lover of honor and modesty and temperance, and the follower of true glory; . . . The other is a crooked, lumbering animal, put together anyhow; he has a short, thick neck; he is flat-faced and of a dark color, with grey eyes and blood-red complexion; the mate of insolence and pride, shag eared and deaf, hardly yielding to whip and spur.
>
> Now when the charioteer beholds the vision of love, and has his whole soul warmed through sense, and is full of the prickings and ticklings of desire, the obedient steed, then as always under the government of shame, refrains from leaping on the beloved; but the other, heedless of the pricks and of the blows of the whip, plunges and runs away, giving all manner of trouble to his companion and the charioteer. [7]

Overlaid as this passage is with Greek idealism, a better description could hardly be found of the anima's task in bringing together the divided soul. Jung called the anima the "archetype of life itself" because of this capacity. *It binds the sexual and spiritual interests of the psyche into one entity*, represents this entity by a more or less specific image, and then projects this image onto another person (the object), accompanied by the powerful effect of love. By this means the anima is the originator of personal love (eros) in all its manifold variations, including both same-sex and different-sex love.

Thus, same-sex love between men involves the same splits and mergers, the same anima functions as different-sex love. But it is my observation that sexual partners who are too much alike in certain important aspects, such as physical gender, have a less stable sexual relationship over time than different-sex partners. In relation to this, there may be a tendency toward depersonalization of the sexual object or an expansiveness in a spiritual direction.

This same observation is the basis of Jung's intuitive evaluation of the effects of the mother complex on the son and its relationship to same-sex love:

> Thus a man with a mother complex may have a finely differentiated Eros instead of, or in addition to, homosexuality. . . . This gives him a great capacity for friendship, which often creates ties of astonishing tenderness between men and may even rescue friendship between the sexes from the limbo of the impossible. . . . Often he is endowed with a wealth of religious feelings, *which help to bring the "ecclesia spiritualis" into reality; and a spiritual receptivity which makes him responsive to revelation.*[8]

Same-sex love especially cannot entirely depend upon sexual desire for its continuity. Because of the gender likeness, there is too much instability in its nature. The likeness can be understood and felt as a kind of incest (based on gender likeness instead of family or blood likeness). Very often, though not always, same-sex love depends on spiritual or transcendent qualities (with or without sex) for its foundation. Besides openly gay relationships, this is evidenced among

schoolmates, fraternity brothers, warrior comrades, team-
mates, teachers and students, mentors and protegés, sons and
fathers, monastic brothers, soulmates, and others. Perhaps
the most famous of such spiritual friendships is the biblical
one between David and Jonathan. When David returned from
his heroic victory over the Philistine champion, Goliath, and
told Saul of his success, then "the soul of Jonathan was knit to
the soul of David, and Jonathan loved him as his own soul."[9]

This spiritual bent in same-sex love (again, with or without
sexuality) is related to its androgynous nature. In such love
both masculine and feminine characteristics are alive and
active in both partners. This tendency to androgyny is, to
quote Jung, "rather a matter of incomplete detachment from
the hermaphroditic archetype, coupled with a distinct resistance to identify with the role of a one-sided sexual being.
Such a disposition should not be adjudged negative in all
circumstances, in so far as it preserves the archetype of the
Original Man, which a one-sided sexual being has, up to a
point, lost."[10]

Robert H. Hopcke, in his excellent book *Jung, Jungians,
and Homosexuality*, has posited masculinity, femininity, and
androgyny as three separate archetypes, bringing them all into
a constantly interacting changing system within the psyche.
He says: "Gay men's sexuality is not simply a one-note affair, a
flight from womanhood, a feminine identification, androgynous acting-out, but rather a polyphonic affair in which father-
son, mother-lover, and the hermaphroditic self all become
actualized and acted upon through physical and emotional
connection with another man."[11] Androgyny becomes then the
mediating principle between the opposing masculine and feminine archetypal poles, allowing in their interplay all the
variations of sexual activity and all degrees of bisexuality,
seen not as aberrations but as medial states, reflecting the
coming together of opposites in a rich, widely diverse, and
androgynous middle ground. Each of these states reflects, as

Jung intimated, a piece of the original spiritual human being, and each has its own degree of sacredness.

In many cultures the value of this state is reflected in the culturally accepted androgyny of shamans, medicine men, priests, spiritual aspirants, and initiates. Mircea Eliade confirms that "we know examples from shamanism in which bisexuality is ritually, therefore concretely assumed; the shaman behaves like a woman, wears a woman's clothing, sometimes even takes a husband. This ritual bisexuality—or asexuality—is believed to be at once a sign of spirituality, or commerce with the gods and spirits, and a source of sacred power," and he concludes that "androgenization is only one aspect of a total process, that is the union of opposites."[12]

These shamans and medicine men, though a small minority of their culture, carry a great deal of accumulated spiritual wisdom; they may be accounted among the wise persons of their societies. Within their ranks, especially between mature practitioner and neophyte, there is a bond of love and intimacy that is necessary for the authentic transmission of their wisdom. There was such a bond between Matsúwa, the hundred-year-old Huichol shaman, and his American student, Brant Secunda[13]; and I found much of that feeling between the Navajo medicine men and their respect and love for their teachers.[14] In order for the student to learn these complicated Navajo chants, much time had to be spent together, the student living with his teacher and repaying the older man with his helpful service. For the men (and sometimes women) in this close relationship, the anima is partly contained in their androgyny and partly projected into the wisdom itself, the anima *sapientia*; this form of the anima (usually imaged as a woman such as the Alma Mater statues on college campuses) embodies the ideals, principles, and aspirations that men have in common. Their love and loyalty to her holds their close emotional relationship in proper balance and allows some measure of impersonality.

And so the basic role of the anima is to bring about a union resolving paradoxes of androgyny toward a realization of the Self. This may be done outwardly in marriage or other intimate relationships and/or it may be done in inner union (coniunctio) symbolized in dreams and visions, and realized in inner ecstatic states. To reach these states one must work through the shadow and negative anima/animus complexes that stand in the way as barriers to spiritual progress.

In the context of this lofty ideal, parts of which, however, are lived out every day on the very earthly plane of love and sex, it matters little whether the other person is man or woman, for the face of the soul is androgynous and can be loved in marriage or in any sexual union experienced as a sacred event, and in same-sex relationships of bonding and initiation. Through this love the most difficult spiritual realization can be made—the need to sacrifice the ego to something beyond itself, which alone allows the blossoming of the soul.

Notes

1. For a review of Jung's ideas on the anima, see James Hillman, *Anima: An Anatomy of a Personified Notion* (Dallas: Spring Publications, 1985).
2. C. G. Jung, *The Collected Works of C. G. Jung* [cw], vol. 9/1 (Princeton: Princeton University Press, 1968), para. 55.
3. Ibid., para. 56.
4. Ibid., para. 57.
5. Ibid., para. 142.
6. Donald F. Sandner and John Beebe, "Psychopathology and Analysis," in Murray Stein, ed., *Jungian Analysis* (La Salle, Ill.: Open Court Publishing Co., 1982), pp. 294–334.
7. Irwin Edman, ed., *The Works of Plato: The Jowett Translation* (New York: Modern Library, 1928), pp. 295–96.
8. Jung, cw 9/1, para. 164. Italics mine.
9. 1 Samuel 18: 1, Revised Standard Version.
10. Jung, cw 9/1, para. 146.
11. Robert H. Hopcke, *Jung, Jungians, and Homosexuality* (Boston: Shambhala Publications, 1989), p. 135.

12. Mircea Eliade, *The Two and the One* (New York & Evanston Ill.: Harper & Row, 1965), pp. 116–18.

13. Joan Halifax, *Shamanic Voices* (New York: E.P. Dutton, 1979), pp. 249–52.

14. Donald F. Sandner, *Navajo Symbols of Healing* (New York: Harcourt Brace Jovanovich, 1979), chap. 2.

Reflections
on Homosexuality
An Interview with Joseph Henderson

SCOTT WIRTH

In May and July 1991, I interviewed Joseph Henderson for three hours on the topic of homosexuality and same-sex love. I was seeking not only to learn his individual views but also to discover a historical flavor on some of the themes running through this volume. As a "first-generation Jungian" who knew C. G. Jung first as an analysand and later as a colleague and friend, Dr. Henderson brings an invaluable perspective to the topic of same-sex love. I feel grateful to Dr. Henderson for allowing me to interview him and to include excerpts from my dialogue with him in this anthology.

SCOTT WIRTH: To begin, I'd like to pose a question that is at the heart of our collection. In which ways might the archetype of initiation show itself differently in the individuation process of gay men or lesbians as contrasted with heterosexual men or women? I remember your saying that in your clinical observation, gay people often seem to have the opposites too close together.

JOSEPH HENDERSON: This is a question I could speak to most comfortably. The fact that the opposites are so close together is certainly true—not just for homosexual people but for anyone who is suffering from arrested development in the early period of life around puberty or later, when the initiation archetype is activated very strongly. When that's activated, the question is, "Is the initiation oriented toward the mother or toward the father or toward both?" If it is both, then there is a conflict. The opposites are too close together. What happens clinically, what we see in many cases of arrested development, is that there is a resistance to meeting the conflict. Young people don't want to. They want to identify with one or the other of these paths and are generally ambivalent about it.

There's an excellent case of this sort in Jung's book *Two Essays on Analytical Psychology*, where he describes the case of a woman who is struggling with resistance to her homosexuality and who dreamed of being pulled back and downward by a crab. Jung described that as the regressive tendency to keep going back to the mother and not acknowledge the full implications of the dreamer's relationship to her woman friend. He said that it would be dangerous for him to activate the unconscious too strongly in this case, because the woman was already in the grip of something that was very regressive. So his program for her was to get her to grow up into consciousness of her feelings about her friend and recognize the homosexual nature of it. That would be one type of case.

The second type, described in the same chapter, was a young man who was already accepting his homosexual feelings toward a certain friend. In his unconscious the relationship had almost a religious quality, whereby he was introduced to something like an initiation. In his dream, the ring that had been given to him by his friend was taken off his finger and given to an older woman. There was a ceremony of some kind, with a little ivory object that he associated with the penis. It might be a phallic object, but it was clearly a symbolic object as well, which meant that his sexuality was seen in a symbolic way as something to be changed or transformed. The danger point in this case would be whether the older woman would represent regressing to the mother or whether the dream meant he was going forward to allow the woman to initiate him into something that would increase his own masculinity and lead him to normal heterosexuality. The implication is that that's what happened.

S . W . : What are the differences in this pattern of homosexual individuation, since each individual is different?

J . H . : The most important thing about all of this is that it depends on the individual case. Every case is a little bit different. That's why I shy away from any generalizations and why Jung shied away from talking about homosexuality, as such, because he was so much more concerned with the individual experience of the unconscious and its relation to these archetypal figures that he didn't talk much about the cultural phenomenon of homosexuality. He was interested in it, and he talked quite a lot about it in a general sort of way as he described those homosexual young men in North Africa that he saw. He saw them as reflecting a very, very early period of culture that we have left behind where the homosexual relation of these men was considered perfectly natural, and he spoke about it with admiration.

He also spoke of the period in Greece when the young men were thrown together in defense of the state, in defense of the polis, so strongly that they established very homoerotic bonds—how sexual they were we really don't know. Presumably they were to some extent. And, of course, some of those young men around Socrates and Plato were presumably lovers and saw the homosexual life as something that had an inner meaning that brought them into a close relationship and was to be highly valued—more highly valued than their marriages to ordinary women, who weren't all that cultivated.

On the other hand, those young men would not have arrived at psychosexual maturity if they had not had a hetaira [companion] to sleep with and teach them what they needed to know about the nature of the feminine. Those hetairas were the most educated women in Greece, and they took young men into their houses and educated them by teaching them manners and poetry, and they acted plays together and so on. So development of the feminine principle was implicit in all of that to avoid an exaggeration of the masculine will.

So far as Jung himself was concerned with homosexuality, I sensed his awareness of the initiatory experiences that were necessary for both men and women. For the woman, however, the initiation is rather different. It's bound to be, and if she has a homosexual attachment, it usually means that she needs more of the mother. There has not been enough mother. She has been thrown too much over into the father world somehow. Or perhaps there's been too much mother so that she wants to continue that into the world and regards men as getting in the way. So there are two different kinds of reaction. I don't know why. I don't know about the origins of these things. I only know the phenomena.

S. W. : Would you care to speculate about what goes on in the psychological dynamics of Lesbianism?

J. H. : There's one case that I describe rather carefully in my book *Thresholds of Initiation*.[1] At the time, I didn't say that the woman was homosexual, because she was still alive and I didn't want to say that about her for fear that she might be recognized. She had a dream in which she was given a package in which there was her mother's liver and there was also some jewelry in it, and she had to cross a boundary into another country and protect this in her journey. Her mother was basically negative. For example, she told me that she had been allergic to her mother's milk and couldn't be breast-fed, so she was brought up by a rather cruel nurse. Thus, everything to do with the mother, even the nurse, was extremely negative to her when she was an infant. One of her initial dreams was about some little lizards that had broken jaws and couldn't eat. She had to put meat into their mouths so that they could eat. This dream showed how injured she was at that very early oral level. She had a fairly strong father and brother and uncles, and so naturally she transferred very strongly to them without, however, becoming unduly masculine herself. She maintained a fairly good feminine persona, but she was certainly over on the masculine side. Her analysis, therefore, had to do with the mother initiation, how to be brought into the mother world in such a way that she could accept it instead of reject it. That was her task.

All this came out in a later dream where there was a treasure in a safe, and the key that opened the safe was in the form of a beehive. Now, the beehive is a typical mother symbol, a symbol of the great goddess, the mother goddess, because of the queen bee as the center of the hive. The bee has six legs, and six is the number of the feminine, of Aphrodite. This was the dreamer's key to the feminine world, a world she had rejected, which was in this safe. With this dream, she had begun to realize that she had to make friends with her own mother and also the archetypal mother, and accept her in a new way. On the personal level it meant accepting the mother more easily, but on the deeper level it meant a whole change from being a father's daughter to being a mother's daughter. Note: not just father, but mother *and* father. As for the effect of all this on her sexual orientation, she never became heterosexual in the usual way. She was in love with men at times, and in her analysis with me she had a very good transference, so that she had the feeling of affirming her feminine response to the masculine, not just being the good girl to me, the father-analyst. But she remained homosexual, although she never came out of the closet.

S. W. : With regard to the question of origins or etiology of sexual orientation, what do you think of the possibility that homosexuality may be innate or constitutional?

J. H. : Oh, I don't know anything about that. I've never seen a case that I thought was constitutional, and, anyway, I've not seen very many cases of early homosexuality. I have no doubt that there may be some, that is, where there *is* a constitutional factor, but I haven't seen them.

S. W. : So what you've seen is a problem of development.

J. H. : I would say rather a psychological problem or even a psychocultural problem. That's how I look at it on the basis of the material that's come my way, which has been fairly consistent.

S. W. : Of what do you think a mature homosexuality might consist?

J. H. : That follows on what I've already said: if the homosexual patient in analysis successfully meets the conflict of the opposites and works with them by separating them, so that he or she feels the tension between them, acknowledging both sides, and experiences that as a kind of initiation, then the person becomes mature. And sometimes homosexual people do better with that than some heterosexual people would, because it's been so difficult for them. They've had to re-relate to or revalue the mother world as well as the father world, and this may lead to a better understanding of the opposites, because the person who's been through that struggle did not just grow up but learned while growing; that's what the growing up consists of. And if he does that, then he's in a position to be able to resolve the problem of the opposites better than someone who hasn't been through that. So that can happen to a heterosexual person or a homosexual person, but the homosexual person is used to having to do it more often because his survival depends on it.

As you know, there are many heterosexual relationships in which the partners are so comfortable that they don't bother to understand the anima and animus problem and work on it, whereas you could say that some homosexual relationships are so dynamic and so troubling that they force people to separate themselves from each other more definitely than heterosexual couples do. So, therefore, in that dynamic of separation and union, they may encounter the Self more dramatically in some ways. But that happens also in heterosexual relationships where they've come to an impasse and they have to separate. So I don't see too much difference, in conscious people, that is. In unconscious people, of course, they are all projecting all over the place. It's hard for anybody to get the anima or animus inside.

S. W. : What do you think about the idea that for some people, and perhaps more often for homosexual or lesbian individuals, the anima could be of the same sex?

J. H. : Well, sometimes it is. But if it is a projection, this is an illusion. The anima must be brought inside.

Even heterosexual people can easily project an anima onto a person of the same sex. For instance, if you ask a heterosexual man if he is attracted to men, he says no, but he can imagine being attracted to a beautiful youth, a beautiful boy, who still has a lot of femininity of varying degrees. He can imagine it. So that would be his ability to project some of his anima onto a man. Some of the stories of ancient homosexuality suggest that that was what certain men did. The emperor Hadrian, for example, had a young man, a boy, who was his lover, or he wanted to be the lover and the boy was always frustrating him. There are a lot of stories of how men have projected the anima onto a perfectly harmless youth who can't, of course, respond in a normal way to that image.

S. W. : Male homosexuality and lesbianism are each classically considered to stem from a *problem* with the mother, rather than a deeper *valuing* of the feminine. What do you think of this idea? What has your experience been?

J. H. : In many cases that I've seen, in gay men the anima has developed before his masculine identity. He knows himself more through the anima than he does through his masculinity. That gives him insight into the workings of the anima. This has both values and disadvantages. The danger is that he becomes imprisoned in the anima andcan't find his way to his masculine identity. But certainly he has that advantage over the man or boy who never discovers his anima until he is faced with love and marriage or something like that. It gives him a sensitivity and it may, in many cases, give him a sense of the unconscious that a more heterosexual boy wouldn't have, because the anima is the link.

S. W. : It's very interesting to hear you say that often the anima development in a gay boy or man would actually precede—or even preempt—the development of masculine identity. Isn't the general theory that anima development would come *later* in life?

J. H. : Yes. Anima *development* can only come in later life. Normally there is a reaching out in the boy away from the mother toward a woman who is not the mother but not *too* far away, like a sister or an aunt or a friend of the mother's, some woman upon whom he can project mother stuff, something of the mother, but she's not the mother. That then creates in him the understanding of soul image, woman as a soulmate. There are many stories about this. Jean-Jacques Rousseau had, for instance, a relation to an older woman when he was a young man—he even called her Mama. They had a sexual relationship. He was not homosexual. It was definitely an affair. She was his *femme inspiratrice*, his inspiring soulmate, you might say. So there tends to be that development. With many men, therefore, it doesn't go straight from the mother to an appropriate young girl. It goes to an older woman before. This can also happen to a homosexual man, and it often is very rescuing for him to establish that kind of relationship with an older woman. I've often noticed that homosexual men have a feminine image who's definitely not the mother but someone else, like an actress. Marlene Dietrich used to be a great one for that. I think it was because of her utter separateness; she was not at all a motherly woman, but a true anima figure.

S . W . : Or women like Judy Garland.

J . H . : Judy Garland, yes, she was another one. And Katharine Hepburn. They're mostly rather masculine women, I would say, not the Marilyn Monroe type, women who are feminine enough but have a rather sharp edge to them.

S . W . : Bette Davis is another example.

J . H . : Yes. So they are attracted to women who have an animus, you see. That counteracts the enveloping mother. It cuts through the mother stuff and awakens something in them that is more responsive to anima development. So the anima is ready to develop in them just as it is in a heterosexual man. But for some reason it gets fixated there. It doesn't tend to move on and become processed in a relationship.

S . W . : So it starts out and remains a very strong inner relationship. This is a little confusing because in the usual sense of anima development, the progression would be to project the anima outwardly and work through it in relationship, bringing the anima back inside later on.

J . H . : Yes, except so many men just project the anima and leave it there with the woman. There are not too many young men who can introvert the anima. They tend to keep it out there. It goes from woman to woman or man to man. It doesn't really want to go inside. They have to be really developed before they can get the idea that it really does belong inside. That's a problem for any man.

S . W . : Which actually leads to what we were just speaking of.

J . H . : You mean whether the anima may be male or female? I think that sometimes the anima does appear to be masculine or almost masculine, but it never can really be *just* that. I think that what is really happening there, when the anima seems to be masculine for a man, is that it's basically hermaphroditic.

This also leads to the question that numerous people have brought up, that anima and animus exist in both men and women. James Hillman, Edward Whitmont, Rosemary Gordon, and various other analysts have maintained such a position, which to my way of thinking wipes out the whole concept. You might as well throw it away, because if there isn't basically an anima in a man and an animus in a woman, why even bother at all? The confusion, it seems to me, is untangled by the fact that you do find in many people this hermaphroditic situation.

S. W. : A kind of blending.

J. H . : Yes, a blending of male and female.

S. W. : I wonder if you might speak on encountering homoeroticism in yourself, if you will.

J. H . : Well, I can answer that quite openly. Of course, when I was young I was attracted to boys as well as to girls, but I wouldn't say more to boys than to girls. I had a special feeling of being in love with one boy who was somewhat older than myself when I was in my teens. I didn't know what had happened to me. I was just completely in love and I didn't know what that was. I never said anything about it. There was no acting out in any way, but there was no doubt that it was a genuine form of being in love. As I see it now, he had just what I didn't have. It was a kind of transference. He had a sort of active, extraverted personality that attracted me as an introvert, and I saw him as a model of what I might hope to become in some way. And then that passed off, but that taught me that genuine love can be experienced between people of the same sex.

S. W. : Did it allow you to find some of those qualities in yourself either then or later on?

J. H . : I suppose it did help me. I think so. I think it was educational as far as it went, though it didn't go very far. Later on I had admiration for older men but not with an erotic feeling about them. That was different. I think that it is natural for men to be somewhat attracted to each other at certain times of life, and very often it does have something to do with an element of transference, with what they need. I'll give an example. The first time I ever flew in a plane was from Paris to London. This was in the 1920s. In those days it was just those little propeller planes, and I had never flown. When I got in the plane, it was scary. Even though it was a short flight, it didn't seem so in those days. So as I sat in my seat, I saw the pilot come, and he was a nice-looking young man and I immediately fell in love with him. That was a transference, you see. He was to guarantee my security. So when we landed in London and we began to disembark, there he was, and he wasn't the same man at all!

S. W. : Only a few hours later!

J. H. : That shows that I needed the transference to give me the feeling of security, you see. Well, that's an example of how one can be attracted to someone of the same sex without its being purely sexual.

S. W. : A very brief involvement!

J. H. : Indeed!

S. W. : Now, to speak a bit of Jung, I think that Jungian theory provides a unique perspective for understanding same-sex love, and yet very little was written by Jung himself about it. Why was that?

J. H. : Well, I think the answer is that Jung was so careful to talk about what is universal in life. The archetypal masculine and feminine he talked about as being universal, not different for some people. He would say, of course, that individuation is the same for everyone. You don't say that some people can individuate and others can't. In fact, he said somewhere that he felt that a lot of time was wasted talking about the different values of homosexuality and heterosexuality. There needed to be a more central understanding of what life and development are all about. I think that was the reason.

S. W. : That's interesting. I also wonder, since Freud's theory was in many respects a sexual theory and he wrote extensively about all sexual matters, including homosexuality, whether Jung paid less attention either because it had already been explicated or because of the difficulty in their relationship.

J. H. : No, I never felt that about him. I didn't feel that he repressed anything of the sexual. He was perfectly willing to talk about any aspect of sexuality. But his quarrel with Freud about the theory of sexuality was that Freud tried to make a dogma out of it. I'm sure that Jung learned more about sexuality during the time that he was related to Freud, and probably opened himself up to his own sexuality in a new way. Certainly one felt that Jung had no prejudice against any form of sexuality. In fact, he said once that nobody can be too sexual. In other words, his attitude was that if you're going to be sexual, give yourself up to it fully and don't hold anything back. So there was no reaction formation that I could detect in that way.

S. W. : Very interesting. How do you view the gay liberation movement and the women's liberation movement in relation to the transformation of culture and in relationship to Jungian psychology? I know that this is a big sweeping question, but particularly having lived for many years in San Francisco, where there is a very large gay subculture, how do you look at that phenomenon?

J. H. : Well, it *is* a phenomenon. And it's far better that it's out in the open than hiding in corners somewhere. When I grew up, it was only possible for a homosexual man—and a lesbian too, but especially the men—to go to Paris. That was the only place. There was no place in America they could feel safe to expose themselves, except in little places like Greenwich Village in New York.

S. W. : North Beach, here, in a sense, was like Greenwich Village.

J. H. : Yes, that's right, Telegraph Hill. Yes, those were the areas of Bohemianism where homosexuality was more or less accepted. But it was not accepted, even there, in a very open way. It was not as it is today. So I think that it has relieved that tension and has brought out into the open the fact that there were all of these people who needed to be acknowledged for what they felt and who they were. And the women's liberation movement also has brought women into a place of acknowledging their own freedom in a way that was not thought of in the early part of this century. And so it has its value. The thing that worries me about the women's liberation movement is that it has, to some extent, had the effect of turning men away from women in a way that is confusing. It's not that men are angry with women. It's that they don't know their role in relation to women. In my generation we were brought up to understand what our relation to women was, how we should treat them and how we should relate to them and help them and be impressed with them and let them have their effect upon us. And we thought that we knew how that should go. But now the shadow side of the liberation movement is that a lot of men simply don't know how to relate to women, though I think that is improving. More and more I see women who were affected by the liberation movement who are now changing and becoming much softer and much less critical of what they call patriarchy or at least accepting that it's a part of history and you can't get away from that. It is a question of the difference between what Erich Fromm called the authoritarian father and the humanistic father. No woman can find any fault with the humanistic father, but not only women but men can find lots wrong with the authoritarian father. So there are different kinds of fathers. The father problem is coming up again for reevaluation, and I think that's a good thing. So I think men are beginning to learn how to adjust to this. The most difficult phase of the women's liberation movement is, I hope, over.

S . W . : You mean the polarization and antagonism?

J . H . : The polarization, that's right.

S . W . : This next question, again, is a personal question. It may be too gossipy, I don't know, but analysts such as Marie-Louise von Franz, Barbara Hannah, Esther Harding, at least those three, have been rumored to be lesbian. Do you feel free enough to talk some about this?

J . H . : I can answer the question quite simply because of what Jung himself said about it, namely, that there was more justification for women's homosexuality in modern life provided it was in the service of the culture. Esther Harding and Eleanor Bertine would be examples, devoted to their work as analysts but very concerned with being, as much as they could, women. They were not feminists. They were women doing work together and loving each other as part of it. And Jung, as the man in their lives, felt that that was similar to life in early Greece, where men were drawn to each other erotically because of their work, because of their having to build a young culture. Their relationship to each other was intimately bound up with their work. In other words, it was not just because they loved each other that they were together. They were together because of something more.

You know that Esther Harding and Eleanor Bertine met when they were both analysands of Jung. Their mutual interest in Jung's psychology was an intimate part of their whole relationship, you see. There was also Christine Mann, who was an intimate friend of theirs. The three of them were the main Jungian analysts in New York for many years. And Christine Mann was not homosexual, but she was dedicated in the same way to the work as they were. I know nothing about von Franz's sexual preferences. She always seemed like a true amazon-type woman. Jung saw that certain women of that type were very important to the development of psychological consciousness in our time. And it was women who were doing that work—not men, you see, at that time.

Note

1. Joseph Henderson, *Thresholds of Initiation* (Middletown, Conn.: Wesleyan University Press, 1967).

Homoeroticism and Homophobia in Heterosexual Male Initiation

DAVID J. TACEY

> Psycho-analytic research is most decidedly opposed to any at-tempt at separating off homosexuals from the rest of mankind as a group of a special character. By studying sexual excitations other than those that are manifestly displayed, it has found that all human beings are capable of making a homosexual object-choice and have in fact made one in their unconscious.
>
> —Sigmund Freud[1]

THE POLYMORPHOUS PSYCHE AND THE SOCIAL CONSTRUCTION OF SEXUALITY

Homosexual individuation processes are not confined to homosexuals but can be found as well in the psychic development of heterosexuals. This psychological fact arose in my own personal analysis, and it challenged my preconceptions about my own identity as a heterosexual, and about the usually hard-and-fast categories "homosexuality" and "heterosexuality." Taking these social categories too liter-ally, in a narrowly conventional way, can be injurious to the psyche and can block the inner processes of both homosexual and heterosexual individuals. This sometimes comes as a shock to heterosexual analysands, who often assume that they *ought* to have only heterosexual dreams and heterosexual individuation processes, and who may become edgy when homosexual elements arise in the analysis, especially if the analyst is of the same sex.

By speaking of "homosexual elements" in heterosexual men, I refer not only to the repressed desire for genital contact with other men, but also, and especially, to the constellation of *images of male-male sexual union* in dreams, fantasies, and psychic material. "Homosexuality" and "homoeroticism" in this paper refer in part to a metaphorical state of soul, in particular to the libidinal situation that arises when a young man's individuation brings him to the stage of reconciliation with the father, and to images of puer-senex intrapsychic union. [2] At first glance I may appear to be taking too much license, but both Freud and Jung understood sexuality in a much wider sense than is popularly conceived.

In her impressive study of Freud's approach to homosexuality, Christine Downing points out that "Freud's understanding of sexuality was always transliteral, always encompassed much more than genitality. . . . Freud saw us as having defined sexuality too narrowly." "When Freud speaks of sexuality he means to include all sensual and affectional currents, all the ways we experience bodily pleasure, all our intense emotional attachments."[3] And in his seminal volume *Jung, Jungians, and Homosexuality*, Robert H. Hopcke writes, "Homosexuality, as Jung uses the term . . . , is as much a psychic state of same-sex attraction as the behavioral expression of this sexual attraction with another man or woman."[4] Metaphorical or psychical homosexuality cannot be reduced entirely to frustrated desire for same-sex genital contact, but must be regarded as a legitimate condition in its own right, a state of soul that both "homosexuals" and "heterosexuals" can and do experience.

Freud believed that homosexuality and heterosexuality were in some degree social constructions. Although he considered heterosexuality to be the norm, and homosexuality to result from an arrested psychosexual development, he nevertheless entertained the (contradictory?) view that we are all psychically bisexual, and that for convenience and stability we repress a part of our sexuality. In *An Autobiographical Study*, he spoke of "the constitutional bisexuality of all human beings,"[5] and in his clinical practice he was constantly alert to the ambivalent nature of human sexuality and its ability to move toward figures of the same or opposite sex. Through social conditioning and through the efforts of the ego, one set of our sexual impulses ends up being repressed.[6] What is very often discovered in the unconscious, as was true in my own case, is a sexual orientation opposite to that which is practiced, professed, and espoused in consciousness. This is not to say that any given heterosexual analysand is "really" a homosexual, but simply that one side of our psychical bisexuality has been repressed and almost invariably comes to the surface in the course of a successful analysis.

Indeed, Freud felt that the fear of encountering one's denied homosexual longings constituted "one of the most powerful elements in resistance to analysis."[7] It is significant that, as Downing has shown, homosexuality, either manifest or latent, literal or metaphorical, figures prominently in every one of Freud's case studies.[8] Reductionists will say that Freud's patients were all latent homosexuals; cynics will proclaim that Freud projected his own homosexual conflicts upon the lives of his patients; but a more appropriate reading is to suggest that the human depths that Freud explored are always and everywhere characterized by an essential psychical bisexuality. In other words, we are metaphorically androgynous, and every journey into psychic depths will yield insight into our unexpressed or latent "other" mode. This means that, for heterosexuals, psychoanalysis is virtually synonymous with an experience of psychical homosexuality. The more ardently or fanatically heterosexual one is, the more actively constellated

homosexuality will be in the unconscious, and—most likely—
the more emotive and fierce is the resistance to psychoanalysis.
This is especially helpful in understanding the long-standing
and entrenched resistance to psychoanalysis in Australia, a
country where, as I shall soon explain, homophobia is endemic
in the prevailing national character.

Freud was aware that in drawing parallels between homosexual and heterosexual development he was challenging the
claims of then contemporary gay men to represent a "distinct
sexual species," a "third sex."⁹ Just here we face a particularly
difficult and sensitive problem, where psychoanalysis and contemporary gay politics appear to collide. The emphasis in the
gay movement on difference and distinction must be considered in its social context. In our political and social discourse it
is important to make real distinctions between gay and nongay
men, since in a society that privileges heterosexuality above
other sexual modes, the excluded and marginalized sexualities
must emphasize their *differentness* in order to survive and to
achieve recognition and moral standing. At the social level,
any bland, all-encompassing, totalizing project is likely to
make homosexuality invisible again and to turn the clock back
with regard to collective understanding and appreciation of gay
lifestyles. But in the realm of the psyche, our sexual categories
may be less important and may be revealed merely as social
constructions. Here I tend to agree with Freud, who felt that
phobias abound whenever our thinking becomes too rigid and
whenever we make a dogma of sexual preference. When we
enter psyche, we enter a very relativistic universe, where the
values, attitudes, and assumptions of our socially constructed
selves are challenged and sometimes even reversed.

HOMOPHOBIC AUSTRALIAN MATESHIP

I grew up in Alice Springs, central Australia, which is possibly the homophobic capital of the world. The social and

psychic situation of present-day outback Australia is similar to that which existed in the "Wild West" of premodern America. We are speaking of a frontier society, with little or no evidence of white civilization, where men gather together to provide mutual support and security, where women are held at a distance, where uneasy or explicitly hostile relations exist between the new settlers and the indigenous people, and where a general sense of siege pervades the psychic atmosphere. In this situation the famous Australian "mateship" is born, that particular kind of behavioral code in which a man will do anything to protect or support a "mate." Mateship, felt Henry Lawson, is not only a code of conduct but a religious creed, something to believe in and to identify with.[10] In Australia mateship reigned supreme for quite some time, but in recent history its shadow side has been exposed by historians,[11] feminists,[12] and sociologists.[13] It was (and still is) misogynist, racist, sexist, bigoted, and repressive. There was a fairly narrow definition of what constituted manly behavior and masculinity. Homophobia is the most recently discovered shadow aspect of this great Australian institution.

For Freud, homophobia is an expression of repressed homosexuality. He sees homophobia as an attempt to reject admission of unconscious homosexual desires by activating "vigorous counter-attitudes."[14] In mateship, the homophobic response stands in direct relation to the intensity with which male bonding is pursued. Precisely because there is so much feeling in the male-to-male bond, society and the ego construct an all-powerful taboo against physical intimacy, sexual attractiveness, and the expression of feeling, whether verbal, emotional, or physical. Men adore their mates, but there will be no obvious caring, no touching, no outward display. Friendship is expressed as it were negatively, by shadowboxing each other, by punching your mate coyly on the arm, by offering terms of abuse, and by swearing at each other when you meet ("You bloody great bastard, how are you?").

Alice Springs is a long way from the San Francisco Bay Area. Here, if two men walked down the street arm-in-arm, well, they would most likely not get to the end of the first city block. If aggressively homophobic "ordinary citizens" did not intervene, the homophobic police force would, since in the Northern Territory (as in the state of Queensland) homosexuality is still a criminal offense. Under sections 208 and 211 of the criminal code, any male found guilty of sexual acts "against the order of nature" can face a maximum prison sentence of seven years' hard labor. It is entirely irrelevant whether the homosexual events took place in private between consenting adults; if the police can prove they occurred, then a criminal sentence is handed down.[15] Homophobia is thus enshrined in our mental attitudes as well as in our legislation, every bit as much of a national institution as the mateship that it unconsciously shadows. Gay men in the Northern Territory and in Queensland go in hiding, develop flawless masculine personae, or move to the inner suburbs of Sydney and Melbourne.

Although I moved south to Adelaide, spending ten years in a "soft male" university environment, the legacy of my upbringing remained. Homophobia has been a strong element in my psychology for over thirty years, and it took a lengthy analysis with the American post-Jungian James Hillman in order to confront this bogey and to work through it. Strange as it may seem to any one of my central Australian "mates," homophobia became a psychological block to my heterosexual masculine development. I am referring in particular to an internalized homophobic response, a refusal to engage in a full and erotic manner with same-sex psychic figures, a resistance to and abhorrence of psychical homosexuality. My university education had effectively banished homophobia from my consciousness (it was considered backward and unliberated), but there it was in the personal unconscious, doing quite well, thanks very much, serving as a censor of internal processes, causing me to "forget" certain dreams, and blocking me off from my own experience of that dark symbolic force *phallos*.[16]

It may sound ironic, or contradictory, but acceptance of homosexual imagery, and a change of attitude in relation to homosexuality itself, brought with it a complete transformation of my character and a more profound experience of my heterosexual masculinity.

DREAMS OF SAME-SEX LOVE AND FATHER-SON REUNION

In 1982 I entered analysis for a second time, still very much an uninitiated male. By "uninitiated" I mean not yet related to the archetypal masculine, not genuinely connected to the father or senex, and also largely unaware that a rapprochement with the father and the masculine was necessary for my psychological development. Like so many young men today who are inflated by their identification with the feminine,[17] I had no awareness of my failure to develop the masculine side until analysis brought me face-to-face with my inadequacies in this area.

The first stage in this process was the realization, tactfully elicited by the analyst, that I carried a totally negative image of my father. This realization itself somehow brought to an end, in my thirtieth year, my oedipal rivalry with the father. Suddenly I experienced a great longing for the father, a desire to reconnect with my personal dad, and I had several dreams in which I was forced to recognize my father's (or my internal father's) talents and virtues.[18] In one dream I entered a room in which my mother and father were sleeping in separate single beds. As an individual with a history of dreams of mother-son incestuous unions, it was with some surprise that I told my analyst that the dream ego approached, and then kneeled beside, my father's bed. The father was in a poor physical condition, and I would have to care for him and nurture him to health. All this was fostered by my positive transference toward my same-sex analyst. Although I did not see it at the time, the analysis began from the start as a healing of the relationship to the father and as an intense exploration of the puer-senex bond.

Homoerotic dreams began to arise. In one early dream a sailor directed me to a house where, he said, I could get my fill of sex. I went in search of the house, found an attractive woman, and began to undress her. When I took off her under-clothes, I noticed she had balls between her legs and then I saw a cock. "You are really a boy!" I said. "Yes," she or he smiled. "But I don't make love to boys," I said. He looked disappointed as I backed away and prepared to leave.

Here the dream ego makes a firm decision that terminates the erotic interplay between itself and the "boy." The transves-tite figure is of great interest since either the anima has become masculinized due to the repression of masculine con-tents into the unconscious or—and this amounts almost to the same thing—the masculine is hiding itself beneath a feminine persona in order to be taken notice of and to arouse the sexual desire of the ego. An alternative interpretation suggests itself: the ego has been led to a deep realm of psychical bisexuality, where the desired love object is neither strictly male nor strictly female, but both, being "polymorphous perverse" (Freud). But however we interpret the dream, the fact remains that the ego cannot cope with what is going on and has decided not to make love to a figure with same-sex characteristics.

What we see here is the effect of an internalized homo-phobic attitude. The fear of homosexuality is so strong that it is introjected into the psyche, where it acts as a prohibition against the commingling of same-sex figures. The ego cannot fully "know" other masculine members of the psyche while it is identified with the homophobic attitude. "Knowing" other psychic figures means, as it meant in the language of the Old Testament, knowing intimately, or "carnal knowledge." Sexual connection is the psyche's favorite metaphor for deep psychic connection, for a bonding that is at once passional, emotional, and instinctual. It is clear that connection with my masculine side involves an erotic embrace and a libidinal investment that the ego is not yet prepared to make.

Other dreams emerged at this time that took me back to childhood, during which I had some prepubertal genital play with a male cousin. This aspect of my early experience had been completely lost to my adult consciousness, or should I say the homophobic censor had "edited out" this childhood homosexual experience from my present image of myself. A number of dreams in which my cousin and I were developed sexually and paraded full erections before each other indicated that the psyche was now calling for a reactivation of my earlier same-sex erotic model into the sexualized atmosphere of adult reality.

At the same time as I was having dreams relating to a reconciliation between the ego and the father figure, a number of explicitly erotic dreams became the central focus of the analysis. Sometimes the dream ego was drawn toward an erect phallus of another male, and occasionally the ego fondled and rubbed the aroused penis. In one dream I watched an erection begin to develop and swell up inside the trousers of an anonymous man, and I pulled down the trousers to release the throbbing erection. In the major dream of this series, the ego was imaged in a state of excited craving for an erect penis. It was not clear who the other male was, since I was unaware of anything above or below the genital region. This was an impersonal, or archetypal, encounter with *phallos*. The dream involved considerable foreplay, and then the ego took the penis into its mouth and, after much oral stimulation, eventually swallowed the hot sperm that was shot out at the moment of climax.

The ego was inseminated with masculine seed and, like the New Guinea youths who must digest semen during their rites of passage into manhood,[19] the sexual fluid contained the

seeds of my own developing masculinity. This dream marked
the birth of my new, or renewed, masculine self.

HOMOPHOBIA IN SO-CALLED
"CONSCIOUSNESS-RAISING" MEN'S GROUPS

Recently I discussed this dream in a large, all-male therapy
group in Melbourne, and it met with a very mixed response.
The atmosphere in the room was tense, and all were listening
carefully, and thank God no Aussie male actually burst out
laughing at the time. But later, during the coffee break, there
was a fair bit of laughter, some of it perhaps a natural response
to a release of tension and seriousness, but some of it decidedly defensive and homophobic. During the informal discussion that followed, a number of burly Australians were
quick to inform the group (of twenty-nine men) that they had
never had dreams like this, and that if they had had such
dreams, they would be very worried about the dreams and
about themselves. The effect of this response was to construct
me as the homosexual other and to relinquish themselves of
their homosexual elements by projecting these elements upon
me. I was not prepared for this transference, but I ought to
have anticipated it, knowing what I knew about the prevalence
of homophobia in Australian men. I was surprised to find that
even a gay therapist in the group found my dreams heavy-
going, possibly because they challenged the stability of his
persona, and possibly because he felt these very explicit
dreams were too highly charged to be dealt with in public.

The homosexual transference of the group challenged my
privileged position as group leader, since (or so it seemed to
me) not a few began to wonder what they were doing submitting
themselves to an intensive course in men's issues in which the
leader was indulging his "poofter" fantasies. My counter-
response was to stand back from the dreams and to emphasize
their "symbolic" dimension. I think I even made a few jokes

about the dreams myself, in order to claw back the authority that I began to feel I was losing. In other words, I attempted to recover power and face by deliberately withdrawing into my own homophobic attitude and by asserting my superiority over the powerfully homosexual dreams.

In the next session we switched to another topic (male violence and aggression), and homosexuality was not mentioned again. All the men came back for future sessions—all except the homosexual participant, who was undoubtedly driven away by the constellated homophobia of the group. I was aware of my failure to contain or transform the homophobia of the group, and I realized later that night how far away I was from the therapeutic reality of the dreams and from the attitude my analyst had adopted toward them.

The main thing I learned, apart from my present inability to deal with any large-scale activation of Australian homophobia, was that defensive heterosexuals are almost incapable of experiencing the healing power that can arise from same-sex psychic imagery. In fact, many cannot even begin to respond therapeutically to internal homosexual imagery, since the homophobic attitude (which should probably be given the status of a complex) is triggered whenever such imagery arises, thus preventing these same-sex symbolic processes from being realized as significant processes of the psyche. No wonder so many Australian men remain boyish or puerile, no wonder they continually seek to prove their manhood, if a precondition to maturity, and to puer-senex union, is the ability to respond to the psyche's unconventional sexual patterns and especially to male-male psychosexual conjunctions.

THE ANALYST'S RESPONSE TO HOMOEROTIC MATERIAL

My homoerotic dreams placed a considerable demand on the analyst, as well as upon myself. Any homophobic residues in him could have proved injurious to my development, and to the erotically charged puer-senex bonding that was taking place in the soul. It was important that the analyst, as bearer of the senex image, became an enabling father figure by adopting a positive, sexualized attitude toward the erotic images. Even a hint of puritanical reaction could have set the process back. But no, he was fully involved in the psychic imagery and able to further the process by his careful attention to the psyche's demands.

After presenting the dream in which I sucked on the penis and ingested the seminal fluid, the analyst simply said, in response, "Go for the cock; grab it; grasp it." Obviously he said more than this during the hour, but these words are the only ones I remembered later. At this stage I dreamed I was discussing sexuality with my paternal uncle, and he spoke warmly to me about male sexuality. As he spoke, my own body seemed more alive, more sensuous, more manly. In reality, my family and relatives were all narrowly puritanical, and they had instilled a fear of the body and an antagonism toward sexuality into me as a child. Now the internalization of this body-denying puritanism, as well as the internalized homophobia, were being dissolved by the dreams, the inner process, and the analysis.

The analyst's response enabled me to experience the erotic imagery fully, immediately, sensuously. There was no attempt on his part to hide behind "Jungian" theory, to emphasize that the homoerotic images were "only symbolic." In the inner world I was being ravished and inseminated by the great archetypal *phallos*, and for this to have any effect in conscious reality, it was important that I allow myself to feel this as a ravishment, as a deeply erotic experience. Adolf Guggenbühl-Craig writes that some Jungian analysts who have not confronted their homophobic attitudes are inclined to withdraw from homosexual images presented by a same-sex client:

Jungian psychologists may, however, try to evade this involvement in eros by not following up veiled or even relatively overt sexual statements by the patient, or immediately trying to interpret such statements on a "higher level." They make reference to the patient's relation to the spiritual-masculine, to his own creative masculinity, etc. A homosexual dream is instantly interpreted as "a search for, and an attempt to understand, one's own masculinity."[20]

Guggenbühl-Craig says that analysts often "clothe [themselves] in an endless variety of theories and run for cover." If the analyst finds the material "painful and repugnant," his use of clever interpretations is "of no use whatsoever to the patient."[21]

What *is* of use to the analysand is a felt, full-blooded, libidinal response to the homosexual images. Chances are that the kind of client who seeks out Jungian therapy already "knows about" the textbook explanations that a defensive analyst would provide. Analysands have read in Erich Neumann or Robert Johnson or elsewhere that sexual imagery in a fantasy or dream is an expression of a symbolic process of union within the soul. The analysand in Jungian-related therapy often "knows" too much—that is his problem and his limitation. The point of therapy is not to collect bits of theoretical information but to experience the psyche. The only kind of knowledge that is important is that old-fashioned "knowing," which meant to know intimately, sexually. What analysands want from therapy is carnal knowledge of the psyche.

Patricia Berry has said that the two golden rules of psychotherapy are: don't repress, don't act out.[22] Some people think that these laws are mutually exclusive, that they cancel each other out. If I cannot repress, and I cannot act out, what on earth can I do? The answer is: *experience the psyche.* Now, in relation to how analysts respond to erotic phenomena in their clients, it could be said that not a few fail to discover this third way of psychic experience. The example Guggenbühl-Craig provides is an example of analytic repression: up go the walls of theory, the pronouncements about higher meanings and archetypes, the body-deadening and eros-refusing intellectual apparatus, which leaves the libidinal ground in favor of psychological knowledge. Here psychology is used against the psyche. The other side of the coin is where analyst and patient go to bed together, the erotic tension so great that only "acting out" can give release and a temporary fulfillment. Here sexuality is used against the psyche.

I was fortunate to encounter an analyst who knew what the third way was about because he knew what psyche was about. The therapeutic attitude consists in being present with the mythic material, in sticking with the images. What repression and acting out have in common is that they impose a reductively personal attitude upon the material and refuse to acknowledge psyche. The analyst represses the homosexual image because he imposes his own homophobic attitude upon it, because he does not want his client to act out the impulse, or because he attempts to forestall or guard against the homosexual advances of his client. Alternatively, the analyst acts out the erotic impulse with his client because he feels the eros constellated in the analysis involves himself, that the dreams or longings of connection are indeed about him and directed to him. These personalistic reductions amount, in Robert Stein's phrase, to a betrayal of the soul.[23]

THE ANALYSAND'S RESPONSE

And what of the analysand's response? If the analysand engages in actual homosexual activity at this point in the analysis, is this acting out, or is this a perfectly natural expression of his homosexual longing? A heterosexual onlooker, perhaps, may see it as acting out (in accordance with his own set of preferences and prejudices), but a homosexual observer may say that he has finally lifted his inhibition and is now exploring the same-sex dynamic in the truest possible way. Interpretation, as every hermeneut and postmodernist knows, is surely a matter of perspective, and largely dependent upon where one stands in relation to the event or thing to be interpreted.

If, for instance, after being implored to "go for the cock" in one analytic session, I came to the next with reports that I had indeed engaged in homosexual relations subsequent to that session, would the analyst think this appropriate? Presumably, he would not be shocked, but would he think it psychologically sound? Of course, much would depend upon my former sexual history, and if the analyst felt that my active homosexuality had arisen solely as a response to a phase in the analysis, then he may be critical of it. Would my homosexuality be read, not as enactment of an archetypal impulse, but as an *avoidance* of the more difficult *intrapsychic puer-senex* union?[24] It would appear that Jung and traditional Jungians would view homosexuality as an acting out of same-sex archetypal dynamics, and therefore as secondary or symptomatic behavior which obscured the primary intrapsychic process.[25] But how come, some of us have begun to ask, they do not apply the same reasoning to heterosexual activity, and see this as obsessive or defensive acting out of the need for the feminine matrix? Why perform a psychological reduction on one sexual mode but not on the other? Obviously, when prejudices govern our thinking we use psychology against whatever it is that offends us or we wish to exclude. The new, relativistic view is that "any sexuality, or no sexuality at all, can be pathological."[26]

Every analysand must arrive at his own individual response, not necessarily as a result of answering these tortuous questions, but by intuitively or instinctively deciding what is right for him. A merely intellectual decision is not enough, and may even be a grave mistake. I must confess that in my own case none of these questions were posed. Such questions only arose years later, when I was situationally outside the analysis and outside the intensity of the puer-senex libidinal reunion. Such questions have been put to me, too, by anxious men in consciousness-raising groups; the same men who said that they would be "worried" if they had dreams similar to mine. Doubts and questionings came to me before and after my analytically assisted passage into masculine maturity, but at the time I found the images so enthralling, the analysis so stimulating, and the inner process so demanding that thoughts about my social classification as "gay" or "nongay" never arose. They seemed, and indeed were at the time, irrelevant. I was in Victor Turner's "liminal" or transitional state, betwixt and between two stages of development,[27] and this sacred condition may have been profaned by a too hasty attempt to impose sociopolitical classifications.

Now I view the process outlined in this paper as a ritualized homosexual phase that was essential for my heterosexual masculine development. My relation to the masculine side was so undeveloped, so deeply unconscious, that nothing short of a powerfully erotic upheaval could have aroused the masculine from its slumber (pun intended) and brought it into contact with consciousness. It is not for me to say that homosexuality per se is a mere "phase" on the way to a more "mature" heterosexual outlook, a view so entrenched in psychoanalytic circles, although not necessarily supported by either Freud or Jung.[28] But I personally experienced a psychical homosexuality in this way, as a powerful initiatory prelude to a profoundly deep and moving encounter with the father and the archetypal masculine.

During this period of my analysis I referred to my analytic hours as "body work" sessions because my body seemed to be responding in definite ways to the analysis. I felt a number of body sensations that are difficult to articulate now. I felt more grounded in my body. I developed a new and very positive body feeling and an awareness of my physical maleness. My body changed shape: I developed muscles where there were before just bony arms and legs; I put on forty pounds in weight and no longer looked like a half-starved student. I experienced as well a new relation to my anger and rage, which had been buried before, but which were now within range of ego consciousness.

Most intriguing of all was the new relation to my personal father, a new sense of warmth and connection, which I had not experienced since I was about eight or nine. During my fourteenth year, my father announced to my astonished family that I was no longer his son, because the gap that separated us was too obvious to ignore. My rivalry and dislike were intense, and I made no attempt to make amends. But after this phase of analysis everything changed; intellectual and ideological differences were still evident, but there was now an emotional understanding and acceptance that transcended these differences. My father related to me as man to man, rather than as parent to wayward child. He sensed the change and seemed to relish the new dispensation.

He once said in Alice Springs that all gay men in Australia ought to be transported to a desert island and left to starve. So I did not or could not explain to him that a psychically homosexual phase had made a man of me. He could not appreciate that the spunk and male energy that had entered me had done so because I had performed fellatio and sodomy in my dreams. My newfound maleness was thanks to my new willingness to "make love to boys," and my masculine energy due to swallowing and ingesting the hot sperm-seed of logos.

Notes

1. Sigmund Freud, *The Standard Edition of the Complete Psychological Works of Sigmund Freud*, vol. 7 (London: Hogarth Press, 1953), p. 145n.

2. For an introductory account, see Joseph Campbell, "Atonement with the Father," in *The Hero with a Thousand Faces* (Princeton: Princeton University Press, 1968), pp. 126–49. For an advanced study, see James Hillman, "Senex and Puer," in Hillman, ed., *Puer Papers* (Dallas: Spring Publications, 1979), pp. 3–53.

3. Christine Downing, *Myths and Mysteries of Same-Sex Love* (New York: Continuum, 1989), pp. 31–32.

4. Robert H. Hopcke, *Jung, Jungians, and Homosexuality* (Boston: Shambhala Publications, 1989), p. 25.

5. Freud, *Standard Edition*, vol. 20 (1959), p. 38.

6. See Downing, "The Universality of Homosexual Desire," in *Myths*, pp. 37–41.

7. Ibid., p. 49.

8. See Downing, "Freud: The Classic Cases," in *Myths*, pp. 51–67.

9. Freud, quoted ibid., *Myths*, p. 44.

10. See especially the later stories of Lawson in Colin Roderick, ed., *Henry Lawson: Short Stories and Sketches 1888–1922* (Sydney: Angus & Robertson, 1972).

11. Humphrey McQueen, *A New Britannia*, 2nd ed. (Melbourne: Penguin Books, 1986).

12. Miriam Dixson, *The Real Matilda* (Melbourne: Penguin Books, 1984).

13. Graeme Turner, *National Fictions* (Sydney: Allen & Unwin, 1981).

14. Freud, quoted in Downing, *Myths*, p. 49.

15. For a recent discussion of these legal issues, see "Bigoted One Day, Prejudiced the Next," *HQ Magazine* (Sydney), no. 12 (November 1990), pp. 46–51.

16. See Eugene Monick, *Phallos* (Toronto: Inner City Books, 1987).

17. See James Wyly, *The Phallic Quest* (Toronto: Inner City Books, 1989).

18. For a discussion of this reversal in father-son relations, see Robert Bly, *Iron John: A Book about Men* (New York: Addison Wesley, 1990).

19. Gilbert H. Herdt, ed., *Ritualized Homosexuality in Melanesia* (Berkeley: University of California Press, 1984).

20. Adolf Guggenbühl-Craig, "The Destructive Fear of Homosexuality," in *Power in the Helping Professions* (Dallas: Spring Publications, 1971), p. 70.

21. Ibid., pp. 70–71.

22. Patricia Berry, *Echo's Subtle Body* (Dallas: Spring Publications, 1983).

23. Robert Stein, *Incest and Human Love* (Baltimore: Penguin Books, 1974).

24. This is the view of Joseph L. Henderson, who claims that the desire for intrapsychic union with the masculine is rarely achieved in active homosexuality. See his *Thresholds of Initiation* (Middletown, Conn.: Wesleyan University Press, 1979), p. 45.

25. C. G. Jung, *The Collected Works of C. G. Jung*, vol. 7, 2nd ed. (Princeton: Princeton University Press, 1966), p. 106f.

26. Monick, *Phallos*, p. 114.

27. Victor Turner, "Betwixt and Between," in Louise Carus Mahdi et al., *Betwixt and Between: Patterns of Masculine and Feminine Initiation* (La Salle, Ill.: Open Court, 1987).

28. See, for instance, Freud's letter to an American woman, quoted in Downing, *Myths*, p. 43.

Individuation, Taboo, and Same-Sex Love

ROBERT BOSNAK

The notion of individuation presupposes that each organism, from its inception, has an innate form that takes visible shape in its subsequent unfolding. This innate form is molded by environmental influences, and it is this interaction that individualizes each organism. A chicken egg becomes a chick, not a turtle; a chick growing up inside a box becomes a different chicken than one running around freely on a large farm. To describe the process of individuation, one has to specify the environment in which this process is taking place. I will talk about modern-day Western civilization, which commonly features a taboo on homosexual activity. Since each gay and lesbian person has to find an individual position toward this taboo, one can actually use the term *homosexual individuation*. In most other ways, it is as useless as the term *heterosexual individuation*: it is too general and shapeless.

What is a taboo?

When Sigmund Freud imported the word *taboo* from Polynesia in 1912, he got much of his wisdom from the *Encyclopaedia Britannica*, written by a Western anthropologist. While the word *taboo* has received ample attention in our post-Viennese psychoanalysis, it is less known that the word is linked to the notion of *mana*. To talk about taboo without talking about mana is senseless.

The United States is fortunate that it can learn directly about taboo and mana, not by way of Vienna, but by way of Hawaii, where the notion of taboo, called *kapu*, is still as vibrantly alive as that of mana.

The word *mana* refers to the spirit of creation, the creative potency that flows through the world and finds a temporary home in certain people and institutions. These people are particularly close to the force (not unlike Darth Vader and Obiwan Canobie in *Star Wars*) of creation and therefore represent a very potent energy field, which is very dangerous to enter for ones with less mana presence. The people with the most potent mana, where the force of creation is of the most pure form, such as queens, kings, medicine men and women, hula dancers, master craftsmen and -women—received either through their direct bloodline or through dedication by a predecessor of great mana—are *kapu*, taboo. To approach them is like approaching the living gods; weaker stomachs would burn up like moths.

Kapu, or taboo, therefore, surrounds creative realms of primordial power. This is clear when we look at the incest taboo. Mother is the source of our creation and therefore of burning attraction. The taboo serves to make us find a position toward the source of all life, our mother.

The fact that same-sex is surrounded by a powerful taboo must point to the existence of a potent mana, a creative energy that can easily burn one to ashes. There must be an inspiring creative fire that destroys the ones who cannot deal with the wringing torture of mana and taboo.

As an example I have chosen a man in the borderland between mana and taboo. Here we can see the individuation process most clearly, since it shows the direct confrontation of the opposing forces more clearly than in the case of one comfortable with himself, living within a group where the taboo has been depotentiated by the grace of social conditions more or less favorable to same-sex (like, for example, a proudly gay man or lesbian in San Francisco or Amsterdam).

Marco is a thirty-eight-year-old military officer from a family of several generations of professional soldiers. When he entered my Zurich analytical practice for the first time in the mid-seventies, referred by an older woman analyst, he was shocked to find me in my late twenties. At first he kept saying that I was too young to work with him. However, since the referral had been by a well-respected doctor with an acknowledged authority in the field, he came back for a second session. Authority was extremely important to Marco. It soon became obvious that he was very attracted to me and that a deep-seated fear of his homosexual urges was at the core of his depression. He would hold himself back from these desires, until they became too strong. Then he'd go to a big city far away and indulge himself in anonymous one-night stands, which left him feeling extremely guilty. He would torture himself for months in a depressive self-punishment laden with feelings of utter worthlessness. After a while the urges became strong once more, and the cycle repeated itself.

During these depressive periods, his life was utterly uninspired, driven by a punishing self-discipline. When he was in these faraway cities, he told me, he felt a tremendous stimulation. He would describe to me in great detail the rooms where the sexual encounter happened, as if he had suddenly been acutely alive, living short electric effusions followed by a power outage. During the blackout he could only feel bitter disgust, the taste of a trespassed taboo.

His father had been a violent man and had beaten Marco viciously when he was young. It was always the inner voice of his father who chided him bitterly, sounding like a belt lashing down on his bare back; this inner voice told Marco he was worthless and despicable. The lashing societal taboo had the face of his father, while Marco's father himself had been an exponent of society's livid condemnation of the infraction against a potent taboo. The most palpable presence of this punishing father occurred at the time of the buildup of pressure just before the breach of the taboo, and right after. The memory, permeated with punishment and pain, of Father and little Marco was the structural arm of the lashing taboo. It would strike at times when the focus around the same-sex desires was most intense. As if the taboo itself sensed infraction and felt threatened, it attacked Marco, propelling him into a state of abject isolation, cut off from the human world by a condemning verdict. A taboo responds like an unconscious organism that attacks when injured.

After a heated description of furtive love in a distant apartment with wicker chairs and red velvet pillows, the attraction between us is pulsing.

We are silent.

Marco sits opposite me. His face looks contorted. He is obviously suffering. After a while I ask him what the matter is. He doesn't answer. His face twists even more.

"What is it?" I ask.

"I want to take my penis out of my pants and show it to you," he replies, blushing crimson.

I get a slight tinge of sexual excitement in my groin, but much less than at other times when I have had, intoxicated by the unspoken passion between us, lewd masturbation fantasies during his confessions of intercourse. I sense deeply down into my penis. Usually bright with pleasure at such moments, now I can only feel darkness. All my physical attention is drawn to my stomach, gripped and twisted with embarrassment. I'm embarrassed about the sexual fantasies I have had about him when he tells me about his escapades. I may be envious that he gets to live these trysts with men while I shelter myself from this gay universe of sexual action by a firm submission to the taboo. I chide myself viciously for enjoying my lewd feelings too much. That is unprofessional. Then I take a step back and look at my emotion. I am full of self-hatred. The image he is presenting me, of showing me his penis, feels hardly genitalized; instead I am filled with feelings of self-flagellation.

He can't stand it anymore and changes the subject. "I dreamed that my father was holding me at gunpoint. All I could feel was terrible shame. Then he shot me, and I fell into a deep dark well. It looked like a sphincter."

At this point we continue working on the extreme sense of shame under the gun from his father. I believe that his desire to show me his penis was a setup for a torture by his father. The tales of erotic exploits had heated the attraction between us, making the taboo assert itself in the guise of his father. A structural force of the soul—the shame bursting forth from a trespassed taboo—is experienced as an attack of self-hatred. While Marco goes through his torment, the taboo individuates by growing ever more personal, the ghost of Marco's childhood father becoming ever more detailed. From now on I must beware of the presence of his humiliating father, who makes Marco enter the sense of being an asshole. Father shoots Marco into the anal underworld, where shame lurks.

When structural forces of the psyche rage through the analytical room—and through any profound relationship, for that matter—it becomes inevitable that the partners in the relationship begin to enact the images belonging to this primal pattern of soul. I could easily become the punishing father and Marco the victimized child dying of shame. Nothing easier than steamrolling my own homosexual embarrassment into Marco. Same-sex desire is universal, living in the depth of everyone's vitality, constantly killed by the patriarchal gun "Thou shalt not . . ."

Where there is a strong taboo, there must be strong mana.

C. G. Jung equates mana with the power of "the Self." This "Self" is described as the nucleus of identity in a field of psychic energy. For an entire lifetime it constantly creates the core of consistent psychological functioning; it creates identity. It makes Marco at any given moment into the man he is. The "Self" is seen as constantly creating new life and destroying old forms. Most of this "Self" functions as unconsciously as our vegetative nervous system, its blind force thrusting us forward from impulse to reflection and/or action. This thrust is mana, the power of libido, the drama of spirit. Sometimes we are aware of its inner forces, but most of the time it is hidden in blind action. Why does same-sex have such great mana that it engenders a killing taboo?

Same-sex satisfies the focus of its love without an association to the realm of physical procreation to distract from the force of its eros, no physical children to spring from its loins. Same-sex gives expression to an unadulterated power of sexual desire, symbolic for pure creative imagination itself, since its creations are not physical beings. It has no physical offspring, but forms other creations of love. As Western society feels deep down that natural sexuality exists for the purpose of human continuity, same-sex is called "unnatural," since its primary focus is directed toward the satisfaction of its love. Love for the sake of love alone is a primordial force of great attraction, powerful mana surrounded by a great taboo.

A visceral response of an entirely different nature comes up a week later as I hear Marco's next dream:

"There is a man closely monitoring my sex life. He finds me a disgusting homosexual. I shoot him."

"What do you feel?" I ask.

"The man is right. I have to admit that I do love men."

Marco had always said that he would never admit to the fact that he loved men with a sexual passion. He'd rather we analyze it away, his patriarchal gun directed at us both in solid denial. I see that look of embarrassment on his face again, and I wait. This reversal of direction, accompanied by the turn of the gun away from Marco, must have repercussions.

"I see an image of a huge erect phallus," he says and looks extremely uncomfortable.

At that moment I begin to feel my breasts develop, and I become all soft and mother-like. I want to pet him and have oral incest with him, to suck him into me.

"I don't hate women. I just like men better," Marco tells me, twisting uncomfortably.

I sense my nipples call out to him and feel like a woman, wanting to seduce him.

Marco begins to talk again. "I see a woman. I am undoing her bra. It excites me. I turn around. I see my mother in a see-through negligee." He is very embarrassed again, ready for self-punishment. This time, because of my feminine erotic response, I go in the direction of his sexual desires toward mother. He tells me how seductive she was, showing off her large breasts.

I am drawn to the large breasts of my own mother, but not in my usual incestuous longing for the breast of my infancy, but *as* her. I have become the nurturing cream and the desire to ingest him; a feeding nipple to suck. Marco and I have both been absorbed by the same maternal force of being.

Why is it that the matrix of creation, Mother, emerges as Marco departs from his homophobic denial, his fear to admit to his homoerotic nature?

By shooting the patriarchal sneer—the silencing voice of repression—the creative force of mother nature can seduce Marco with her milky breasts, feeding him with her desire to draw out his creative juices. The life force herself has been awakened by his conversion. The rest of the hour is spent in reminiscing about the attraction to Mother, to the playfulness of childhood, to the inquisitive mind of Marco the child.

The third vignette comes about three months later.

"Do you love me?" he asks me.

I feel instantly very distant from him and don't answer.

"I want you to tell me that you love me," he repeats.

The sense of distance grows, and I feel very bad about this. I didn't realize I felt this distant from him. In fact, there have been, also recently, moments of intimate closeness in our relationship. But I can't feel any of it at this moment. Just the distance. Then I suddenly remember a memory he once told me about his father spanking him. The image becomes stronger, until it is all that matters.

"I am reminded of the memory of your father spanking you," I say, realizing that it is an awful response to his request for love.

He is immediately inside the memory, as if he had forgotten all about his demand that I tell him I love him.

"I see myself lying on your lap," he says. "You're spanking me and my pants are down. You stop spanking me and then you put your finger up my rectum."

I feel a pressure on my sphincter myself, as if I have to go to the bathroom. Then it feels as if Marco enters me. At once we are very close.

"I've always wanted my father to do that to me," he says, without shame. "I've always wanted him inside me." The question about whether I love him or not seems answered. He never asked me again for the rest of our work. From then on the feeling between us is genuinely intimate. The distance between Marco and his father has been bridged. As long as Father was the threatening repressor, ready to pull his gun at the slightest offense against his authority, Marco could never feel a sense of his own authority, of himself as an independent decision maker.

Soon after this event, the military decided that Marco was to transfer to another position, one he did not want. His usual behavior was to pack his bags and go wherever he was sent. This time, however, he decided to ask for a transfer to a position he really wanted, even though it would hold up his career for some years. But it was what he wanted, so he stood up against his father and the military hierarchy, standing up for himself in the face of general derision. When he won his way into the new position that made sense to him, he left Zurich for another city. Soon thereafter I left Switzerland to come to the United States. I don't know what happened to his life in the closet, whether he ever came out or not. All I know is that when he found his way to the love of his father, when he could let Father enter, he was free to find his own value.

Same-sex is a primal urge of creation. It leads to itself: to relationship and sexuality. Its offspring is nonphysical. Its mana is the power of invisible, intangible creation. Its spirit does not follow nature's path of multiplication, thus giving birth to imagination. This is its mana, creative and strong; this is the source of its potent taboo.

A woman or man opting for same-sex will, at some point or other, feel the power of imagination clash with the taboo against its enactment.

In Marco we can see the agony of this head-on collision. A sense of self-value and self-authority can only develop through an experience of this clash without a repression of the shame involved. Then individuation leads to the ability to stand up for oneself in whatever lifestyle one ultimately chooses.

Mirroring Affirmation
With Special Reference to Psychoanalysis and to Men

EUGENE MONICK

The concept of mirroring has a long and rather forbidding history in psychoanalytic literature. Mirroring implies narcissism, which in its simplist form has to do with the fixation of psychic energy, libido, upon oneself. Narcissism characterizes an infant's initial self-discovery and early childhood ego emergence, but it is substantially displaced, over time, by interest in what Freud called "the object." As a child's ego coalesces, self-love and self-interest become established through a natural narcissistic process. Socialization and maturation then move the focus of the child's attention to others. Psychological development shifts away from a preoccupation with oneself—in a way, one begins to take oneself for granted—toward genuine concern about someone or something else. Holdover primary (early, as in original ego-building) narcissism in an adult ordinarily indicates a problem in the movement of psychic energy from oneself to another.

Psychoanalysis has produced extensive vocabularies and systems of interpretation based upon this very simple, yet very complex, dynamic of human reflection. In early childhood, a mirroring parent, usually the mother, has a godlike authority over an infant's initial experience of his or her self. The child "believes" information reflected back by a parent. As a child's ego forms, its unconscious simultaneously develops, and mirrored information becomes the primary data registered below the surface of the ego's perceptions. For example, if an infant perceives his or her basic human need for affirmation as met with coldness by a mirroring mother, the child will register that coldness in its nascent unconscious as rejection. Thus a condition of self-doubt begins that is experienced throughout life as an undertow of personal inconsequentiality.

As I write this essay, there is a picture on the front page of the *Scranton Tribune.* An eleven-year-old boy, on the edge of puberty, is shown at the grave of his Marine father, killed in the Persian Gulf war. His eyes are sunken, terrified, his mouth agape. His head sinks into his chest. Life has thrown back to the lad a frightening image, portending a lonely walk into incipient manhood bereft of masculine model and support. Such is the dynamic of mirroring, plunging the subjective self into a turmoil of complexity in the process of self-definition.

Same-sex erotic attraction—from this point I focus upon males—has been suspect in psychoanalysis from its outset as a perverse, if not clearly pathological, condition. The notion of pathology finds its focus in a supposed signal sent by the mirroring parent to the boy-child in the earliest months of his life. An adult man, therefore, might find himself lacking in masculine substantiation because, say, his mother wanted a girl-child and unconsciously communicated her wish to him as an infant, imposing a feminine reflection rather than one that is gender-appropriate. As a man, he might find himself obsessively searching for an outer mirror that will serve to reverse the anomaly of his inner message. He is male, but he was originally and foundationally mirrored in his infancy as female. He needs to find a way into authentic self-love. *Authentic* here means an inner sense of identity appropriate to body gender.

The characteristically narcissistic feature of homosexual

desire, according to psychoanalysis, is a man's "oblique strategy for loving himself" as a male.[1] The homosexual love object, then, is never really seen as an object, a genuine other, but rather as a means of repairing the misimage the boy child saw in his determining infantile mirroring. The homosexual man consequently relates to his lover so as to reassure himself that he is male, rather than to express and contribute his core masculine sexual identity to a gender-opposite object. According to this mythologem, the homosexual man did not pick up a male message about himself at an early age and spends his erotic adulthood seeking to redress the loss. Body and psyche are at odds with one another, split, and thus pathologically related.

A kind of narcissistic demeanor often noticed in homosexual men can support such a diagnosis. One might observe an aspect of the anxious feminine, a not-quite-right feminine quality, seemingly diminished and out of place. Fussiness, overattention to surface detail, hysterical reaction formation, emotionality, and demand for privilege are some of the stereotypic manifestations. Such narcissistic conduct suggests a disjuncture in mirroring, as I have described it. The film *Longtime Companion* depicts a gay world enmeshed in trivia, a superficial and panicky preoccupation with parties, romance, and frivolity, until the plague struck.

So much is common knowledge, seen from the conventional psychoanalytic perspective, richly enmeshed as it is with cultural bias. But there is considerably more to the matter, even from the perspective of mirroring and psychoanalysis. However much one might conjecture about early childhood mirroring, one simply does not know to what extent those conditions create a foundation for a synergetic relationship between a gendered body and a similarly gendered interior identity—what I have called one's "masculine grid,"[2] or how they contribute to the building of masculine consciousness, for which sexual arousal is the erotic manifestation.

It is clear that a range of potential stimulation exists in every man, as Kinsey pointed out decades ago. In a man with conscious bisexual interests, where both masculine and feminine attract, the line of differentiation is close to the center of the erotic personality. On what basis, then, does one proceed to pathologize—not the obsessive behavior of a person, but the condition of bipolar appeal itself? Does one attribute a man's interest in a woman to gender-appropriate mirroring and his interest in a man to failed mirroring? One is caught in a quagmire.

Freud, I think, understood and respected the confusion surrounding sexual preference when he wrote, "In the psychoanalytic sense, the interest of the man for the woman is also a problem requiring an explanation, and is not something that is self-evident."³ Many of Freud's followers have been less reticent in their declarations of truth, and this has stamped the entire psychoanalytic school with an attitude that clings tenaciously to any discussion of homosexuality within its framework. The concept of the mirror and the literature of narcissism that flows from the phenomenon of reflection in human interaction has resulted in claims and counterclaims, depending upon viewpoint. One must remember that "facts" in psychoanalysis are actually theories, that surety in depth psychology follows fashion as in every art.

One thing seems to be clear. A man's need for an opposite as an erotic partner tends to interfere with a superficially narcissistic flow of energy. It moves him "out of himself." The subject's eyes—whether *eyes* here indicates concrete vision or metaphorical implication—grasp an image that demands attention because of its difference from an inner perception of himself. But the question is: what is an opposite? What is difference? A man might look into a mirror, see his own reflection, and compute that reflection as strange and exotic. His attraction to what he sees, then, is a factor of his distance from himself, what might be called his self-alienation. He himself is something of an opposite to what he perceives in the reflection.

But self-alienation is a factor in all of human experience. By no means is it peculiar to eroticism. Freud's preoccupation with sexuality was his particular focus, and an enormously valuable one. But opposition is not only sexual, as Jung profoundly knew. Because of our gender split, opposition draws primal energy from the psyche in one's attraction to, or avoidance of, an "other." But the question remains: what, in an individual's experience of himself, constitutes that other?

The question of the other is fundamental in latter-day Freudian object relations theory, in Kohut's "higher forms and transformations of narcissism,"[4] in Jung's belief that an archetypal substratum undergirds human experience. If a nascent person enters the human scene with a psychological inheritance that precedes and predisposes gender-syntonic/dystonic parental mirroring, as Jung claimed, assumptions about what ought or ought not to be that person's experience of an "other" must be broadened. Introversion enters the picture as well as the extraverted object-mirror-reflection. An introverted perspective is impossible if one is locked into one of the many doctrines of an outer-oriented psychoanalysis, an oxymoron if ever there was one. This does not mean that depth psychology is an obsolete art. It does mean that it is speculative.

Jung's crucial notion that archetype and instinct are correlative concepts provides an opening. One moves beyond stasis with the idea that archetype as predisposing pattern is psychic, instinct as predisposing pattern is physical, that psyche and physis are themselves mirror images of one another. What a man receives back, then, as he looks into a mirror, even if the image is of his own physical likeness, may not be only a reflection of an outer attitude toward himself, as though inner perception were only a product of external influence. The pattern suggested by the mirror may be one that undergirds appearance. It may be slightly odd, out of joint, of a strange texture and tone as judged from outer convention. It may actually be archetypal, and indissolubly enmeshed with instinct. We presumably know that individual instinctual drive experience varies enormously from person to person. And while the pattern in rough outline is consistent, even as housing structures are uniform in their ability to provide shelter, peculiarities in design and decoration are ubiquitous.

Jung was drawn to the odd. He saw in oddness not something to be extruded because of its difference—as if it could be—but that which belongs in the human definition simply because it exists, strange or not. His breadth of attraction to the unconventional undoubtedly had something to do with his being quite an odd fellow himself, subject to strange and inexplicable images he saw in his own mirror, his own self-reflection. In order to affirm himself, the *sine qua non* of the narcissistic process, he took seriously the figures and feelings he saw in the permutations of his inner gaze. He came to feel that the *meaning* of the image was more important than its correction, that the unconventional image served a purpose in his own life saga. Such a point of view made him quite unpopular in the world of doctrine, even among those who were already on the outside of cultural conformity. (Certainly ego possession by archetypal images/instincts that are totally out of control requires radical attention. I do not attend to that issue in this small essay. Under ordinary circumstances, what is called for is integration of the archetypal/instinctual upsurge into a functioning ego, which Jung assumed was a necessary base for psychological work. Integration is a broadening of the ego's smallish grasp of life, rather than an effort to root out the strange. Integration is a looking beneath the surface of the image to discover the message inextricably interwoven into the strangeness.)

Psychoanalysis itself is a rather odd discipline, standing as it does beyond the confines of convention. Convention takes a dim view of self-reflection in any case. The deeper reflection becomes, the more it challenges a "correct" way of being and looking, tending to redeem the incorrect way, which convention has nudged into the unconscious to live, obliquely hidden. It is oddment built upon oddment that psychoanalysis has maneuvered itself into enforcing an understanding of life that is attitudinally oppositional to its own nature. One suspects that a mirroring fault is at work within the structure of a vocation committed to the reversal of mirroring faults. Distortions are inevitable under such circumstances, and should be expected, without invalidating the value of the whole.

The seemingly odd situation of a man's desiring a sexual partner who reflects back to him an image of his own gender probably indicates his need for masculine affirmation. How this need, which every man has in one way or another, becomes focused in eroticism is an issue involving archetypal patterning, early childhood narcissistic gratification, and cultural conditioning or anticonditioning, itself influenced by one's archetypal configuration. Genetic inheritance, also an aspect of archetypal/instinctual patterning, may be another element of the blend. Negative father archetypal elements, for example, exist in the ocean bed of the psyche, as available for appearance in a man's psychic constitution as are positive father elements, all mixed into the relationship a man has with his personal father. A preponderance of negative father energy in a male's archetypal inheritance influences the mirroring process in the child and is a constituent part of the formation of his superego. Whether a son tends to be obedient or rebellious regarding his erotic object choice is at least partly contingent upon this archetypal influence.

To return to otherness: in February 1991, I was privileged to be invited by a group of three men who have met for years engaged in a process of masculine self-discovery and celebration, based upon Native American practices. This particular meeting was designed to acknowledge the end of winter and borrowed from the ancient bear ceremonies of the Lenape tribe

of New Jersey and Pennsylvania. We drove to a house in the
woods on a cold night. Winds howled. We sat in a circle on the
floor by the light of a candle, smudged each other in a ceremony much like blessing with incense, invited our male an-
cestors to be present. We drummed for an hour, went twice
around the circle with personal stories told in the third person
as we passed the "talking stick," a pipe. We undressed,
anointed one another with the grease of a deer that had been
killed weeks ago on the property (we had no bear), then
danced with drumming for another hour. We began at 8:00 PM
and ended with a supper of deer at 3:00 AM. The seven hours
went by almost unnoticed. My invitation read: "We have two
'intentions' in doing this: renewed personal commitment to
embody male energy, not only for ourselves but also in the
name of all those men who would love to join us if they knew
what we were about; and to do so specifically in the face of the
Middle East madness."

The ritual and the sharing were deeply moving to me, but
strangely beyond the agitations of emotion. I felt that I had
entered a larger dimension of time and meaning, a liminal
place, that I had touched a threshold of manliness only hinted
at in ordinary male interchange. We were all over fifty, currently or previously married, professional, Christian, but
burnt-out ecclesiastically. We were men who had worn through
the games and illusions of patriarchy, and/or had been worn
through by them. We were bearers of sacred phallos; we knew
that, yet we needed to know it better and more deeply.

We returned to our source. We became supplicants in a way
that I had never experienced before: strong, clear, structured,
with an admixture of muscled and unsentimental feeling,
using our five senses to affirm our brotherhood and the brotherhood. There was intelligence in what we did, yet a simplicity,
gentleness, directness, and unselfconsciousness that was star-
tlingly refreshing and, in its way, as new to me as was the
remarkable setting in which it occurred.

Everything about the event was erotic, as *eros* means infusion of love. The aspect that I worried about in advance—the nakedness, anointing, and dancing—passed as though it were the most natural thing in the world. We dipped our hands in the grease and touched each man's back, chest, and genitalia. Men don't do such things together. How could this happen without embarrassment and excitement? Well, it did. There was a flicker of arousal at one point, a sigh or two escaped some lips, but the particular took its place within the whole as an ordinary concomitant of serious affection and shared labor. The evening was not easy, sitting together for so long a time; neither was it difficult. I found anew a kind of work I am meant to do, a kind of trust I am meant to give, an embodied spirituality, a spiritualized banquet of sensation.

The wind spoke to our fragment of the masculine search, and one man spoke back to the wind. A critical juncture for me was the blessing of one man's new pipe stem. As we had with our bodies, each of us in turn held the long stem, anointed it with the substance of the deer, and spoke to it, passing on his hold on spirit to the wood. As I was doing so, seated on the floor, I became aware that I had joined the stem to my own masculine organ. The stem became an extension of my tumescent nature. I touched it; it touched me. My hand went back and forth upon it, as though I were masturbating, as masturbation is, according to James Hillman, a construct of introversion.[5] Quite a different thing, really, from touching another man's erection, yet not so different when grasped from within the context of phallic archetypal emergence.

Affirmation this most assuredly was, as also it was mirroring. The image in the reflection was not my face, not my body, not my particular hold on masculinity. Nor any other man's face, body, hold on masculinity. Both mine and the others' needed to be present for the ritual to occur; that, plus mutual need and knowledge of tradition. The image beneath the image was aided by sense, even dependent upon it, but it plumbed a depth in which the sacred nature of human gender finds its source and its expression. For some time it has been clear to me that gender, sexuality, and spirit cannot be separated, that they never are separated. Our fear of the daemon of sexuality clouds the spirit.

I speak of the archetypal affirmation of human nature that is mirrored in erotic attraction, whether this attraction is particularized, as in desire, or generalized, as in ritual. When one considers same-sex love, perhaps it is not enough to imagine two men making love to each other. One must also imagine the image behind the image in the mirror provided by the lover, as though Narcissus bent over to kiss the look in his own eye, containing a deeper reality than his surface reflection. The image of the Self, understood in a Jungian sense, is constellated by the idiosyncrasies of a man's psychic and historical conditioning. Since eros is of the gods and therefore strikes where it will, one is, perforce, in the realm of the holy when one falls in love. The provoking image is not only the effectual fallout from a mother's appropriate or inappropriate reflection. That god is too small. At the same time, anyone who has fallen in love knows how the archetype overwhelms.

Same-sex love for a man announces his entrance into a mysterious place dominated by certain archetypal elements and not by others. It is quite a lofty thing for a psychological professional working out of a doctrine to determine just how a man's response to his archetypal underlayment "should" work. It is also quite unconvincing to the man, which is a reason why this book has appeared. Because therapists are human, with ego needs of their own, it is almost impossible for such judgments not to happen. Good analytic training, as well as good raw material to start with, should build in brakes against what the old Zurich Jungians called "god-almightyness" in the therapist.

Human affirmation is more than a matter of interpersonal interchange, whether at a young age or an old. The root of desire seeks out archetypal waters and feeds upon a nourishment that finds its reflection in one who is loved. Without this essential element in a consideration of same-sex love, one is in danger of universalizing one's own personal judgment, reflecting, pro or con, the habit of society, rather than psyche.

Notes

1. Kenneth Lewes, *The Psychoanalytic Theory of Male Homosexuality* (New York: Meridian, 1988), p. 38.

2. Eugene Monick, *Castration and Male Rage: The Masculine Wound* (Toronto: Inner City Books, 1991), chap. 1.

3. Sigmund Freud, "Three Essays on the Theory of Sexuality" (1905), in *The Standard Edition of the Complete Psychological Works of Sigmund Freud*, vol. 7, ed. James Strachey (London: Hogarth Press, 1961), pp. 123–246. Quoted in Lewes, p. 35.

4. Heinz Kohut, *Analysis of the Self* (New York: International Universities Press, 1971), p. 220.

5. James Hillman, "Towards the Archetypal Model for the Masturbation Inhibition," in *The Reality of the Psyche*, ed. Joseph Wheelwright (New York: C. G. Jung Foundation/G. P. Putnam's Sons, 1968), p. 121.

The Uncharted Body

SUSAN GRIFFIN

The body. What body? The uncharted body.

The unexplored body.

And how can one describe what is unexplored?

Language contoured according to the lines of a map in which this territory is missing.

The map creating the fiction that every possibility is drawn there.

The uncharted never mentioned.

And yet.

Yet it is there in the borderlines, in cipher.

A memory: I am nine years old. I am going to the circus. It is sometime in the fifties, a time of repression, dullness, near sleepwalking. These are the last days of the travelling tents. I am very excited to be going. I have read about it, heard about it all my young life. And what draws me the most, more even than the lions or the clowns or the flying trapeze, all of which I love, is the freak show.

People with three arms, two heads, limbs petrified to wood. The man who can bend pipes with his mind; the bearded lady.

That sense of thrill, of amazement when considering what lies outside the predicted, the expected.

Under those tents, people flying through space, ten clowns emerging from a tiny car.

In the earliest years of the first circuses there were no

public zoos. People had not seen circus animals before. Elephants, tigers, gorillas then were all marvels, new discoveries.

At the turn of the century, the circus was the most popular form of entertainment in the small towns of America.

All those confining assumptions about the nature of female sexuality and gender, abundant in this period, entrenched in rural America.

The classic dream of the small-town girl or boy: to run away with the circus.

Huck Finn, Madame Bovary, the desire to escape from a stultifying atmosphere into a wider world.

A body outside the defined body. The larger realm one dares to imagine only in secret.

Arm of the anatomical drawing. Of "standard" proportions. Classical proportions. The arm of a man with white skin who is young. A soldier's arm. The arm of a woman, a certain class, a certain weight, height, color of skin, bearing, stance.

The arm of function. That lifts. Or commands. Or carries. Or cooks.

Is my arm when I extend it, hover, slide over the breasts of another woman, my lover, a lesbian arm?

The arm neat in its outlines. A straight line, sharp edge, undeviating as the wooden ruler I inherited from my grandfather, border of skin defining where I begin in space.

And then I shut my eyes. And I let the idea of an arm drift away. I begin to explore what I feel in that area of my body I call an arm.

Energy. Moving out in every direction. Elongated sphere of radiance. No clear line. A pulsing motion even in stillness. Arm.

The idea of a limb as a tool, an instrument, almost as if designed for a purpose. Plotted and graphed. Convenient, the physiological placement of hands.

The idea of the sexual body as an implement of reproduc-

tion. Vagina existing, then, for the insertion of the penis.
Uterus for childbearing. Breasts for milk.

Homosexuality according to this utilitarian vision, a waste
of energy. Counterproductive. The body not used as "intended" in the design.

The author of the design anonymous. A god. God.

And the actual sacred experience of the body. The awe that
can be felt, entering the experience of the body, which, by
contrast to the restrictions of utility, is infinite.

Strict categories of sexuality. The man. The woman. The
heterosexual. Homosexual. Bisexual.

Do these categories really exist? (Like arms, like breasts?)

Another memory: I am fifteen years old. I am invited to a
party. I bring a boy from my geometry class with me. I like the
olive color of his skin. His black hair. His kind face. We
quickly become friends in class; I help him to pass his tests by
letting him see my answers. At the party I drink two or three
glasses of wine. I am exhilarated, by the wine, the party, the
other guests. A group of students on vacation from college
have come, and they read us poetry from the Beat generation.
This seems to me to be what I have been looking for, seeking.
A door. An opening. My friend and I go to his car. He touches
me below my belly and moves his hand downward. I love the
feeling. I am happy. I have never been touched in this way
before. It is an adventure. My body grows in size and starts to
swirl about me. The utter largeness of sexual feeling. We
return to the party. Drift apart, even then. The next day we see
each other in geometry class. Still friends. But I did fall in
love that night. She is one year older. Sixteen. The party was at
her house. I do not call myself a lesbian. She never touches me
on my breasts, below my belly. I never touch her.

By what category or name does one label one's feelings,
the sensations in the body, mingled with ideas, memories,
emotions?

The words used for definitions not like numbers but like

natural objects, whales covered with barnacles, trees with moss, altered by context, surroundings, history.

Memory: I am sixteen. The girl I met becomes my best friend. We talk about the boys who are our lovers. Laugh. Weep in each other's arms. It is our way of making love to each other.

The construction of the question, if I do this, or think that, then am I really a lesbian?

The idea that many girls pass through a lesbian "stage." And this stage is not "real."

Her real life beginning when she is married. Which is when the story ends. Happily ever after.

The power of the word *lesbian* deriving from silence.

A phenomenon at the periphery of vision. Exogenous. Outside (yet also inside) oneself.

Memory: the implication in the words of a well-meaning adult that my friend and I were in some kind of danger. That our friendship was not healthy.

Charts on the wall representing three kinds of food one should have on one's plate in order to be healthy.

The power of the word *lesbian* deriving from speech.

The power of words which through delineation makes visible, and palpable, what has always been present. Present and yet unrealized. Nascent. Half-born.

The real substance of any human life is experience itself.

But an experience which is unnamed and unrecognized is not only invisible, it is also truncated.

Human experience is so intricately woven with consciousness, with knowledge and self-knowledge.

Like any kind of organic life, an experience develops. Perhaps it begins as a wish, or as something imagined. A hunch. Or perhaps it begins with a touch and then proceeds to a wish, and an intimation of the future.

She touches me.

She touches my breast. Then I feel desire.

Memory: I am twenty-two. For the past several months I have shared a bed with a friend. It began innocently, I would have said then. Though looking back now, I see in myself the force of desire from almost the moment I met her. It must have been many times before that, turning in bed, she brushed against my breasts. But this time the possibility of intention occurred to me. And I wanted her with an intensity I could not ignore.

Ringed by an alliance of institutional and cultural prohibitions, silence, or rather, the muting of speech, it is a miracle every time the desire of one woman for another is pronounced.

Memory: After the first few times we made love, I look into the mirror to see a different face. As if I have returned to myself. I find a wholeness.

The history of the word *whole* meaning wholesome meaning what has been described by authority as good.

The idea that someone is or is not "one of our kind," belonging to the whole, an exclusive "whole."

A prohibition against "unnatural acts."

A man's hand against a woman's vulva "natural."

A woman's hand against her lover's vulva "unnatural."

That common sentence spoken by so many women just after their first experience of making love with another woman, said with a tone of surprise, "But it felt so natural."

Nature like a ferocious beast kept under the tent, and behind bars.

To ask once again, what is sexuality? What do I feel? Where does my desire take me? To ask in a field of perception that has been opened.

This in itself would be an event. For in sexual experience, perception is an activity. Perception of one's own feelings, of what transpires between two lovers, the meeting, the penetration, the knowledge.

Year after year approaching and retreating from freedom within myself. Certain states of mind and body entering me as if by grace, old presuppositions falling away, transmutations.

The ignorance of certain definitions. Thinking I knew the parameters of my body's capabilities and then, a door is nudged open, and a whole new world appears, for which there ought to be a new vocabulary, a new dictionary.

Moving beyond the old anatomical drawings, the old ideas of who we are. The wholeness which exists beyond what is charted.

The ideas of the masculine, the idea of the feminine. Barriers to knowledge. Boundaries beyond which are uncharted lands.

Not only knowledge of the body, but intimacy itself.

The first real intimacy with a lover found with another woman.

Not that intimacy is impossible between men and women. But that the roles men and women play truncate being and thus militate against a real meeting.

Lesbians, gay men as explorers. Opening up new worlds for a civilization grown tired of itself.

The avarice for the land of other people's being perhaps a misplaced longing for a wider range of being.

Violence an expression of imprisonment.

The shaman, the berdache, the poet, artist, heterodox, androgynous, lesbian, gay, slipping out of the prescribed role and in this slippage, learning the secrets.

That secret knowledge.

Whispered. Dreamed. Glimpsed in a moment of waking.

The whole body. That mansion with many houses.

Where, nevertheless, we dwell, all of our lives.

Note

I owe a great deal in my thinking for this piece to Emily Conrad Da'Oud and her work with movement, "Continuum."

About the Contributors

JOHN BEEBE, M.D., the editor of the *San Francisco Jung Institute Library Journal* and the American editor of the *Journal of Analytical Psychology*, is a Jungian analyst in practice in San Francisco. He is the editor of C. G. Jung's *Aspects of the Masculine* and the author of *Integrity in Depth*.

ROBERT BOSNAK is a Dutch Jungian analyst in practice in Cambridge, Massachusetts. He is a graduate of the C. G. Jung Institute in Zurich and the author of *A Little Course in Dreams* and *Dreaming with an AIDS Patient*, which was adapted and produced as a play.

KARIN LOFTHUS CARRINGTON is a writer and psychotherapist in private practice in the San Francisco Bay Area. She has contributed to various Jungian journals, including *Quadrant, Psychological Perspectives*, and the *San Francisco Jung Institute Library Journal*, and has taught and lectured in the United States and Europe. She is currently working on a book entitled *Speaking the Truth in Love: The Alchemy of Women Loving Women*. She lives in the country northwest of the Golden Gate Bridge and enjoys the company of good friends, wild animals, the wilderness, and silence. She is devoting her creative energies to music, photography, and writing, as well as to her clinical practice.

LYN COWAN, Ph.D., is a Jungian analyst practicing in St. Paul, Minnesota. She is the author of *Masochism: A Jungian View* as well as several essays, and has lectured throughout the United States. She is currently Professor of Psychology at the Minnesota School of Professional Psychology and Adjunct Professor in Women's Studies at the University of Minnesota. She really *is* a romantic, and A.D. is her real flesh-and-blood muse.

CHRISTINE DOWNING is Professor and Chair of Religious Studies at San Diego State University and past president of the American Academy of Religion. Her previous books include *The Goddess: Mythological*

Images of the Feminine, Journey through Menopause, and *Psyche's Sisters: Re-Imagining the Meaning of Sisterhood.* Her most recent books are *Mirrors of the Self: Archetypes That Shape Our Lives,* which she edited, *Myths and Mysteries of Same-Sex Love,* and *Women's Mysteries.*

MORGAN FARLEY, Ph.D., is a writer and a psychotherapist in private practice in Santa Fe, New Mexico. A graduate of the University of London, she has recently completed a book on the sense of wonder, combining literary and psychological perspectives. Her first chapbook of poems, *Name Yourself Feast,* appeared in 1980; her second, *Her Radiance Everywhere,* an expanded version of the poem sequence in this anthology, is forthcoming. Morgan lives in a house warmed by the sun, where she is at work on a full-length collection of poems.

SUSAN GRIFFIN is the author of several books, including *Woman and Nature* and *Pornography and Silence.* Her play *Voices* won an Emmy in 1975. Her recent book of poetry, *Unremembered Country,* received the California Commonwealths Medal for Poetry. Among many other awards, she has received an NEA grant and a MacArthur Grant for Peace and International Cooperation. Her latest book is *A Chorus of Stones, the Private Life of War.* She is currently at work on a novel and a prose work on the body and social justice.

JOSEPH L. HENDERSON, M.D., is a Jungian analyst in private practice in San Francisco. He took his medical degree at St. Bartholomew's Hospital Medical School in London, and C. G. Jung was his personal analyst. He is the author of *Thresholds of Initiation* and coauthor of *The Wisdom of the Serpent* with Maud Oakes. He also wrote the chapter "Ancient Myths and Modern Man" in Jung's last book, *Man and His Symbols.*

ROBERT H. HOPCKE is a Licensed Marriage, Family, and Child Counselor in Berkeley, California, and serves as Coordinator of the AIDS Prevention Program at Operation Concern, a gay and lesbian counseling agency in San Francisco. He is the author of *Jung, Jungians, and Homosexuality; Men's Dreams, Men's Healing;* and *A Guided Tour of the Collected Works of C. G. Jung* (Shambhala Publications) and has written numerous articles on homosexuality and men's issues for collections and journals worldwide.

ROBERT JOHNSON is a teacher and a psychotherapist in San Diego, California. He is the author of several books including *He, She, We,* and most recently *Transformation*, a study of Goethe's *Faust*. He lectures widely throughout the United States and the world.

EUGENE MONICK, M. Div., Ph.D., is a Jungian analyst in private practice in New York City and Scranton, Pennsylvania. He is a graduate of the C. G. Jung Institute, Zurich, a professional and faculty member of both the New York and the Inter-Regional Society of Jungian Analysts, and the immediate past Vice-President of the Inter-Regional Society. He is the author of *Phallos: Sacred Image of the Masculine, Castration and Male Rage*, and *Evil, Sexuality and Disease: Grünewald's Body of Christ*. He has lectured widely on the subject of phallos as an antidote to patriarchy.

SUZI NAIBURG, Ph.D., is completing a book entitled *The Appalling Other in Henry James*. She is an associate in the Harvard Women's Studies Program and a candidate at the Massachusetts Institute for Psychoanalysis. She was the Executive Director of the C. G. Jung Society of New Mexico from 1989 to 1991 and has presented her research at the C. G. Jung Institute of San Francisco, the C. G. Jung Foundation of New York, the Modern Language Association, the Association for the Study of Dreams, and the International Conference for Literature and Psychoanalysis.

WILL ROSCOE, Ph.D., is an affiliated scholar with the Institute for Research on Women and Gender of Stanford University. He is the author of *The Zuni Man-Woman*, which received the 1991 Margaret Mead Award from the American Anthropological Association and the Society for Applied Anthropology, as well as a Lambda Literary Award. He has been active in the gay men's spirituality movement since 1979.

DONALD F. SANDNER, M.D., has practiced as a Jungian analyst in San Francisco for over thirty years and has been past president and member of the teaching faculty of the C. G. Jung Institute of San Francisco. He has lectured in most of the Jungian training centers worldwide and has written twenty-five articles and book chapters on Jungian psychology and cross-cultural healing. He is the author of *Navajo Symbols of Healing*.

CAROLINE T. STEVENS, Ph.D., is a Jungian analyst in private practice in Chicago and a training analyst at the C. G. Jung Institute there. She loves music, dance, and drama on the stage and off, sunlight and firelight in her home, furry creatures, admirable friends, her work, her children, and her life's companion, Rosemarie. She has published several articles in *Chiron*, the *San Francisco Jung Institute Library Journal*, and *Quadrant* and has contributed to several anthologies including *Mirrors of the Self: Archetypes That Shape Our Lives* and *Psyche's Stories*.

DAVID TACEY, Ph.D., is a Senior Lecturer in English and in Interdisciplinary Studies at La Trobe University in Melbourne, Australia. He is the author of *Patrick White: Fiction and the Unconscious* and of essays on literary and cultural studies in British and Australian journals. He has written for *Psychological Perspectives* on men and incest and for the *San Francisco Jung Institute Library Journal* on the contemporary men's movement, and is currently at work on a book concerning Jung and men's issues.

HOWARD TEICH, Ph.D., is a psychologist in private practice in San Francisco and Sonoma, California. His lectures on solar and lunar psychologies have included a presentation at the Friends of Jung Society in San Diego and the Los Angeles Jung Institute's conference on "Women and Men: Revisioning Gender Identities." Dr. Teich has led classes and workshops on dream psychology and twin-hero mythology and is currently at work on a book entitled *Beyond Gender*.

SCOTT WIRTH, Ph.D., is a Jungian analyst in private practice in San Francisco and a Staff Affiliate Psychologist at the California Pacific Medical Center Department of Psychology, also in San Francisco. He has published several articles, including an afterword to the book *Beyond Acceptance* and a Jungian Chapter in the anthology *What to Do about AIDS*. He is a member of the C. G. Jung Institute of San Francisco, where he completed his analytical training.